TRUTH FOR TODAY

Truth for Today

Bertha Munro

BEACON HILL PRESS
Kansas City   Missouri

Truth indeed came once into the world with her divine Master, and was a perfect shape most glorious to look on.—MILTON.

I'am the Truth.—JESUS.

DEDICATION

To my co-workers, the Sunday-school teachers of the Church of the Nazarene, who gave the original inspiration for these notes.

FOREWORD

The writer of the devotional readings which make this book is known, loved, and trusted by an ever enlarging circle composed of her fellow-laborers in the work of Christian education—both teachers and students who have known her personally during past years. To this group the following pages will come as leaves from the tree of life, and they will be forward in securing and using the book and encouraging others to do likewise. To those who have not been so fortunate as to know Dean Bertha Munro, we send these few words of explanation and exhortation.

Dean Bertha Munro is a scholar, and, which is more, she is a Christian scholar. Her interest in God is the interest of a true worshiper. Her interest in people is the interest of a soul-seeker and a soul-saver. Her interest in the Bible and Christian thinking is the interest of one who would know the will of God in order that she may do it. Dedicated to quality work, Dean Munro is an example of her own philosophy of life.

The material of this book is the product of a life lived in the heights, and is useful to those who would ascend into the hill of the Lord. The substance is of the highest order, and the form is carefully wrought out. The object is to help the reader to think clearly, to love God supremely, and to serve faithfully in all places where the providence and Spirit of God may direct.

I commend this book to all who sincerely desire to be good and to do good. May it serve to bless its thousands directly and its millions indirectly in all the days to come.

In Jesus' love and service,

JAMES B. CHAPMAN

Kansas City, Missouri,
January 24, 1946.

ACKNOWLEDGMENTS

The material of this book is a rearrangement and reorganization, with the addition of Scripture readings and hymns, of material published in the "Truth for Today" column of *The Bible School Journal* (for teachers) of the Church of the Nazarene. Hence, the somewhat arbitrary choice of subject matter and Scripture references.

Grateful acknowledgment is made to the following publishers of permission granted to quote lines from well-known hymns:

To Lillenas Publishing Company for hymns too numerous to list, and for assistance in securing other permissions.

To Rodeheaver Hall-Mack Company for the use of "Alone," "God's Way Is the Best Way," "He Lifted Me," "I Know He's Mine," "Lead Me to Calvary," "Take Up Thy Cross," "The Glory of His Presence," "The Way of the Cross," "Then Jesus Came," "Transformed," and "Where the Gates Swing Outward Never."

To Hope Publishing Company, Chicago, for lines from "Faith Is the Victory," "God Will Take Care of You," "I Am Redeemed," "I Remember Calvary," "What Will You Do with Jesus," and "Will There Be Any Stars."

To Rev. George Bennard, Albion, Michigan, for lines from "Speak, My Lord."

To the Standard Publishing Company, Cincinnati, for permission to quote from "Calvary."

To the Theodore Presser Company, Philadelphia, for portions of the song, "I Met My Master Face to Face."

To Mrs. Arthur Ingler for lines from "There's a Path to the Hearts of Men."

Acknowledgment is made also to the following of permission to quote from poems published by them: The Sunday School Times, Philadelphia, Pennsylvania, and the Brethren Publishing House, Elgin, Illinois.

To Houghton Mifflin Company, Boston, thanks is expressed for permission to quote from Whittier and Thoreau, and from Lloyd Douglas, *The Robe;* to D. C. Heath and Company, Boston, for permission to quote from J. L.

Borgerhoff; to Harper & Brothers, New York, for permission to use the title, "I Have a Rendezvous with Life," copyrighted by Countee Cullen in *Caroling Dusk;* to the Union Seminary Review, Richmond, Virginia, for permission to quote from "The Meridian Test of the Minister" by Ralph G. Turnbull.

For use of the few poems whose authors or owners I have been unable to identify, or communicate with, I request indulgence.

BERTHA MUNRO

Gifts

The wise men came, that far-off winter dawn,
And brought their gifts—gold, myrrh and frankincense—
To Christ the King. But as they turned to go,
Their pathway changed into a road of gold,
A heavenly fragrance to their garments clung
And songs of praise set all the world aflame.
Blessing the King, themselves were blessed indeed.

I too brought treasures to my Lord Divine.
I brought my gold—my wealth of human joys,
My friends, my gathered store of truth, my work.
I brought my myrrh, the bitter griefs of years;
And frankincense, the worship of my heart.
I brought them to His feet, and laid them there.

But lo, He touched my gifts, and gave them back
Radiant, transformed, a royal gift to me.
His joy transmuted mine to living gold,
Gave my frail work pledge of eternity;
His peace breathed on my griefs, and perfumes rare
Of sympathy and faith and hope distilled;
His love on my soul's altar kindled there
An answering flame, and showed my Saviour's face.
In the King's hands poor gifts wax infinite.

BERTHA MUNRO

CHRIST—WHAT THEN?

Read: Matt. 2:1-10; John 1:11-13.

Text: *If any man will do his will, he shall know of the doctrine, whether it be of God, or whether I speak of myself.* John 7:17.

Christ—what then? He is the Fact that every person born into the world must face. Admit it or not, we reveal ourselves by our reaction to Him. And we condition ourselves for receiving Him.

Many know of His coming, but not all care. Sometimes those with the best opportunities to know care the least. The scribes knew every promise by heart; the Magi must read the stars. But the scribes were indifferent; the Magi traveled weary miles to find the Christ. I would not let great opportunity make me careless, nor great light make me blind. Both have been mine.

Some men oppose and would destroy—they are the Herods, the vested interests. Jesus would ruin their business. Their antagonism reflects on them, not on Him; it brands them as insincere. Your own stubbornness—does it proclaim a pet sin that Jesus would interfere with?

Some have a good substitute for Jesus: their own counterfeit coin—these are the scribes, the religionists. Back of their humanistic religion is a secret pride of self. Look into the past experience of almost any "liberal" thinker, and you will find he has once known the truth, but somewhere has refused to walk in the light. Men do not reject Christ unconsciously.

Some, thank God, are earnest seekers, glad finders, wholehearted worshipers—these are the wise men. Too wise to be satisfied with a human religion, too humble to be self-sufficient, they recognize Jesus as the Desire of Nations, and bow at His feet. The sign of wisdom is humility.

> *O come to my heart, Lord Jesus;*
> *There is room in my heart for Thee.*

CHRIST—WHAT THEN?

Read: Matt. 2:11-23; John 12:31-50.

Text: *If any man serve me, him will my Father honour.*
  John 12:26.

But God has something to say. He let Jesus come to
earth apparently unprotected; but He never forgot, never
closed His eyes, never took His hand off the wheel. He
sees what we do with His Son; and He acts accordingly.

He leads every humble seeker surely and safely, and
gives him the desire of his heart. He has guided many a
heathen to the light by strange, unexpected ways. He
will lead you to complete satisfaction if you are earnest
and sincere.

God foils the selfish enemy of the truth utterly, as-
toundingly. When he thinks himself most secure he is
nearest his overthrow. Instead of harming the cause of
Christ, he will only fulfill prophecy. Don't fear the persecutors. God can deal with them. And He will.

God is silent to the "scribes"—most terrible fate of
all, perhaps. They have chosen a substitute and He lets
them have it. They know the most about Jesus and get
the least from Him. Hardest to reach with the gospel is the
man who has a "good religion of his own."

Herod had not long to live. He died and was forgotten. The scribes were cursed, and passed the curse
on to their children. The wise men were blessed, and
passed their blessing on even to us. Blessing and cursing
are in God's hands; which we receive depends on how
we treat Jesus.

> *What will you do with Jesus?*
>   *Neutral you cannot be;*
>   *Some day your heart will be asking,*
>   *What will He do with me?*

CHRIST—WHAT THEN?

Read: Matt. 2:9-11; John 7:32-39; John 10:19-30.

Text: *He that believeth on me, as the scripture hath said, out of his innermost being shall flow rivers of living water.* John 7:38.

The world is full of notions about religion. The birth of Jesus shows us what real religion is. Real religion is not a human scheme. It is not "God made in the image of man." It is revelation from above; there was light from a star. It is power from above; there was a Heavenly Child born. God made the first move.

Real religion is not cold creed. It has a creed, but it starts with personal experience. For it begins with the love that sent Jesus to earth, and the heart hunger that sent the Magi journeying. It is consummated when that hunger meets that love.

Real religion is more than formal ritual in a fine church. The Christian religion began in a stable where the only form was spontaneous adoration. It began when men met God sincerely. It continues so.

Real religion has at least three elements: heart satisfaction (a personal seeking and finding of God); worship (a personal adoring of God); consecration (a personal giving to God). Real religion is a personal relationship. Wise men will recognize Christ; they will worship; they will give. A test for every one of us.

What have I to give my Lord? Just what the wise men gave. Gold—all the things that are wealth to me: money and health and strength and friends. Frankincense—the first intensity of my heart's love and loyalty. Myrrh—my sorrows, my hurts, my trials—and my power to suffer. When I give Him these, I give Him all. And He is worthy.

> *Well of water, ever springing,*
> *Bread of life so rich and free,*
> *Untold wealth that never faileth,*
> *My Redeemer is to me.*

THE GREAT PHYSICIAN

Read: Matt. 8:1-17.

Text: *And Jesus went about . . . . preaching the gospel of the kingdom, and healing every sickness and every disease among the people.* Matt. 9:35.

Jesus was always giving. Out from Him went a steady stream of blessing and healing. We stop helping when helping costs us a little too much. We draw the line when helping is "inconvenient." We are eager to help those we know, but rather indifferent toward those we do not know. Some of us bleed for the suffering multitudes, but neglect the individual next door; others are strong in personal work, but uninterested in revivals. We can be more like Him—but it costs.

Jesus makes no distinctions of sex, class, or age. Jesus has a rendezvous with every person on earth. He has business to do with every one. Rich and poor; young and old; man, woman, child; aristocrat and social outcast— He overlooks none. So insignificant that society thinks they do not matter, Jesus knows each has a soul; for He bought it at high price.

Jesus sees all alike. In our relations with Him we all stand on the same plane. None is "superior." All are infinitely below an infinite God; but, as seen through His infinite love, all are infinitely worth saving.

Jesus' look is always kind. He could well hold grudges against us; for He knows our past, and that past is full of rebellion and neglect. But He does not break the bruised reed. If we are fearful, we can be assured that He is saying, "Fear not."

> *On the land or wave*
> *Jesus waits to save—*
> *He never turns a soul away.*

THE GREAT PHYSICIAN

Read: Matt. 8:18-32; 9:1-8, 20-22.

Text: *Whether is easier, to say, Thy sins be forgiven thee; or to say, Arise and walk? Matt. 9:5.*

Jesus sees a need in every human soul whom He has not touched. His look is searching. Until we meet Him we are fairly well satisfied with ourselves. We think we are pretty nice persons. He sees the weak spot; and He puts His finger on it. Our wisest prayer for a seeker is that the Spirit will talk to him and show him his need definitely. Then there will be real seeking and real finding.

We thought our need was comfort; He saw we needed cleansing from carnality's rebelliousness. We thought our need was physical: health, sound nerves; He saw our need was spiritual: the peace of the abiding Spirit. His diagnosis is correct. When we come to Him for help we should let Him speak first. Always diagnosis before remedy. It is only a quack that will let you select your own remedy.

So many men, so many needs. But Jesus handles every one as a Master. You have got yourself into an impossible tangle? Admit it. Then put it into His hands, and see Him work. When you come to Him you come to Power.

What is your peculiar difficulty? Social maladjustment, like Matthew? Disease, recent or of long standing, like the woman who pressed her case? Blindness or dumbness, "normal" sickness or devil-possession? Face it—then let Jesus work on it. Remember He never loses a case.

> *The great Physician now is near,*
> *The sympathizing Jesus.*

THE GREAT PHYSICIAN

Read: Matt. 9:9-13.

Text: *I am not come to call the righteous, but sinners to repentance.* Matt. 9:13.

Jesus counts on what He can make us rather than on what we are in ourselves. "I called to preach? I never could talk!" Neither could Bud Robinson, but Jesus saw in him, under His touch, a winsome soul winner, and He was not afraid to take the risk. "I go to school? I'm no student." No, but Jesus can stimulate minds as well as blood cells. "I be a Christian? With a temper like mine?" You are forgetting that something happens to a jangled spirit when the wounded hands of Jesus are laid upon it.

Jesus sees possibilities in the most unpromising. Everyone has some talent, gift, ability, that will be released by His touch. He sees it latent as the sculptor sees the head in the block of marble, and He is eager to make it actual. Some of us never will find out what we are capable of in life until we meet Jesus.

Unpatriotic, betraying his country to Rome—yet later Matthew wrote his Gospel for the Jews, his own countrymen. Jesus always has specialized in transformed lives; no one is unpromising to Him.

The socially unfit—so there is hope even for the down-and-outs of the city missions. The rich, neglected by most of us—Jesus knows the gospel will fit them too. The habit-ridden—"just one touch" from Jesus will break the fetters that years of "trying" only fastened tighter. The blind can grasp a promise and see with the eye of faith. The devil-possessed can achieve a clear, sane testimony. These miracles are not too much for Jesus.

> *O Lord, take up the tangled strands,*
> *Where we have wrought in vain;*
> *That by the touch of Thy dear hands*
> *Some beauty may remain.*

THE GREAT PHYSICIAN

Read: Matt. 9:18-36.

Text: *When he saw the multitudes, he was moved with compassion on them.* Matt. 9:36.

Jesus looks at men with divine sight rather than human. So He looked when there was no arm to save, no eye to pity. So He came to earth to seek and to save that which was lost. Because He cares and because He can, we are saved. Because He sees where men would pass by and because He can save where men could only sympathize, no case is hopeless. My case never will be hopeless. I have a Saviour!

"Where Power and Will are one" (Dante) and Love—that is our Christ. To have someone always watching, always understanding, always caring—life holds no richer blessing. But when that Someone by your side is always strong to help, life holds only blessing. The sorrows are more than shared; they are healed.

There is no dead-end street for the wayfaring Christian. The All-Seeing Eye will open every door before him in the nick of time.

Jesus is looking our way today. He is looking at our world, our town, our community, our homes, our hearts. What does He see there? And what would He do? Can I look as He looks, in loving concern? Can I give Him free right of way to act, with power?

Jesus came to save every one. There is no favored or preferred group. I wonder how glad He will be to see me if I come without the others whom I have allowed to die in ignorance. Have I shoved away someone else at the feast to make room for myself? Have I misappropriated wealth which was entrusted to me to share with others?

The world's Burden-Bearer is Jesus,
Your Jesus and mine.

FOLLOW ME

Read: John 13:1-17.

Text: *I have given you an example, that ye should do as I have done.* John 13:15.

Jesus lived on earth the ways of heaven. Jesus was controlled by an unseen set of values. He was no social pragmatist. His actions were not governed by apparent laws of success.

Knowing Himself to be Lord of all, He chooses to become a humble Servant.

Leaving His friends poor and defenseless, He bequeaths them as the best gift—clean hearts.

Betrayed by His own, He chooses to love.

Crucified in shame by His enemies, He promises peace on earth and a royal heaven. Here is a mystery, the mystery of the long view and the heavenly vision.

Stranger yet, He enjoins these values upon His followers. As Lord, He commands them; as Way, He is our Example in living by them. If we live by any other standards, we are living in another kingdom than His and under other laws. We are aliens.

Jesus' humility is not a mere form; He washes feet to teach a truth. Real humility has a sincere desire to help others. It is possible to bend double in self-abnegation with a proud heart. The humility that is Christlike is a loving self-forgetfulness in service.

> *O Master, let me walk with Thee,*
> *In lowly paths of service free;*
> *Tell me Thy secret, help me bear*
> *The strain of toil, the fret of care.*

FOLLOW ME

Read: John 13:18-21; 33-35; John 14:1-6.

Text: *Whither I go ye know, and the way ye know.* John 14:4.

Christ is grieved if one professed follower of His is controlled by other principles than His. Have you ever felt checked in some good deed and made to examine your motives? Christ was searching you out. He expects absolute sincerity. He does not hold with those who say, "The end justifies the means."

Jesus is less concerned about what we must suffer than about the state of our hearts. He is content to leave His disciples in a hostile world without political or social influence; He is not content to leave them with uncleansed hearts. He knows that sin will betray them; it will be their worst enemy.

Jesus' love is not in words only, but in deeds. He loves well enough to tell the truth, well enough to warn of sin. I am glad He does. I will appreciate His rebukes; I will hate sin worse than I fear human disapproval. And I will be a friend whose word can be trusted.

Jesus' promise of heaven is no sleight-of-hand jugglery; it is no magic gift of a wishing-ring or a fairy godmother. It is the natural end of the journey for those who will walk the narrow way. He will keep their steps; He will meet them and carry them over the last dark, bridgeless river; He will welcome them home. For He has given them pilgrim hearts.

He will lead me safely in the path that He has trod,
Up to where they gather on the hills of God.

FOLLOW ME

Read: John 14:19-31.

Text: *Peace I leave with you, my peace I give unto you: not as the world giveth give I unto you.* John 14:27.

To live by worldly ways is to belong to this world, not to Jesus and heaven. What are our values? What is our working rule of conduct? Happy are we if we do as He does. We all endorse the Christian code; we praise the beauty of humility and love. But we are saved if we *act* as though we believed. In fact, if we live by other values we really have not Jesus—the Jesus of the Bible.

The world system: to dominate, to get all you can and keep all you get, to demand adulation, to keep everybody busy waiting on you, to play favorites, to "pay back," to work for self, openly or subtly—but to be restless, unhappy. Can we imagine heaven made up of people ruled by such principles? It would cease to be heaven.

Christ's system: to serve, to prefer others in honor, to avenge not yourself, to overcome evil with good, to humble yourself to walk with God, to love never-failingly, to seek not your own—and to be happy. Yes, and a good citizen of heaven.

To live by the ways of heaven is to find peace on earth. Your Christian experience cannot be an adjunct to an otherwise full life. It is revolutionary. It comes first. Become a real Christian, and all the rest of your doings and holdings become secondary and subject to Christ's call. But it is worth it.

Only one thing can keep hearts singing in our troubled world—Jesus' "Let not your heart be troubled." When He says, "Let," He can bring it to pass.

Peace, perfect peace, in this dark world of sin?
The blood of Jesus whispers "Peace" within.

CREATION'S STORY

Read: Gen. 1:1-10; Isa. 40:12-15.

Text: *In the beginning God.* Gen. 1:1.

The world needs to read Creation's story afresh. The doubters and skeptics need to read, "In the beginning God." For there all questions are silenced. Faith rests in the Person of God.

The humanists and moralists need to read, "The Spirit of God moved." For spiritual life we are still dependent on the work of the Spirit. A "religion of man" is as dead and cold as was chaos before the blessed Spirit brooded.

The nations who forget God need to read God's charge to the man He had created. Man was given a good world to manage and he has made a failure of it. He will have to give account of his stewardship.

Those who are confused and think there is no way out need to read, "Let there be light." God's first gift was light. In light there is certainty and clear direction. In God's truth there is salvation even for this evil day.

"The first creature of God, in the works of the days, was the light of the sense; the last was the light of reason; and His Sabbath work ever since is the illumination of His Spirit. First He breathed light upon the face of chaos; then He breathed light into the face of man; and still He breatheth and inspireth light into the face of His chosen." —Bacon.

We are walking in the beautiful light of God.

CREATION'S STORY

Read: Gen. 1:11-28; Ps. 19.

Text: *Even from everlasting to everlasting, thou art God.* Ps. 90:2.

The story of Creation gives us a true picture of our God. Thank God for Genesis 1. It is one of our greatest treasures: no "myth," but glorious, beautiful certainty.

Genesis 1 *takes God for granted.* It does not try to demonstrate His existence, but it proves Him in experience. The best way—and it still works.

He is *infinite* in power. He did not have to toil and scheme to create this vast universe; He said "Let," and willed it all into existence. The morning stars came into being with a song. What is "His power to usward who believe"?

He is *eternal,* and is Himself the answer to life's ultimate question. He is from before the beginning. If His voice conflicts with all other voices, He is right. His is the perspective of eternity.

He is a God of *order and system.* There is nothing haphazard about His doings. I am not guessing or chancing when I obey Him. His dispensations are timed exactly right—for the great universe and for my little world.

He is a God of *providence* and kindly thought. Everything is provided for the well-being of man—and what a bountiful and beautiful provision! Why did He not make all the trees and grass and sky a dirty gray? Why did He not make all the fruits and vegetables taste alike and insipid? He gave more than He had to; He planned for us to be happy. He always does.

> *Frail children of dust, and feeble as frail,*
> *In Thee do we trust, nor find Thee to fail;*
> *Thy mercies how tender, how firm to the end,*
> *Our Maker, Defender, Redeemer, and Friend!*

CREATION'S STORY

Read: Gen. 1:24-28; Ps. 8.

Text: *What is man, that thou art mindful of him? and the son of man, that thou visitest him? Ps. 8:4.*

God is always at work, creating. He only can make something out of nothing. He did it the first of all days; He does it now. We are afraid of what God will do to us if we yield. We run away and try to "make a life" ourselves. We fail, always. Then we come to Him, feeling our helpless nothingness, ready to hear His words, "I will turn my hand upon you."

God creates; the devil destroys. Who would not rather trust himself to God? The devil is not satisfied until he has torn a man to pieces. He will dull his mind, degrade his emotions, weaken his will. But let God lay His hand on a man, the work of repair begins.

God made man the climax and ruler of His creation. He too is dust, but he is something more. Man is more important to God than all the worlds of infinite dimensions, for he has a soul that is not material. Man is related to God in a sense that the animals cannot be; he has a God-faculty. He must not live on the animal plane, eating and drinking and reproducing without a thought of his Maker.

God's good work of creation is being repeated in lives today—in my life, in yours. Chaos is turned to cosmos, confusion to order. Before God spoke, mind and heart and conduct were in a hopeless muddle. But "there is a simple remedy for life's confusion: (1) *Trust* God, (2) *Obey* God, (3) *Do right* as defined by God. So life becomes plain and orderly."—E. S. Mann.

> *Made for a better world than this,*
> *Made for a home on high;*
> *Not made for the fleeting things of earth,*
> *But to live eternally.*

CREATION'S STORY

Read: Gen. 1; Job 38: 4-11.

Text: *God, who commanded the light to shine out of darkness, hath shined in our hearts.* II Cor. 4: 6.

Darkness is turned to light. Left to myself, I lose my way and wander in circles. When God's light shines in, I find a goal, a purpose, a direction. That light will never leave me so long as I use it to walk by. We have a bit of the light of heaven here—and that light is Jesus. Earth's shadows cannot dim His face.

Discord becomes harmony. The morning stars sang together at the creation, and they have been singing ever since. Men of old spoke of "the music of the spheres": that harmony the planets make as they revolve in their orbits, doing their appointed task at the command of God. God puts a song at the heart of life—just common, ordinary life. He turns the jarring discords into music for our hearts and for His ear.

Disproportion becomes symmetry and beauty. When our lives are centered in God, other interests and other people find their true relative position. Nothing is so ugly as deformity. He will make us straight and poised if we will let Him.

Deadness becomes life; the dead void springs into living green. Into our dying clay has been breathed a spark of eternal life. We begin to plan for eternity.

Barrenness becomes fruitfulness. He shares with us something of His own creative energy. No one whom God has made a new creature is useless. Every Christian is a fruit-bearer. His barren soul is transformed into the garden of the Lord.

From shades of night to plains of light,
Oh, praise His name, He lifted me!

CREATION'S STORY

Read: Gen. 1:1-5; Ps. 104:24-31.

Text: *And God said, Let there be light.* Gen. 1:3.

God's creative work in lives proceeds by clear, definite, recognizable principles and methods. First, *the divine fiat*: "Let there be." The power is God's. Man co-operates, but his share is to lay hold on the resources of God; and he lays hold by committing himself absolutely to the will of God—without question and without reservation. No yielding, no life; no consecration, no creation.

Separation, God's method. If God is to create a new world in our spirits, we must be willing to have all evil banished. He separates light from darkness, the waters above from the waters beneath. He is light, and in Him is no darkness at all. Postponement, evasion, compromise will not do. The separating line of the will of God is drawn sharply.

The Holy Spirit, God's agent. He breathed on the face of the deep that first morning, and darkness and death gave way. It is that same Spirit that I have to deal with; the same Spirit that has been sent to purge my heart and empower my life. How can I be dead or fearful while I have Him? Or how can I trifle with Him and escape?

A day with God is a creative period; it marks a section of His will accomplished. I would offer Him each one of my days; and when I come to its close I would have the sense—or the glad faith—that He pronounces it "good." And I would have my whole life "one of God's days": the work He chose for me accomplished, pleasing in His sight.

Holy, Holy, Holy, merciful and mighty,
All Thy works shall praise Thy name in earth and sky
    and sea!

CREATION'S STORY

Read: Gen. 1; Isa. 40:25-31.

Text: *He is strong in power; not one faileth.* Isa. 40:26.

The God manifested in creation is the God I can know today—my heavenly Father.

Let me look about me and marvel at that which He has given me, and be grateful, and trust. Let me not take my world for granted. Let my constant mood be glad surprise at the ever fresh wonder of His creation.

"God is not the author of confusion, but of *peace.*" Any topsy-turvy conditions that make me feel "the world is all wrong" are of man's choosing, not of God's making. And man can choose to undo them.

God is the infinite *Provider.* Providence is His name. He took thought for man in general; He made the earth useful for man in every detail—in uncounted ways. He takes thought for me. To meet every need He has a provision that exactly fits—made ready ahead of time and beyond my understanding. The reverent biologist will preach a sermon to us Christians.

God made the sun with a gift of healing and invigoration for man; He made the moon to govern the salt ocean waters in their "task of pure ablution round earth's human shores." "He made the stars also": innumerable, vast worlds which should speak to us of the limitless might of our God. Will His everlasting arm give way under my weight?

All that God makes is *good.* It has beauty, order, usefulness. Beauty as the eternities define beauty; order as the stars in their courses know order; usefulness in fulfilling the eternal plan of God. Make my life "good." I commit my soul to Thee, as to a faithful Creator.

> *The Hand that bears all nature up*
> *Will guard His children well.*

THE NEW COMMANDMENT

Read: Mark 12:28-34.

Text: *A new commandment I give unto you, That ye love.*
John 13:34.

The New Commandment is a new life. "When Jesus
says, 'Behold, I make all things new,' He lays his hand
on the heart of a man."—C. E. Jefferson. Everybody
chooses his own philosophy of life—consciously or unconsciously. His life is made what it is by the value he
sets at its heart. His *summum bonum* practically determines the policy by which he lives. Money? Then fraud.
Power? Then force. Popularity? Then compromise.
Pleasure? Then self-indulgence. Jesus? Then love. We
do well to weigh our values.

Society well-nigh compels us to keep the Ten Commandments—or most of them. We must be law-abiding,
or else pay the penalty. The New Commandment we
choose—or reject—for ourselves. The New Commandment is *inward*: it reaches us where we live; it makes
us new persons.

The New Commandment is *life on a higher level.* No
one will force it upon me, but I may have it for the choosing. It is a superhighway where I may travel if I will.
Who would not choose its light and freedom in these days
of congested traffic and stuffy conveyances?

The New Commandment makes a *unified personality.*
It puts one command in the place of ten—that one fundamental. It emphasizes the flow out from one source, not
to ten goals. It gives one spot to watch; it says only, "Keep
the fountain pure." It allows for one concern and only
one. It banishes cross-purposes and rebellious passions.
It reduces all of life to a single ruling motive—love.

> *Now rest, my long-divided heart,*
> *Fixed on this blissful center, rest;*
> *Nor ever from thy Lord depart,*
> *With Him of every good possessed.*

THE NEW COMMANDMENT

Read: John 13: 34, 35; Deut. 6: 4, 5; Lev. 19: 18.

Text: *The fruit of the Spirit is love.* Gal. 5: 22.

The New Commandment is the eternal way—new only to us. Truth is not new. The Old Testament taught the same standard of love for God and neighbor; but it could not be seen clearly—till Jesus came and embodied it. It is not a human way of life, the human imagination could not grasp it—till Jesus came and showed how it worked. Then we saw love doing good to evil and conquering it. And we understood.

If you find yourself making excuses—"But that's more than human; I can't do that"—you are still living in the dusk before Christ's coming, the dusk and the deadness. For this Commandment is new life as well as new light. You can do it because Christ did it.

It was always right to love. Right never changes. But it was not always possible for sinful man—not until Jesus came, and died, and sent the Holy Spirit. Now "the fruit of the Spirit is love."

Love was always true. Love was always right. It is "new" to us only because our moral sight is dim. Love will never be superseded by anything better. It "abideth." There is no true "modernism," no "relativity," no greater revelation yet to come. We never shall find a higher standard than Jesus—and holy love.

> *Near the Cross, O Lamb of God,*
> *Bring its scenes before me;*
> *Help me walk from day to day*
> *With its shadows o'er me.*

THE NEW COMMANDMENT

Read: John 15:10-12; Gal. 5:13-15.

Text: *These things have I spoken unto you, that my joy might remain in you, and that your joy might be full.* John 15:11.

The New Commandment is the best way. Love is the normal way. Supernaturally natural, it is furnished from above. One glimpse of the Cross, and love springs up for the God who "so loved the world," for the Christ who "gave himself for me," for the others for whom He died. Grateful love and deeds that show it are spontaneous, natural. Gratitude is no burden for the man who has been redeemed; formal obedience would mark him a base ingrate.

Love is the normal *family atmosphere,* and the family is the normal unit of human society. As Christians we belong to a heavenly family unit. That family will never be torn apart by war, never invaded by death. Let us cultivate those family ties that cannot be broken.

Love is the *joyful* way of living. Try it and see. Jesus was the Great Lover; and He had joy to give away.

Our joy in loving is not gay cheer, not even the natural pleasure of making others happy. It is Jesus' joy that He gives us, a deep calm, independent of circumstances or people's appreciation. If we love God and our neighbor in His way, His joy remains whether God treats us as it seems He should, or not; whether people praise us or blame us.

Jesus' joy is not natural to us, but it fits our natures. His joy makes our joy full. It is what we have been looking for all our lives. Would you know satisfaction? Then learn to live by love.

> *Living for Jesus, oh, what rest;*
> *Pleasing my Saviour, I am blest.*

THE NEW COMMANDMENT

Read: John 15:13, 14; Rom. 5:1-8.

Text: *Love one another; as I have loved you.* John 13:34.

The New Commandment is Christ's own way. Christ's love is the *measure* of ours. Love others as He loved us. The lengths and depths and breadths and heights of that *as?* Love without end: forgive to the "seventy times seven." Love without bottom: share to the depth of need, stopped by no sin, no shame, no problem, no perplexity. Love without limit: reach to the last man, every race and every color, every class, every social or intellectual group. Love without self: lift everyone toward God, toward heaven, toward his own best possibilities. Lift without dragging. Love from the Cross.

Love is the mark of our *identification* with Christ. We wear it as the defense worker wears his badge. "By this shall all men know . . . . my disciples." Our case is desperate if we lose our love. We don't really work on His job again until we get it back and display it again.

Love is *sacrificial,* but not poor. Love gains the life that lasts. Love lays down its own dying life, but wins a new, undying life. Love is in essence eternal life.

Sacrifice? Love knows none. Enough to be friends of Jesus.

> *Love of God, so pure and changeless,*
> *Blood of Christ, so rich and free,*
> *Grace of God, so strong and boundless,*
> *Magnify them all in me.*

WHAT DO YOU WANT OF LIFE?

Read: Ps. 4: 3-8; Matt. 5: 1-12.

Text: *Thou hast put gladness in my heart.* Ps. 4: 7.

"Dost thou love life? Then do not squander the stuff that life is made of." The purpose in Christian living is to make every day count for God and heaven. Our days are numbered. We are foolish if we throw away one of them—one hour of them, even. We shall show good sense if we make certain that we are really getting something out of life. Only a fool would live at random.

What do you want out of life? Happiness? You will find true happiness in God. Most people try to find satisfaction in money or in good times. But good times are good only while they last, and they don't last long. And the happiness money can buy doesn't go deep enough. The smile of God reaches the heart and puts a song there.

"The smile of God"? Does it sound poetic and perhaps capricious? His approval is solid reality, and is to be gained by very definite, practical means. God is not arbitrary nor incalculable. And best of all, the attitudes that He requires of us are the attitudes that are for our own best good. We would have chosen them voluntarily if we could have seen clear through.

Righteousness and trust are the two poles for the electric current of happiness. Obey God's laws and trust God's love, and your life will know fullness of joy.

Joy in God is steady and dependable. It is independent of changing circumstances. "Earth changes, but thy soul and God stand sure." Its flow is continuous, self-sustaining. Righteousness stimulates trust, and trust stimulates obedience: an endless chain of blessing.

> *Trust and obey, for there's no other way*
> *To be happy in Jesus but to trust and obey.*

WHAT DO YOU WANT OF LIFE?

Read: Gal. 5:22-25; Heb. 4:12, 13.

Text: *Man doth not live by bread only, but by every word that proceedeth out of the mouth of the Lord doth man live.* Deut. 8:3.

What do you want of life? Reality? You want to make certain that you do not drift through the days of your years without ever touching life's depths. You want to know you are not spending for trifles the precious coin of your counted heartbeats. You want to know that you will not come to the end of your allotted time only to find you have missed the real thing—life itself. If you don't want this, you should.

If we want reality we must make use of the only means God has given us—His Word. Without His revelation we should not know true values. Without the Bible we could not find the way to God. And the Bible has something to say to me personally. Only when its words become a personal revelation to me, shall I ever find reality. I must live by them. Every word of God has meaning for me.

The realities of life are not the things we see and hear and smell and taste and handle every day. The realities are the things of the Spirit: the love, the faith, the hope, the courage, the joy, the God-contact, the peace, the devotion—those attitudes that are independent of time, that vitality of the Spirit which is eternal life. These are the things men live by. Beside these "bread" is cheap.

All the earth took on new beauty
When mine eyes beheld the King.

WHAT DO YOU WANT OF LIFE?

Read: Ps. 16: 5-11; Isa. 55: 1-3.

Text: *He that cometh to me shall never hunger; and he that believeth on me shall never thirst.* John 6: 35.

What do you want out of life? Satisfaction? Variety? Fullness? You tend to become bored? You need excitement to keep you interested? You will not find what you need in the movies, not even in travel, not in seeking new and stronger thrills. You will come there to a dead end; everything human has an end. "She that liveth in pleasure is dead while she liveth." You will find what you seek by believing in Jesus. He is infinite, exhaustless, ever-varied, ever new to fit your varying moods. He will engage you in a program that ends only in eternity—and what that means who can say?

"Wherefore do ye spend money for that which is not bread, and your labour for that which satisfieth not?" This inscription should stand over every movie theater, every dance hall—perhaps over every department store and every restaurant—until people begin to weigh values. Over how many colleges and business houses—wherever men are trying to satisfy immortal hunger with earthly, human bread.

To believe on the Lord Jesus Christ is to take Him literally. It is to trust His blood for salvation; it is to trust His words for counsel. It is to find in Him your all for this world and the next. He is all to you, or He is nothing. You don't get something for nothing, but you get a greater bargain: for your poor all you get His mighty All.

> *There's no thirsting for life's pleasure,*
> *Nor adorning rich and gay;*
> *For I've found a richer treasure,*
> *One that fadeth not away.*

WHAT DO YOU WANT OF LIFE?

Read: Rom. 12:1, 2; Col. 3:1-14.

Text: *For what shall it profit a man, if he shall gain the whole world, and lose his own soul? Mk. 8:36.*

What do you want to get out of life? Full development? You have decided you cannot find satisfaction in things of earth; you have begun to experience reality in God. Go clear through. Your life will find its completeness only in the perfect thought of God for your individual life. That comes by way of an entire consecration. The miserable man is the man who goes half way.

The world doesn't stop pulling on you when you start for heaven—it pulls harder because you are pulling in the opposite direction. The price of heaven is giving up the world. What is worldliness? You know. Whatever pulls you away from God is for you worldly.

God isn't going to kill you. He isn't going to numb or deaden a single natural faculty or appetite. Swinburne was ignorant when he said Jesus had made the bright pagan world go gray and gloomy. Give all your powers to Him and He will enable you to realize every one to the full. You will be a truly "living sacrifice."

You cannot know, until you have tried it, the joy there is in living at the center of God's will. That is the normal life. The bird with wings was made for the skies.

> *All discords hushed, my peace a river,*
> *My soul a prisoned bird set free—*
> *Sweet will of God.*

WHAT DO YOU WANT OF LIFE?

Read: Rom. 13:10-14; 14:7,8.

Text: *Light is sown for the righteous, and gladness for the upright in heart.* Ps. 97:11.

What do you want of life? Light or darkness? The good or the evil? The fine, the essentially beautiful, or the coarse, the essentially repulsive? The true or the false? There are two forces battling as different as day and night, and we have to choose. We cannot be neutral. Life isn't static. In the long run one or the other gets us.

We all would turn in horror from the demons of darkness. But to escape them we must turn from their "works." We would shrink in disgust from their finished works: rioting, strife, debauchery. But to be certain of escaping them we must shrink from self-indulgence in its harmless beginnings. The only way to avoid living for the flesh is to live for Christ. The only way to escape the darkness is to live in the light.

Any amusement, any activity, in which you feel the hand of Christ taken off your shoulder is a dangerous one for you. He should always be at the controls of your life.

After all, we do not show our love of life by "taking all it can give." The truth is that we get the most out of life only as we *give*. And we can give only as we take from God; of ourselves we are frail and empty. "All our springs are in him."

We walk in the Light when we follow our Guide;
The Light of the world is Jesus.

TEACH US TO PRAY

Read: Jas. 5:13-18; Luke 18:1-8.

Text: *Lord, teach us to pray.* Luke 11:1.

More of us should have an ambition to pray effectively.
It is really possible to "move men through God by prayer
alone." Men in every age have found it so—men like us.
And it is the best way to move them. Every real achievement of the church has come through individual prayer;
every failure can be traced to lack of prayer. Why, then,
is there so little prayer?

"Prayer changes things," our mottoes say. "It doesn't
make much difference," Satan whispers. Which tells
the truth?

The first-century Christians were said to be *power-
conscious.* We are *problem-conscious.* What did they
believe about prayer? What do we?

"Praying Hyde" had a compact with God, that each
day he should have at least four souls. Was he God's
pet? Or did he just care more?

I wonder how many souls would be saved today if
we had really believed in the power of intercessory
prayer—in *our* hands.

I wonder if when we stand before the Lord to give an
account of our stewardship we shall find that some souls
are lost for lack of our prayer and faith.

Can we fail to be "alert" and escape tragedy?

> *I can no denial take*
> *When I plead for Jesus' sake.*

TEACH US TO PRAY

Read: Gen. 18:1-8; 16-22.

Text: *The effectual fervent prayer of a righteous man availeth much.* Jas. 5:16.

The first step toward effective praying is to qualify as a pray-er. Who can pray? An ordinary man—but a friend of God. For his job is to get heaven and earth together.

God said of Abraham, "I know him, that he will do what is right." A consistent, faithful Christian life is prerequisite to successful prayer. Without obedience to God's known will for ourselves we can do a good deal of wishful thinking for our friends, but no real praying. For God is not paying attention.

The man who would pray for others must himself be free from the condemnation of those for whom he prays. He cannot live in Sodom. Transparent sincerity is the atmosphere of God's presence. The minutemen of prayer are those who keep their hearts constantly under the cleansing flow.

The habit of entertaining God prepares us for the special sessions of intercessory prayer. If I take Him into all my doings, if my heart is hospitable to all His needs, He gets the habit of telling me things that need prayer and I get the habit of expecting the miraculous because I have seen what He can do. I cannot wait for an emergency, to learn to pray. I shall be unable to come for a great thing if I have not been carrying "everything to God in prayer."

Unanswered yet? Nay, do not say ungranted;
Perhaps your part is not yet fully done.

TEACH US TO PRAY

Read: Gen. 18:23-33.

Text: *If thou wilt forgive their sin—; and if not, blot me out of thy book.* Ex. 32:32.

Intercessory prayer demands man's utmost. It costs in time. The reason most of us are not better intercessors is that we haven't time to see it through. We ring the doorbell, then run away before the door can be opened.

It costs in self-denial. "Lack of time" is really an alibi. If we do not pray, it is because some other things seem more necessary: sleep or rest or work or friends or clothes or food or good times. No one can be an intercessor whose sense of values is askew. The intercessor is spiritually-minded; he really puts first things first.

It costs in unselfishness. We give up our ease for another's good. We must often pray for those who neglect or scorn us. (Abraham prayed for Lot's city that should by rights have been his own.) The moment self-interest enters, the prime leverage of intercession is gone. Even in praying for our own family we must pray for their good and God's glory, not to make life easier for ourselves.

It costs in persistence. The only way to pray through is to pray through. Try it. Take on a "prayer job," and stick to it until you know God has undertaken the case. Pray, if you must, as if the Lord were an unjust judge. Pray humbly, but desperately. When it matters everything to you, it will matter something to God.

It costs in spiritual energy and physical vitality. For it is born of burning desire and ripens into the urgency that wrestles and prevails. It risks life itself to get God's best for others.

> *Pray your way through, pray your way through:*
> *If you want victory, pray your way through.*

TEACH US TO PRAY

Read: Gen. 18:17-29; I Kings 18:41-46.

Text: *If we know that he hear us, we know that we have
the petitions that we desired of him.* I John 5:15.

*True intercessory prayer always comes to an understand-
ing with the King.* If you will pay the price to be a
friend of God, you can spread blessing as far as your
prayers can go. Do not waste a single audience. Really
believe that every word counts when you talk with the
King.

Faith grows with intimacy. But it does not depend on
maturity. A heart wide open to the needs of men and
filled with the love of God will find a way to get its
prayer through. Do not wait for a faith like that of some
mother in Israel you have known. Use your own. It will
work.

The basis of all genuine prayer is the will of God. It
is impossible to speak face to face with the King and be
other than humbly yielded to His higher wisdom. And
if we are sensitive to His voice in prayer, we shall recognize His check and stop asking when He stops encouraging.

Why does God sometimes say "No" to an earnest, im-
portunate prayer? Perhaps He has a better way to give
us what He sees we really desire. Perhaps He knows
that to give exactly what our human wisdom asks would
harm us more than help.

Is the prayer wasted when the request is denied? By
no means. It has made it possible for God to give us
what we really desire; it has frustrated the schemes of
the enemy. If we go our limit in prayer for the unsaved,
God will save every one that is savable.

> *Thou art coming to a King;*
> *Large petitions with thee bring;*
> *For His grace and power are such,*
> *None can ever ask too much.*

THE WORD OF GOD

Read: Luke 4:16-22; Ps. 119:89-96.

Text: *For ever, O Lord, thy word is settled in heaven.* Ps. 119:89.

Jesus set His seal on the Old Testament. The notion has somehow got afloat that the Old Testament is less inspired than the New, less authoritative, less of a Bible; that the New Testament only contains the truth. Actually the Bible is a whole; the Old Testament points to the New; the New fulfils the Old; and God speaks in both to the human heart.

Jesus loved the Bible; and His Bible was all Old Testament. *Deuteronomy,* the wonderful Book of the Law, which He quoted more than any other; *Psalms,* those songs of personal experience of the soul with God; *Isaiah,* the matchless vision of the suffering Saviour— He loved them all and lived by them. He taught of Moses and Jonah and Job. That Bible was more to Him than food. Surely I cannot outgrow it or become too spiritually fastidious to find truth there.

Jesus fulfils the prophecies and the types of the Old Testament. To understand Him rightly I should see Him promised from the very beginning; I should see Him filling full the types and putting an end to the temple sacrifices. I should see God's purpose being carried out through the centuries. Jesus towers highest and shines brightest when we see Him as the climax of divine revelation, as the Promised Messiah. Read rightly, the Old Testament is our best introduction to Jesus.

Nothing strengthens faith in God, or reverence for God, much more than to study Old Testament prophecies of Christ and see how exactly they were fulfilled to the letter and to the minute. The Bible is a book that shows God at work behind the scenes—with awful power.

> *O truth unchanged, unchanging,*
> *O light of our dark sky.*

THE WORD OF GOD

Read: II Pet. 1: 19-21.

Text: *Thy testimonies have I taken as an heritage for ever: for they are the rejoicing of my heart.* Ps. 119: 111.

The Bible is the great miracle. Many different authors wrote at widely different times in widely scattered places on varied subjects in varied styles. Yet their work fits together perfectly. Their interpretation of life is identical; their writings form an ordered whole, an epic of redemption with Calvary as its climax, the Resurrection its crisis, the new heaven and new earth its denouement. This could not just happen. This Book is the work of the living God.

The Bible is a Book of many authors; it is a Book of one Author. It was written by holy men; it was dictated by the Holy Spirit. It is beautiful literature, but it is more: it is inspired by God. We cannot comprehend fully how this could be. It is the unforgettable example of the way God allows men to co-operate with Him in His great saving work. He lets us write, but His big, sure hand guides our little, clumsy hand.

"The words that I speak unto you, they are spirit and they are life," Jesus said. "The seed is the Word." That electric spark which is life is resident in every word of God. A phrase that you have read a hundred times will suddenly come alive in your spirit, become a part of you, and make you forever different. The tiny seed and the tiny stone look just alike; but one has life. The seed of wheat found in King Tutankhamen's tomb after forty centuries will produce a whole wheat harvest. So of a single word of God.

But the word of God shall stand forever—
Earth with all its glory soon must pass away,
I'm standing on the never-failing word of God.

THE WORD OF GOD

Read: Ps. 119:129-136.

Text: *The entrance of thy words giveth light; it giveth understanding unto the simple. Ps. 119:130.*

The Bible is the great answer. It gives all the answers. Our heathen Saxon ancestors, when the Christian missionaries came to them, suddenly saw their lives as like the swift flight of a sparrow out of the darkness of the night through their lighted hall, in at one window, then quickly out at another—so brief, with such a dark unknown before and after. That is life without the Bible. But, they said, if these men can tell us anything of what went before and what will come after, it seems that we should heed them. Thank God for the Book that tells us why we are here and where we are going.

Because the Bible tells us the truth about the past and the future, it is the one eternal Book. It has the sweep of an everlasting kingdom. It covers time and eternity. It has been verified by history; it will be verified by history yet unmade. Perhaps, rather, we shall come to see that it verifies history. Every day it interprets history for those who read both attentively. God is working as He said He would work.

The Bible has the answers because it is written by the One who knows. To God the future is as the past; the darkness shineth as the light to Him. Foolish to question God's omniscience when we read His prophecies and His promises from Genesis to Revelation, and see them fulfilled or being fulfilled to the letter. As foolish to doubt His care, His power, His faithfulness to provide for His children to the very end.

> *Word of the ever-living God,*
> *Will of His glorious Son;*
> *Without thee how could earth be trod,*
> *Or heaven itself be won?*

THE WORD OF GOD

Read: Ps. 119: 105-112; Prov. 2: 1-9.

Text: *Thy word is a lamp unto my feet, and a light unto my path.* Ps. 119: 105.

The Bible is the perfect guide. The Bible contains everything one needs to know to come through life safely and successfully. You may be young and inexperienced, you may not be very wise, but if you build your life on Bible principles you will come out ahead of many a cleverer man.

Dare to trust the Bible standards. They are right; they are there because they are absolute and unchanging. Perhaps they seem unreasonable; sometimes they are costly; but they work every time. Much cheaper for a young man than the trial-and-error method is to obey the Bible red lights and green lights.

I really believe God knows more than I do. That is why I trust His judgment on my problems. That is why I look for His solutions. I believe I shall find in His Word a principle to fit every problem. I should fear to run my own life at random.

The Bible has the answers because it deals with the moral and spiritual issues of life. Those are the questions that really bother us. We can live and die in peace and safety without measuring the distances of the stars or counting the ages of the glaciers; but we must know how to recognize and meet temptation, how to fight the battles of today, how to live with our fellow men, how to face our God at last. For every moral problem—for every problem you must have solved—the Bible will not fail you. It was written for you.

> O teach Thy wandering pilgrims
>   By this their path to trace,
> Till, clouds and darkness ended,
>   They see Thee face to face.

THE WORD OF GOD

Read: II Cor. 3:1-8.

Text: *The letter killeth, but the spirit giveth life.* II Cor.
3:6.

The Bible is living seed. The history of the Bible translations is a thrilling story of heroes who have risked
their lives. We are proud of the beauty of our King
James Version, of the accuracy of our modern versions.
But the best of all translations is the translation into human lives; without this all others fall short.

The Bible is translatable into everyday living. And
many can read this translation who could read no other.
Many are reading this every day. By this translation
each of us has an opportunity to preach the gospel daily,
hourly. With what care must we read our Bible. With
what prayer and faith and love must we water the seed.
For this translation is in terms of life; these are living
epistles we are writing.

Not only is the Bible translatable into lives; it must
be so translated. It is alive, but it remains as good as
dead until it is tested, tried, acted upon, proved. The
glorious Word of God will remain a dead book to us
until we make it ours, and the truth we profess to live
must pass through us if it is to mean anything to others.

The Bible is dead if not translated into lives; more
than that, it is deadly. If we know the Word of God and
fail to act on it, the savor of life unto life becomes to us a
savor of death unto death. If we "hold the truth of God in
unrighteousness"—misinterpreting, holding back, just doing nothing with it—we bring upon ourselves "the wrath
of God." It is dangerous to have the Bible and do nothing
with it.

> *Words of life and beauty,*
> *Teach me faith and duty—*
> *Wonderful words of life.*

GREAT MOMENTS

Read: Mark 9: 2-8.

Text: *They saw no man any more, save Jesus only with themselves.* Mark 9: 8.

Life's great moments are its high mountains. In every Christian experience there are a few great moments that stand out from all the rest, moments that have changed the course of our lives. They are the moments when we managed to forget our crowd and their ideas, ourselves and our own wishes, and got a revelation of God and His truth and His will for us, of Jesus Christ and His love and its meaning for us. We saw the Cross; we saw heaven. We breathed heavenly air and looked from a higher point of view. That view has not changed; only we have come down into the dust and confusion.

They are poor indeed who never have had great moments of revelation. Great moments are reality. For behind the scenes is eternity. Faith is not believing what isn't so. It is shutting your ears to all the lying things that are not so, and opening your eyes to the things that are gloriously, eternally real. Faith sees Jesus.

Faith is living logically. *If* the unseen, eternal things are the real and lasting, then what? *If* Jesus is God and is with me always, then how should I live? Faith dares be consistent. Faith accepts the challenge and lives as if Jesus were who He is.

> *Since my eyes were fixed on Jesus,*
> *I've lost sight of all beside;*
> *So enchained my spirit's vision,*
> *Looking at the Crucified.*

GREAT MOMENTS

Read: Isa. 6:1-8; Ex. 24:12-18.

Text: *And look that thou make them after their pattern, which was shewed thee in the mount.* Ex. 25:40.

Great moments make great service. Life exhausts faith; vision renews faith. And without faith we are defeated: "This is the victory that overcomes, even our faith." Would you increase your faith? Take a fresh look at Christ.

Vision conditions service. Work without vision is treadmill drudgery. How many are working hard—at good things, but all the windows of their souls are shut and the blinds are down. Christ would make us sharers; He would tell us something of what it's all about. His servants have free souls.

We can perpetuate the vision of our great moments by keeping saturated with the Word of God and the presence of the Holy Spirit. Day by day, as we read the Bible under the Spirit's guidance, Moses and Elias can constantly testify to the deity of Christ. Day by day we can be conscious of the living Christ with us. We can keep the glow of the vision constantly renewed. For we are on this side of Pentecost.

"Up on the mountain" and "down in the valley" do not represent for the sanctified Christian a vacillating "up-and-down experience." His mountain is not the mountain of ecstasy, but the mountain of vision; his valley is not the valley of the dumps, but the valley of service. Mountain and valley are the normal intake and outgo of the Spirit in the Christian's life; if either is lacking, he stops breathing spiritually.

> *Vision without service is a dream;*
> *Service without vision is ashes.*

GREAT MOMENTS

Read: Mark 9:17-27.

Text: *Bring him unto me. . . . If thou canst believe, all things are possible to him that believeth.* Mark 9:19, 23.

Effective service is service in the presence of Jesus. "Bring him to me." What does it mean that we bring our problems to Jesus? It means that in every conflict with Satan we have the power of the shed Blood to plead; that in the moment when Satan lays claim to the soul we are praying for, we remind the enemy, "There is a fountain filled with blood."

What does it mean that we "bring him to Jesus"? It means that we can confront Satan with the authority of the Name of Christ. He fears that Name. It means that we confront the world and tackle our problems with the spirit of Christ. That spirit melts hearts and untangles human snarls.

What does it mean that we "bring him to Jesus"? It means that when our prayer seems inadequate, we realize the Christ praying with us at the right hand of God. It will clinch our faith.

It will mean everything to our service if we realize Jesus with us—if we begin to realize what that means.

Where is your "If" placed? "If Jesus can do?" Or, *"If* I can believe?" Jesus transfers the responsibility to us. The "If" is not with Him. As we live much in His presence, we shall find ourselves surer and surer of Him and His power. We shall be willing to accept His placing of the *If.*

> *Tempt not my soul away—*
> *Jesus is mine.*

OVERCOMING TEMPTATION

Read: I Peter 5: 6-11; II Cor. 11: 14, 15.

Text: *Resist the devil, and he will flee from you.* Jas. 4: 7.

The first step in overcoming temptation is to recognize your adversary. Do not think the devil is dead, or a myth. He is a powerful enemy set on ruining you, and he knows you better than you know yourself. Reckon with him.

Satan does not always speak in a diabolical whisper. He often uses worldly-minded people as his instrument. The "world" is "society organized apart from God." Its spirit is defined in Jesus' words: "How can ye believe, which receive honour one of another, and seek not the honour that cometh from God only?" Watch that spirit and beware of it.

Jesus' temptations were those of a sanctified man. They were all to do legitimate things at the wrong time or in the wrong way. Do not ever think entire sanctification ends temptation. The devil now hides his bait in seemingly good things; he words his suggestions in Scripture language. He knows you have no desire for evil things; he will try to poison your good.

My one desire is to do God's will and to advance His kingdom. Nothing would please Satan better than to see me using his weapons to do this. For after all, he knows better than I do that the Kingdom is of the spirit, and if I conquer with the wrong spirit I have hurt the Kingdom more than I have helped it. That is why propaganda and unkindness and display and insincerity seem out of place in the work of the church.

God does not need success so much that He must see truth or love or purity go by the board.

> *We will not fear, for God hath willed*
> *His truth to triumph through us.*

OVERCOMING TEMPTATION

Read: Heb. 2:9-18; Luke 4:1-3.

Text: *God is faithful, who will not suffer you to be tempted above that ye are able; but will with the temptation also make a way to escape, that ye may be able to bear it.* I Cor. 10:13.

The second step in overcoming temptation is to believe God is with you. Real temptation is to the limit of our endurance. When the unendurable, impossible trial comes, the blinding, confusing situation that makes God seem unjust and you utterly mistaken in all your faith and hopes —in that hour hold steady and remember: This is not abandonment nor despair; this is temptation—and God has a way out.

Anything less acute than this utter failure of human resources might be difficult to bear, but it would not be the severe test through which I must be put to toughen my spiritual fiber and display the grace of God. Jesus went through this kind of temptation, and I ask no less. God's eye is upon me and His arm underneath. I will endure temptation.

Jesus was tested as a man, and as a man at his weakest. We excuse our failures because we were "tired" or "nervous." But He conquered not as a strong man but as a great believer. The body is closely connected with the mind and spirit; admit that, and then remember grace. When human resistance is low, divine grace is available, if we count on it.

Watch Satan's "If." It is that "If" that makes temptation deadly. *"If* you belong to God, surely He will not want you to suffer"; *"If* you belong to God, surely—."* When Satan has instilled in your mind a doubt of God's care or wisdom for your case, he has you blinded.

I need Thy presence every passing hour;
What but Thy grace can foil the tempter's power?

OVERCOMING TEMPTATION

Read: Rom. 8:1-9.

Text: *The carnal mind is not subject to the law of God, neither indeed can be.* Rom. 8:7.

The third step in overcoming temptation is to obtain and keep a sanctified heart. Self is crucified at the mourner's bench, but Satan would resurrect it. We keep self dead in everyday living by continually choosing God's will, not ours. There is a cry of the body, a cry of the mind, a cry of the spirit—a legitimate cry to be heard. The body cries for ease: Satisfy self. The mind cries for understanding: Justify self. The spirit cries for action: Do it yourself. But not out of God's will. Satan must know that we act now under God's direction only.

There was needed a Saviour for the Kingdom before the King could ascend His throne. Jesus was scheduled for a cross; He could not get by with a crown. If you are called to preach, you cannot get by with making money to pay some other preacher's salary. Death once for all to your own preferences, and that death confirmed daily, is the price of victory.

Temptation will try to reach you through every part of you—and temptation will not be over for you until you have been proved in body and mind and spirit, and have finally satisfied Christ's claim to be Master of your whole self. He is watching, and for your help He has sent His Spirit.

> *Did we in our own strength confide,*
> *Our striving would be losing,*
> *Were not the right Man on our side,*
> *The Man of God's own choosing.*

OVERCOMING TEMPTATION

Read: Matt. 4:1-11.

Text: *Then was Jesus led up of the Spirit into the wilderness to be tempted of the devil.* Matt. 4:1.

The fourth step in overcoming temptation is to see that God is using temptation to test and prove your Christian character. The temptations of the Christian worker: (1) God has forgotten me. (2) God will do it all. (3) I must do it all.

"Sooner or later every preacher must face the bread-and-butter problem and fight it through."—E. E. Angell. Yes, and every Christian; for he cannot give whole-hearted service while he is anxious about himself. And there is always the possibility that he will some day sacrifice truth for bread.

Sooner or later every Christian must face that "sin of presumption" which would have you cast yourself into the abyss of the day's cares and pleasures without the parachute of prayer, and expect God to keep you; have plenty of time for the funnies and the radio but none for Bible study, yet expect to have Scripture in your mind to defeat Satan in the hour of temptation; invest nothing in the means of grace, yet expect to become a strong Christian.

Sooner or later every Christian worker must settle whether he is to win his world by compromise or by conquest. Begin to give up some of your convictions in order to win your unsaved friend, and you have to go farther and farther; you have made a Munich pact. Christ owns no half-victories.

"Christ's temptations contained in essence all temptations known to man: (1) misuse of power, (2) misapplication of faith, (3) misappropriation of means."—H. Orton Wiley. Think it through.

To him that o'ercometh
God giveth a crown.

OVERCOMING TEMPTATION

Read: Luke 4: 4; Ps. 119: 11; Ps. 19: 7-14.

Text: *Stand therefore . . . . taking the shield of faith, wherewith ye shall be able to quench all the fiery darts of the wicked. And take . . . .the sword of the Spirit, which is the word of God.* Eph. 6: 14, 16, 17.

The fifth step in overcoming temptation is to know and use your Bible. Use God's "It is written." There is a command to fit every situation. It sounds very plausible: "How do we know what is right today? Different groups lay down different standards." Satan can quote Scripture texts, but he never gives the sense of the whole. There is a *Bible principle* by which to settle every question.

"You can't always think your way out of a spiritual tangle; you can always obey your way out." Stand on conviction, on the known command of God, whatever seem the complications, and you cannot be defeated spiritually.

Finally, and always, *use the shield of faith.* Remember Andrew Murray's rules for times of temptation or trouble. Say:

> I am here—
> By God's appointment
> In His keeping
> Under His training
> For His time.*

We can overcome some temptations so completely that the devil will not bring them again. In fact, complete victory is permanent victory. We should be advancing and fighting for new territory.

> *God's truth abideth still;*
> *His Kingdom is forever.*

*From *Young People's Standard*

56

MY MIGHTY DELIVERER

Read: Mark 4: 35-38.

Text: *He was in the ship asleep . . . .; and they awake him.* Mark 4: 38.

Jesus is more than a match for all our circumstances. Having Jesus in my life is no insurance against trouble or distress. In fact, I may have more trouble just because I am a Christian. Certain it is that I could escape some persecution and reproach by not following the Master too closely. But having my Lord in the boat of my life is assurance that the schemes of Satan cannot destroy me. God is not going to abandon His Son, nor any who are loyal to His Son. He will bring me through.

Do not let the devil scare you when he blows up his hurricanes. The Lord is *always* going to let circumstances be too much for you. It is true there is no way out: your work is gone, your business is ruined, your health has failed. But God—God is there.

Temptation is real, and it is stronger than we are. There is no way out, humanly speaking—else it would not be temptation. God must make a way of escape; and He said He would. Remember to look for His way out. Look up, not around.

"It is when we find ourselves in a situation which we cannot meet without God that we really pray. If we can get along without our petition, we do not really pray."—S. Young.

We are not always very brave in our dark hours; all too often we get panicky. But so long as we keep Jesus with us, we shall not despair and jump out of the boat. Christians do not commit suicide; they pray. It pays to stay within hearing distance of Jesus.

No waters can swallow the ship where lies
The Master of ocean, and earth, and skies.

February 13

MY MIGHTY DELIVERER

Read: Matt. 8: 26, 27; Mark 4: 39-41.

Text: *Why are ye so fearful? How is it that ye have no faith?* Mark 4: 40.

If we will look at Him and not at the circumstances. Have the difficulties piled up until it seems as if Jesus has slept too long? Hold steady and trust. We have said it before, we will affirm our faith as long as we live: Help will come "in the nick of time." (Heb. 4: 16).

Scared? Panic-stricken? Jesus says that means little faith. Eyes on the waves? Then very much like us; for circumstances often seem to determine our faith! Or was the poet speaking for some one else when he wrote:

How easy when sailing the sea in a calm,
To trust in the strength of Jehovah's great arm;
But somehow I find when the waves swamp the boat,
It takes some believing to keep things afloat!

The disciples did not know their Lord very well; they had not lived through Easter nor Pentecost. We should hold steadier than they did. Sanctified faith sings and rejoices; for it has been purged of doubt and it sees a mighty Christ.

Is your name "Little Faith"? Then sometimes your Lord looks at you with disappointed eyes and speaks in a reproving tone. It is not for your weakness He condemns you, but for your failure to trust His power. His command was to receive the Holy Spirit of power.

"Faith is ever bold. Unbelief is always timid." Loud praying can be a sign of timidity or panic. Faith has the quietness of confidence, the poise of assurance.

"Hold fast to faith; what else is there?"—R. Babson.

> *Keep on believing—Jesus is near;*
> *Keep on believing—there's nothing to fear.*

58

MY MIGHTY DELIVERER

Read: Mark 5:1-19.

Text: *For this purpose the Son of God was manifested, that he might destroy the works of the devil.* I John 3:8.

Jesus is more than a match for the devil's power in human lives. He is not mocking when He gives His preacher the message for you, "Look unto me and be saved." The habit that binds you fast He can break. If you even look His way with a sense of need, He will come and find you. For He loves and prizes *you*.

If men really want His kind of deliverance. Jesus knows that spiritual miracles cost heavily in material wealth—and He believes they are worth it. This is not a popular idea. Rather, my business first, and the odds and ends of my time and money for God. No miracles are wrought in lives that want them cheap. By our choices we open the way for Jesus to make our lives miracles of His grace, or ask Him to go away and leave us our ease, our security, our wealth. It is not by accident that some Christians' lives are perpetual miracles; they let go of things and let God work.

Not always is it deliberate, calculated selfishness that hinders Christ from working miracles. Just the multiplicity of legitimate business and plans and programs can so fill our vision that we do not recognize Him when He would come among us. Our lives can become so crowded that we scarcely feel the Spirit's urge to prayer for revival and for souls. Lord, stay with us. Do not depart out of our coasts because of our dullness and deadness to the spiritual needs about us!

> *Here I give my all to Thee,*
> *Friends and time and earthly store—*
> *Wholly Thine forevermore.*

SELECTED—CONTACT WITH CHRIST

Read: Luke 6: 12-16.

Text: *He called unto him his disciples.* Luke 6: 13.

Jesus trained His disciples in a threefold relationship: to Himself, to needy men, to material things. I too would learn of Him in all three aspects; for life will soon apply the same threefold test.

Jesus teaches by personal contact. The best education is personal contact with a great teacher. We still can have that kind of training from Christ. We can hear Him speak through His Word; we can see how He meets the demands upon Him of trying situations; as we watch His work we can catch glimpses of our own. Let us never divorce our Christian work from Christ; never do Christian service with methods Christ would not own.

Jesus selects His own class of learners. You cannot use Him as Teacher till you have found Him as Saviour and accepted Him as Lord. Many would claim His teachings today, but He owns only those who come through the Blood of the Atonement.

The Christian who has had a call to Christian service must first of all maintain direct contact with Christ. Otherwise the call becomes vague and irksome. "Jesus is all I need"—but I need Him real.

Jesus prayed before every crisis in His life and ministry; He prayed before He "met His class." Surely I should do no less. Time spent with God gives perspective, clear insight, right judgment, poise of spirit, strength of purpose. If Jesus needed to take time to ascertain the will of God, what can be said of us who dash into our most momentous undertakings half-cocked and self-confident?

> *To walk with God no time is lost—*
> *Walk on!*
> *To talk with God no breath is lost—*
> *Talk on!*

SERVING—CONTACT WITH MEN

Read: Luke 6:17-19.

Text: *There went virtue out of him, and healed them all.*
Luke 6:19.

Jesus teaches by the laboratory method. "A charge to keep I have"—words for every Christian, not merely for the preachers. Christ has more to teach you if you still think salvation all privilege. Your relation to Christ involves responsibility and a sense of obligation. You are saved to serve; He is Master as well as Saviour.

The Christian never can pass by on the other side. Jesus taught by example that every needy person encountered must serve as a test case in the laboratory of grace. His follower must never lose the sense of the challenge of need. How did you react to the last person who told you his trouble? Did it worry you, bore you, or challenge you? Grade yourself accordingly.

If you will first go up into the mountain with Jesus, He will come down with you to the valley. If you have the assurance that He has called you and commissioned you, you can endure as seeing Him who is invisible. Before prayer the wheels dragged heavily; after prayer the grind is illuminated and the routine transfigured.

Do not forget when you face the impossible case that you are not just yourself. You are yourself plus all the resources of God that you have faith to claim. The point of view that Jesus teaches is inner sufficiency: face every ugly fact and every overwhelming situation with victory, He says, for "I am with you."

> *Faint not nor fear, His arms are near;*
> *He changeth not, and thou art dear.*

SACRIFICE—CONTACT WITH TRUTH

Read: Luke 6:20-36.

Text: *Blessed be ye poor: for yours is the kingdom of God. Luke 6:20.*

Jesus teaches by direct instruction a new standard of values. Sacrifice is the key word for the Christian worker's attitude to earthly things—and every Christian should be a "worker." Should missionaries be expected to sacrifice all and we nothing?

The photograph of Christ's representative is supposed to resemble His followers in any age. See if it looks like you. He lives in the Beatitudes: he is humble, hungry (for truth), mourning (over the world's sin), unpopular (with a certain crowd); yet he is happy and rejoicing. His reward is in the future; his only wealth is the spiritual satisfactions of the kingdom. "Poor, yet making many rich"—he comes of an ancient, noble line. What would Jesus have to say today to those who are preparing for Christian work, yet are full of frivolity, fashion, worldly ambition?

Lord Beaverbrook, owner of the most influential London newspaper, peer and millionaire, is quoted as saying recently, "The evangelist is the man who has the greatest opportunity for doing good, and if I were in a position to influence the life of a sincere young man today I would say to him, 'Rather choose to be an evangelist than a cabinet minister or a millionaire.' When I was a young man I pitied my father for being a poor man and a humble preacher of the Word. Now that I am old I envy him his life and career."

> *In Thy service pain is pleasure;*
> *With Thy favor loss is gain.*

SHARING—CO-OPERATION WITH JESUS

Read: Luke 6:37-49.

Text: *And why call ye me, Lord, Lord, and do not the things which I say?* Luke 6:46.

Jesus pays most attention to the morale of His disciples. More important in preparation for service than homiletics or theology is training in fundamental attitudes. You settle that you are not going to fear poverty nor people enough to compromise with evil, that you are not going to fight with the devil's weapons of harshness, censoriousness, retaliation. You bargain for poverty, reproach, unkindness; you pledge in return patience, faithfulness, love. No enemy can down a man who has no self-interest.

Jesus is fair and wise. He tells us the worst at the outset. He invites us to cold, hunger, weariness, pain. And He knows He cannot scare us with these, for He is offering us something to live for and something to die for.

Jesus tells His men that they are engaged in a co-operative, profit-sharing enterprise. They are to invest all they have in the Kingdom; but they can know that the Kingdom belongs to them finally. They are not hirelings but part-owners, and their spirit must show it.

Jesus trains His disciples to look to the end of the way. Wendell Phillips' friends were begging him after a lecture engagement not to return home that night. It was late, cold, and stormy, they reminded him, and he must travel several hours to make it. "But at the other end," he returned, "I shall find Anne Phillips." The other end will be worth all the sacrifice and strain; Jesus would have us strong in the thought of it.

> *Just one glimpse of Him in glory*
> *Will the toils of life repay.*

63

SPECIFICATIONS FOR SERVICE

Read: Luke 10:1-9.

Text: *Behold, I send you forth as lambs among wolves.*
Luke 10:3.

The Servant Spirit. Jesus cares as much how we do our Christian service as what we do. Our spirit counts for more than our doctrine. The worst enemy of the full gospel has been the harshness or selfishness of some of its exponents. As soon as Jesus thought of sending out His preachers, He "therefore" thought of their preparation.

Jesus gives ten maxims for "servants." Are they *your* Ten Commandments?

1. Prepare the way for Jesus—do not attract people to yourself.

2. Learn to do things by prayer—use prayer as your first resort, not your last.

3. Keep the vision of lost, but savable souls—see the world with the eyes of a reaper.

4. Work by love and gentle means—win rather than drive.

5. Die to selfish ambition—yours is not a money-making job.

6. Concentrate on your job—you're not in it for a social good time.

7. Avoid partiality—bring blessing wherever you go.

8. Do not fight your own battles—let God defend you.

9. Die to your independence—be willing to "live of the gospel."

10. Do not be fastidious or fussy—learn the lesson of contentment.

"These are they who, being poor, depend only upon God; being humble, they obtain strength from on high; being meek, they have that courage which does not require outward show to bolster it up to meet any danger—not even death itself. The meek both live and die as becometh men who have an understanding with God."—J. B. Chapman.

> *Gladly will I toil and suffer,*
> *Only let me walk with Thee.*

SPECIFICATIONS FOR SERVICE

Read: Luke 10: 17-20.

Text: *Behold, I give unto you power, and nothing shall by any means hurt you.* Luke 10: 19.

The Conqueror's Tread. Expect victory over the devil. Or the old adage will catch up with you in your undertakings for God: "Blessed are they who expect nothing; for they shall not be disappointed." Carey's motto is better: "Expect great things from God; attempt great things for God." The pessimists are not the most effective Christian workers.

But base your confidence on a firm foundation. *Learn to conquer through the name of Jesus.* Pray not hopefully because conditions look better, but believingly because Jesus died for sinners and sent the Holy Spirit to fight your battles. Get a seeker through, not by using effective psychology on him, but by pointing him to the Blood. Be bold in proclaiming the Word, not because you have influential friends in the community, but because you have the authority of Christ behind you. Use His name.

Never preach to others what you do not know in your own experience. Always keep your own connection clear with heaven. Sincerity is power.

Christ has no favorites, but He fights at the side of the man who keeps His commandments. Rather, that man has built his life into the eternal, unshakable Rock; he has enlisted in the army of the Invincible Leader. Nothing can cause to fail the man who actually shapes his life by the principles of God.

> *Conquering now and still to conquer,*
> *Rideth a King in His might;*
> *Leading the host of all the faithful*
> *Into the midst of the fight.*

SPECIFICATIONS FOR SERVICE

Read: Luke 10: 21-24.

Text: *For it is not ye that speak, but the Spirit of your Father which speaketh in you.* Matt. 10: 20.

The Child's Faith. "We need no greater message than this: Jesus Christ, the Saviour of the world." Do not expect substitutes to improve on it.

What the Word of God says is really true even when it seems preposterous. "What my daddy says is so *is* so even if it ain't so!"

Of course the "old-time religion" of the gospel of Christ is "good enough"; for it is real and eternal. Some people think they have got away from this "conservatism." They are "modern"; they will find a message better adapted to this modern age. Really they are only contemporary, and their religious fad will die like every other fad.

"Every occupation, plan, and work of man, to be truly successful, must be done under the direction of Christ, in union with His will, from love to Him, and in dependence on His power" (Mueller). How much more our work for God.

"He took it upon himself"—the oft-told story of those men and women of missions who have accepted the challenge of a country without the gospel, a leper field, an unopened continent. "He took it upon himself"—it is the description of the Christlike Christian. He can escape responsibility, but he will not. Every new need met is a new burden, but he accepts it. What have you "taken upon yourself" of late to do for God?

> *Were the whole realm of nature mine,*
> *That were a present far too small.*

GOD'S GOOD PURPOSE

Read: Eph. 2:1-7; Gen. 12:1.

Text: *According to the eternal purpose which he purposed in Christ.* Eph. 3:11.

The upward climb of the redemption of the lost race from sin and its penalty. Let us trace the steps. We still are traveling this road.

First God. A God who sees the end from the beginning, whose thought spans a vaster scope than our finite minds are capable of grasping. His plans are for the ages and for eternity.

God purposes to redeem the race from the slavery into which it has sold itself. His own Son must break the chains; but to spread the news He purposes to use men. Men had failed Him before—had failed themselves; now men must be found who will appreciate and co-operate. We can have a share in helping Him save His world from itself.

God purposes to found a nation which He can use as a witness. He succeeded once. We owe the Jews a debt which never can be paid; for they brought us one God— a holy God; a purposeful God; a saving God. Since Pentecost His "nation" is His Church. May we do as well our task of bringing Christ to the world.

God purposes; but He doesn't stop there. He brings to us what He purposes. He selects His men; He guides them; He uses them. He works with them and for them; and sometimes He must accomplish much with very faulty human instruments. "That the excellency of the power may be of God and not of us." It rests me to know that the real work is done by God. I need not be feverish in my activity.

> *The way the holy prophets went,*
> *The road that leads from banishment,*
> *The King's highway of holiness,*
> *I'll go, for all His paths are peace.*

GOD'S GOOD PURPOSE

Read: Gen. 18:17-19; Heb. 11:8-10.

Text: *By faith Abraham . . . . went out, not knowing whither he went.* Heb. 11:8.

When God honors a man with His choice it is because He sees both what the man is and what he will become as he walks with Him. He sees a man who will appreciate God's blessing, who will trust God's judgment, who will obey God's command without knowing all the "whys." He sees a man who will "command his house," a man who can wait and be patient, a man who will keep God first in his life. He is choosing men like that today wherever He can find them. With such He can work—and they are not so common.

Great as God is, strange to say, men can thwart all God's gracious purposes or they can actualize them. The promise is good, but it is not fulfilled unless men show resolution and action. "They went forth to go into the land of Canaan; and into the land of Canaan they came." It has a businesslike sound. And we have to do good business with God to get results.

"He went out, not knowing whither he went." A fearsome risk—except that God was holding the map. Abraham was a man like us—no stronger, no bolder— and he took the risk that every one takes who sets out to walk with God, a risk that turns into a simple formula: *Trust and Obey.*

The one permanent thing in all our changing world is a personal relationship with the unchanging God. And the only way to this relationship is a personal covenant of righteousness. We keep His ways; He keeps our feet.

> *When we walk with the Lord*
> *In the light of His word,*
> *What a glory He sheds on our way.*

GOD'S GOOD PURPOSE

Read: Gen. 11:26-32; 12:1-5.

Text: *Surely blessing I will bless thee.* Heb. 6:14.

It is a great day in a man's life when he begins to walk alone with God. For God is certain to catch him up into His purposes. He has begun to make something of him above the "effortless average."

What a host of "family" Abram has (Gen. 11:26 ff.); but only Abram hears God's call. Abram's obedience brings blessing to all the rest. So will yours if you are faithful. The rest do not realize it now; perhaps they think you are the black sheep. Hold steady. Give God time.

God's call is always a call to greatness. Eventually the faithful Christian becomes great. "They that be wise shall shine as the firmament."

Walk with God, and you will have influence! Hold steady, and people you never dreamed of will turn to you for help—for they will recognize in you a strength that is more than human.

Always God's call is a call to be blessed. The faithful Christian is inside the promise, "All things work together for good to those who . . . . are the called according to his purpose." This is not "Christian science, falsely so called," which denies the reality of evil, but Christian chemistry, which transmutes persecution into strength of soul, and sorrow into new knowledge of God; which gives beauty for ashes, the oil of joy for mourning, the garment of praise for the spirit of heaviness. "Who is he that shall harm you if ye be followers of that which is good?"

> *He comes to make His blessings flow*
> *Far as the curse is found.*

69

GOD'S GOOD PURPOSE

Read: Gen. 12: 6-9.

Text: *Thou shalt be a blessing.* Gen. 12:2.

Always God's call is to bless others. The promise seems extreme? "In thee [in one man] shall all the families of the earth be blessed." But it proved true. Through Abraham came the moral law, and through Abraham came Jesus. No promise of God is extreme if we will wait to see it through. Through the weakest of us God will start circles of influence and blessing that will go on forever. There are humble prayers that have saved souls at the ends of the earth in heathen lands, prayers that have transformed kingdoms. One such might be yours.

Abraham an ideal? Far from it, from our point of view. But what wonderful things God has accomplished with persons who seem to their fellows—and justly—to be full of faults. Let us not be quick to discount the work of any man whom God is using.

A promise delayed is not a promise broken. Build another altar and remind God that you are depending on Him. Stay put.

It is great to own a future as well as a present. Sinners cannot do that; even the present becomes the past, and they lose it. Get adjusted to God's eternal future, and you have something that will last.

Suppose Abraham had failed anywhere along the line. Suppose he had stopped at any point on the journey —tired, apprehensive, disheartened, fearful. He had every excuse—but too bad for us! No alibi is weighty enough to justify a man for ruining a plan of God.

Let Goodness and Mercy, my wonderful God,
*   Still follow my steps till I meet Thee above;*
I seek, by the path which my forefathers trod
*   Through the land of their sojourn, Thy kingdom of*
*   love.*

70

A SECOND-GENERATION CHRISTIAN

Read: Gen. 26:1-6.

Text: *I am the God of Abraham thy father: fear not, for I am with thee, and will bless thee . . . . for my servant Abraham's sake.* Gen. 26:24.

The story of Isaac is the story of a "second-generation" Christian. Most of us are second-generation Christians. History tells us that has been the danger period in every church. Can we learn anything from Isaac?

The son of a godly father starts life with an advantage. Blessing was promised to Isaac because Abraham obeyed. I thank God for the prayers, the faith, the example of righteousness and consecration and answered prayer and joy in the Lord that are my heritage. They have gone far toward setting my feet in the right way. I was born as it were tabernacling on the road to Canaan; shame indeed if I turn aside to lesser privilege.

The second generation need not have a second-hand experience. A choice is set before me as definite as ever was set before my father. It is for me to choose whether or not I will have my father's God. And when I choose Him, He becomes my God as really as He was my father's. I have a revelation on my own account. I find my father's God still answers prayer.

You have taught your children the way of the Lord, you have lived the Christian life before them, you have prayed for them—but you cannot be saved for them, nor bring them up into the Kingdom. Every individual has to meet God for himself and make his own covenant with God. He must choose the blessing or the curse. God help parents to make so strong an impression that children will see what they are choosing.

> *Faith of our fathers, holy faith,*
> *We will be true to thee till death.*

71

A SECOND-GENERATION CHRISTIAN

Read: Gen. 26: 7-16; Ps. 118: 5-9.

Text: *Trust in the Lord with all thine heart; and lean not unto thine own understanding.* Prov. 3: 5.

The story of Isaac is the story of "Everyman." He fights the battles we all must fight. He faces the temptations we all must face, and learns the lessons we all must learn. He is very human, but he wins his fight through grace. Watching him, I take courage.

It is one thing to choose God's way; it is another thing —and a longer process—to learn God's way. He does not adjust His way to my human point of view; I must adjust my nature to His thoughts. I learn slowly, sometimes even by "trial and error"; but if I hold fast to Him, every experience will bring me new understanding of the way God works.

I learn from Isaac that a promise must be won by faith and patience. It is not human nature to wait. We think God should work overnight. God cannot be hurried, for He is doing it right.

Isaac is human enough to worry about the future, and to scheme to protect himself—before he thinks to ask God's help. We are never in such danger that we need do anything shady in order to escape.

Sinners see the folly of Christians' driving sharp bargains or making elaborate excuses. They expect God to fight His children's battles, and are surprised that they do not use Him more. There is a simple dignity about the man who really trusts God, which the world admires in spite of itself.

After centuries of God's care for His children we should know better than Isaac. We should be less "human"; we should trust God's protection first. But do we?

> *I loved to choose and see my path; but now,*
> *Lead Thou me on.*

A SECOND-GENERATION CHRISTIAN

Read: Gen. 26:17-25.

Text: *Now the Lord hath made room for us, and we shall be fruitful in the land.* Gen. 26:22.

The story of Isaac is the story of every humble, sincere Christian. He chooses to be a "pilgrim"—and that in a day when "adjustment to environment" is the popular slogan.

He is not ashamed of the "old-time religion," not afraid of being called an "old fogy," not trying to be "modern." For he has seen his father's religion work, and he knows he has hold of the real thing.

He counts on meeting with opposition if he is to follow the Lord's program. He knows the world is no friend to grace.

He refuses to fight back or defend himself. He has learned that if a man is in the Lord's will he can trust God to give the necessary favor with men.

He refuses to grab for himself. He knows that when God gives "room" there is real peace and lasting; when a man—or a nation—tries to corner more than his share, there is only insecurity and resentment.

He is a real peacemaker. We usually think of the peacemaker as the go-between who patches up a quarrel between two others. That ideal might encourage the busybody. The real peacemaking is to keep flowing from your own life a current of peace and love that will cause peace and good will to spring up wherever it comes.

> *If I live a holy life,*
> *Shun the wrong and do the right,*
> *I know the Lord will make a way for me.*

A SECOND-GENERATION CHRISTIAN

Read: Gen. 26: 26-30.

Text: *We saw certainly that the Lord was with thee.*
Gen. 26: 28.

*The story of Isaac is the story of a conqueror, who won
out by holding on.* The inner victory comes always before the outer. If the circumstances of life are proving
too much for you, get a fresh vision of God, a fresh sense
of His presence, a fresh reminder of His unchanged
covenant. It is like God to give you that reassurance
after trial and patient endurance. Then,

> *Keep holding on, keep holding on;*
> *The victory will soon be won.*

Hold on with confidence. It is astonishing how quickly things work out once you get the victory in your own
soul over your circumstances.

Hold on when your persecutors are the most pro-
voking. If you can stand it a moment longer, you will
find they were just on the point of yielding when you
thought them the strongest.

Hold on until your enemies can see how your God has
delivered you. Sinners admire a Christian when they
have tried him out, and they are convicted of their own
need. This trial is your opportunity to glorify God.
Perhaps you will never have another like it. Hold on a
little longer!

> *He'll take you through, however you're tried,*
> *His tender care is never denied;*
> *Then always trust His promise so true—*
> *He'll take you through.*

A SECOND-GENERATION CHRISTIAN

Read: Gen. 26:31-33; Heb: 6:11-20.

Text: *Blessed are the peacemakers; for they shall be called the children of God.* Matt. 5:9.

The story of Isaac is the story of a knight who has won his spurs. He has gone through the series of tests of faith, devised by the enemy and permitted by God, and he has come out on top. The greatest wealth he has gained is not his flocks and herds, but his knowledge of God. He has earned the right to add his name to his father's. Henceforth men are to speak of the "God of Abraham *and Isaac.*"

We must every one of us go through our probationary period of testing when we prove our own purpose and God's faithfulness. What will our title be?

Our God is the God of the grains of sand as well as the God of the interstellar spaces. Every jot and every tittle counts with Him. What I do today will have its bearing on the vast whole of God's purposes; what I sow today will be yielding its harvest tomorrow. My obscure little strand will perhaps show up all too plainly in the finished web.

The world often gets its judgments crossed and tangled. Eternity will straighten them out. Only be sure what you are writing up there is all you will want it to be.

The battle is not always won with shouting and blare of trumpets. Many quiet, unobtrusive lives all over the world are winning victories that will swell the song of triumph of the Lamb. Enough that He gets the record.

> *Not to the strong is the battle,*
> *Not to the swift is the race;*
> *But to the true and the faithful*
> *Victory is promised through grace.*

75

CLAIMING THE BIRTHRIGHT

Read: Gen. 25:29-34; Gen. 27:18-34; Heb. 12:14-17.

Text: *Esau despised his birthright.* Gen. 25:34.

"A calm hour with God is worth a whole lifetime with man."—R. M. McCheyne. We all can have the birthright of Jacob. We can choose to have God, whatever else we lose. It is a good Jewish bargain!

The making of every life begins with a choice. For that freedom to direct his steps Godward is what lifts man above the brutes. What have you done about your birthright?

Everyone would like, in general terms, to have God with him. Every army of the world would be glad to have "God on our side." That is, we want God when we need Him to help us out. But there are times when His presence would be inconvenient; and always it is costly.

The first step toward having God in our lives is setting a true estimate on His blessing. Jacob was full of faults, but he appreciated God; and God stood by him. The real rose, bedraggled and torn, has a living quality which the perfect artificial rose lacks. The sincere Christian with all his faults is ahead of the best "moral man." He has reality.

Why is it that God burst into your life when you were going on your way not thinking of Him at all? It was not accidental; He is not partial; He does not waste His grace. Perhaps your parents had sent you out with their prayers and faith; perhaps God had read the real desire for Him in your heart. Every outreach to Him is noted and answered.

> *I have made my choice forever:*
> *I will walk with Christ my Lord.*

CLAIMING THE BIRTHRIGHT

Read: Gen. 28:10-15.

Text: *Behold, I am with thee, and will keep thee in all places whither thou goest.* Gen. 28:15.

"If you lose your sky, you will soon lose your earth." "Realizing the presence of God"—to many people the phrase suggests some vague mystical rapture, some ecstatic trance unrelated to living, a waste of time, nonsense to the "practical" man. Actually, relationship with God is intensely practical; it counts in living as does no other force. *Practical* is not a synonym of *seen* or *material*. *Practical* is *workable*. Electricity and radio are practical; so is God.

God with us is *prosperity*—in the long run, when all the reports are in and all the upheavals past.

God with us is *influence*. How much one man's choice of God can mean! It can open the gracious privileges of the gospel to a whole family line, to a whole generation, to a whole nation. Suppose John Wesley had not insisted on knowing God—or John Knox—or Dr. Bresee— or Charlie Soong. Or that person back in your family somewhere who headed it Godward.

God with us means that life has a *guiding star* and a sure destination. It means hope, it means a purpose in living, it means confidence through all apparent contradictions. Men are hungrier for that than for food.

And being in the presence of the living God is certain to make us different persons—bigger, finer, truer.

> *My Father is rich in houses and lands,*
> *He holdeth the wealth of the world in His hands—*
> *I'm a child of the King.*

CLAIMING THE BIRTHRIGHT

Read: Gen. 28:16-22.

Text: *Surely the Lord is in this place.* Gen. 28:16.

"No public feast with Him can compensate for the loss of the private interview." "One short hour" in His presence will transform our whole outlook on life. "We kneel, how weak; we rise, how full of power." When we are up against life there is nothing that will give us morale like realizing God. Why do we blunder through our days without that reassurance?

The life that has been touched by the presence of God bears the marks. It reacts in:

Awe. It is not boisterous, loud, overbearing. For it has seen its own littleness and God's greatness.

Gratitude. It is not self-confident, self-assured. For it has realized its dependence on God.

Worship. It is not slow to seek the place of worship. For God has become real.

Giving. It is not stingy. For it recognizes its great debt and wishes to return something to God.

Our fathers found glory and joy unspeakable in personal communion with God. Must we settle down to a formal religion of church-going and social service? Jacob found the same face-to-face relationship that Abraham and Isaac had known.

And it looks as if not one generation need be skipped. For now it is the God of Abraham, Isaac, *and Jacob.* Have you left a gap where *your* name should come?

> *Pass me not, O God my Father—*
> *Let Thy mercy light on me;*
> *Even me.*

CLAIMING THE BIRTHRIGHT

Read: Gen. 32:1-12.

Text: *The angel of the Lord encampeth round about them that fear him, and delivereth them.* Ps. 34:7.

God's host. "God's host"—many never see them, nor dream that it is possible to live a life over which heavenly agencies keep watch. The angels of God can be on your track—behind and before; they will be if you have chosen a God-related life.

Jacob had many faults, but he could not live without God, and God did not forget him. Perhaps you are discouraged with your failures; you cannot forgive yourself your shortcomings. But if you know you have to have God, God knows it too, and so long as you hold to Him, He will not let you go.

"I've got to look out for myself. If I don't, nobody else will." It has a strangely familiar ring. Self-preservation is our first instinct. Like Jacob, we first "send messengers." "Nobody else is going to look out for me." But perhaps God will!

Well for us when we face life's "impossible" circumstances—and we all face them—if we have the habit of prayer. Pity the man facing his emergency who has not cultivated the prayer habit when things were going fairly smoothly. It is hard to learn to use your weapons after the attack is on.

The leverage in prayer for God's protection can never be our worthiness. Faith's leverage is our knowledge of God: past help, past guidance, past revelation, past promise yet unfulfilled—all tell us God will not fail us now. God's mercy is our only plea.

> *Thro' many dangers, toils and snares*
> *I have already come;*
> *'Tis grace hath brought me safe thus far.*
> *And grace will lead me home.*

CLAIMING THE BIRTHRIGHT

Read: Gen. 32:22-32.

Text: *I will not let thee go, except thou bless me.* Gen. 32:26. *Thy name shall be called no more Jacob, but Israel.* Gen. 32:28.

God's X-ray diagnosis. When we reach the place of helplessness before God, He can show us what He sees in us. The picture is not flattering, but it is as accurate as any X ray. See it, recognize it, acknowledge it—and the next step is transformation.

We do our utmost to make things right, but after our best doing we are conscious of a desperate lack; the fundamental help we need must come from God only. Life's tangles are too stubborn to be unraveled by human skill.

God's love tells us the truth. Do you want to know the worst of your case? Or would you rather be comfortable without being right? You can know by the kind of preaching you like best. When we are in earnest with God, He will be in earnest with us.

A blessed heart makes it possible for God to bless a man with things. And He loves to bless. But He will never put second things first.

There is blessing for each of us to the limit of our need. The world, the flesh, and the devil, and most of all our sluggish self, will struggle to make us rest contented short of that best. God has the "Prince" nature and a "Prince" life for us if we will refuse to take anything less.

> *Like Jacob in the days of old,*
> *I wrestled with the Lord,*
> *And instant with a courage bold*
> *I stood upon His word—*
> *I would not be denied.*

THE PRINCIPLE OF FORGIVENESS

Read: I John 4: 7-11; Matt. 5: 23, 24.

Text: *Then said Jesus, Father, forgive them; for they know not what they do. Luke 23: 34.*

Forgiveness is a fundamental, necessary principle of our sinning, erring world. Like the rhythm of ebb and flood tide is the rhythm of offense and forgiveness. Christ makes the prayer for forgiveness one of the essential petitions in His model prayer. I cannot overlook it.

The one who will not forgive hinders God in His great work of forgiveness. He obstructs the flow of healing to his own heart and he retards its flow to other hearts. For any man finds it hard to believe God has forgiven him so long as his offended brother is nursing the offense.

Forgiveness—or the need of it—does not depend on time. Forty years does not heal a wrong. Sin is never settled until it is forgiven.

"I never beg anybody's pardon." But you need forgiveness just as much. You will always be in debt until you ask.

Christians must forgive. For to forgive makes us truly Godlike. It proves us children of the God whose favors are not dependent on our deserving. Our readiness to forgive stands in direct ratio to our desire to be like our Father.

"If he hadn't done so much," you say. But forgiveness is not in ratio with the injury done; rather, with the size of the heart and its inner resources.

> *Five bleeding wounds He bears—*
> *"Forgive him, oh, forgive," they cry,*
> *"Nor let that ransomed sinner die!"*

81

OUR NEED OF FORGIVING

Read: Gen. 45:1-4; 9-15; 47:11, 12; Eph. 4:29-32.

Text: *I will cry unto God . . . . that performeth all things
for me.* Ps. 57:2.

Christians can afford to forgive. Foolish not to forgive,
foolish to hold a grudge, when we know nothing done
to us can really harm us. God has assured us that all
things—evil as well as good—shall work together for
our good. We can afford to forgive if we have faith in
God's providence. In fact, our failure to forgive would
make it impossible for God to include us in His good
purposes.

Unforgiveness stems from unbelief. If we must nurse
a grudge, we do so because we do not believe God fights
for us; we want to work out the "vengeance" ourselves.
So we put ourselves outside the pale of those who are
"the called according to his purpose," for whom "all
things work together for good."

We cannot afford not to forgive. We need to forgive
more than others need our forgiveness, for the most important thing to a man is his own spirit. He cannot afford to have a heart that is filled with rancor.

We cannot afford to be bothered with an accumula-
tion of hurts and grievances. They will only rankle and
fester until our capacity for joy will atrophy and our capacity for pain will increase. And we do not have to
stoop to pick up every hurt.

"In many things we offend all." We come from different backgrounds and have different notions; we shall
all need forgiveness at some time. Let us lay up a store
of kindness. And we must forgive others before we can
be forgiven by God; the man with a grudge in his heart
is unable to receive forgiveness.

> *Man may trouble and distress me;*
> *'Twill but drive me to Thy breast.*

THE GRACE FOR FORGIVING

Read: I Sam. 24:4-19; Acts 7:59, 60.

Text: *Who forgiveth all thine iniquities.* Ps. 103:3.

We can't forgive without God's help. Circumstances will always be bigger than we are; and they will wreck our lives if we let them. We are defeated without God. We need to count on God—and we can.

It is one thing to talk of loving your neighbor as yourself—loving and forgiving; it is quite another thing to make it concrete when the actual life situation arises. The Golden Rule isn't exactly automatic, self-starting, self-adjusting; it has to be worked. How about a program to build up the "Golden Rule habit"? You set the switches, and keep them set. God will furnish the power.

We do not have to stay hurt. Christ came to heal the broken-hearted as truly as to save from sin. It is part of His work; and we can claim it definitely. We can soar above life's hurts.

Healed of the Lord, the spirit of healing can flow from your life. That is forgiveness. It does not wait until men repent before it feels the disposition and the desire to forgive.

Forgiveness cannot be forced; it flows from within spontaneously. It comes from a heart of love. It is of no use to preach the duty of forgiveness; but we may well live its beauty, until men grow hungry for a forgiving heart.

> *More about Jesus would I know,*
> *More of His grace to others show.*

THE MANNER OF FORGIVENESS

Read: Gen. 45:5-8; Col. 3:12-17.

Text: *Now therefore be not grieved, nor angry with your-selves . . . . ; for God did send me before you to pre-serve life.* Gen. 45:5.

Forgiveness "blesses him that gives and him that takes." Forgiveness heals the wounds the devil has made; for-giveness breaks the fetters the devil has forged. For-giveness plays a joke on the devil, and sets two souls free.

There is something cleansing about the act of forgive-ness, and something liberating. The man who forgives puts himself out of reach of the harm of false friends, un-just criticism, unkind treatment. He is bigger than them all. Forgiveness is part of "the glorious liberty of the children of God."

It is a big-hearted man who forgives, and a big man who asks forgiveness. And it is a great moment when these two meet.

There is a right way to forgive. "But he was wrong!" Of course he was wrong. Forgiveness is not calling wrong right; it is not condoning sin. But it is not your job to show him his wrong. That is the Lord's job. Let Him do it.

There is a graciousness about real forgiveness. It does not "rub it in" nor make the offender feel small. It makes him feel that you love him. It somehow turns his mind to God rather than to you and what you have suffered.

Forgiveness shows itself in deeds as well as in words. It treats the sinner as if nothing had happened. It does not pretend to forget, but in remembering it overcomes evil with good.

Forgiveness is love in action.

> *There's a wideness in God's mercy,*
> *Like the wideness of the sea;*
> *There's a kindness in His justice*
> *Which is more than liberty.*

March 11

ALL THINGS FOR HIS GLORY

Read: Gen. 41:46-52.

Text: *For God hath caused me to be fruitful in the land of my affliction.* Gen. 41:52.

There is a Christian use of all things. Most of life is spent outside the church. But "Egypt" is used in God's plan. We are still on a physical earth, still inhabiting earthly bodies, still eating and drinking and wearing clothes, still carrying on God's work with the currency of this world, still worshiping God in buildings of wood and brick and stone. There are practical needs to be met and practical decisions to be made. The better our religion, the more workable it should be for earth as well as for heaven.

We are expected to make such use of the natural resources of this life as will honor God. There is a loose, slipshod, careless way of daily living that is "a scandal to the gospel" (Moulton's version of Titus 2:5).

The governing principle for the management of our everyday affairs is *stewardship.* God has given me wealth —in many forms; I am not free to waste, nor even to spend according to my fancy.

The governing principle for the use of the good things of this world is *temperance.* I do not for conscience' sake shut myself up in a monastery, eat bread and water, and wear a plain garb. But neither do I revel nor gormandize. From harmful indulgences, total abstinence; in good things, self-control—this is the God-given rule, and truly wise men follow it.

Back of all true stewardship is *gratitude.* In prosperity the sincere Christian remembers his debt to God. Some men God cannot trust with prosperity; for they forget. "How much I owe!" Dollars cannot pay the debt, but they can express something of our gratitude.

> *How much I owe for love divine—*
> *I cannot tell how much I owe.*

March 12

ALL THINGS FOR HIS GLORY

Read: Gen. 41: 53-57; 45: 16-28.

Text: *And we know that all things work together for good to them that love God.* Rom 8: 28.

God works through all things. Much of life is made up of disappointments and upsets. But God will use "famine" for our good. Without the famine, the long-lost son never would have been found, nor the family reunited. Without the famine Joseph's brothers would have lived and died with a weight of unforgiven sin on their consciences. Without the famine Jacob's sons would have remained petty patriarchs and Abraham's line would have become obliterated. Without the famine the family would not have been unified in a foreign land—unified and made family-conscious. Without the famine God's plan for Israel and the world could not have been carried out. Thank God for famine if God is in it! And when tempted to complain, remember that God sees to the end.

A wonderful testimony, that of Joseph, as he looks back over the years of his long apprenticeship—and how often we chafe under the strain of such years: "God hath made me *forget* all my toil and my father's house"; "God hath made me *fruitful* in the land of my affliction." That double divine marvel of forgetfulness of evil and fruitfulness in spite of evil changes for the believing heart all loss to gain.

The man who has followed God's directions in prosperity is safe in adversity and has strength to hearten others. God's Word has many promises for the day of famine; but they are always for those who have been true to Him in the time of plenty.

> *In the midst of affliction my table is spread;*
> *With blessings unnumbered my cup runneth o'er.*

ALL THINGS FOR HIS GLORY

Read: Gen 46:1-7.

Text: *Fear not to go down into Egypt; for I will there make of thee a great nation.* Gen. 46:3.

God turns all things to blessing for His children. Most of life is spent among sinners and worldlings; most of the world is non-Christian. But God will use Egypt to feed us.

There is a sense in which our enemies, and God's, will become bread for us. We must not hope to escape contacts with sinners, for we are living in a sinful world. But we are not here to be fearful, cowardly, shrinking, longing to flee away to heaven or to the wilderness. We are here to face temptation and grow stronger. We are here to witness for God, and in doing so to strengthen our faith and kindle faith in others. Egypt is not to dominate us; we are to dominate her.

It is easier always to crumple and cower. It is not sinful to be timid; it is sinful to yield a principle because of timidity. The man who is utterly Christ's need fear for no future; no circumstance can prevent your bringing glory to God if you insist. The scarecrows are all of Satan's making.

We Christians never can be supercilious or superior in our relations to those who do not know the saving power of God. "But for the grace of God"—that marvelous grace we never shall fathom—we are no better than they. And we owe much materially, socially, politically to the efforts, often to the sacrifice, of men who are not Christians. We shall always be debtors. But, thank God, we can be servants, ministers, feeders. Such as we have we can give.

> *His might thy heart shall strengthen,*
> *His love thy joy increase;*
> *Mercy thy days shall lengthen;*
> *The Lord will give thee peace.*

CONSISTENT CHRISTIANS

Read: Jas. 1:17-25.

Text: *Of his own will begat he us with the word of truth, that we should be a kind of firstfruits. Jas. 1:18.*

More than human. What do we mean by a "consistent Christian life"? With what is it consistent? A Christian life is consistent when it is worthy of God's supply and of faith in that supply. A king's son is not consistent when he lives like a beggar.

Our Father is perfect—God. What kind of representation do we give of Him? Poise? steadfastness? dependability? Or whim? uncertainty? changeableness? unreliability? God expects us to build a life in His likeness. "A truly religious life is a mirror in which Christ sees His own image."

God has invested largely in us. He has given us everything, and He looks for returns in Godlikeness. Everything God gives us is perfect; let us give Him in return as near perfection as we are capable of. Let us not soil the beautiful light of God as it passes through the prisms of our lives.

We were "born again by the word of truth"; we trusted the Bible absolutely in order to find God. We shall grow in grace by trusting the same Word. Therefore let us be "swift to hear." Bible Christians are consistent Christians.

Following our own notions and the notions of others will make us one-sided and unbalanced. If we build by the Word of God we have some chance of poise, proportion, symmetry in our Christian character. It is not enough to admire the Bible. Act on it; graft it into your very nature. Make it a part of you. Live by God's plan.

Make me more like Thee, Saviour, make me more like Thee;
That others in my conduct Thine image clear may see.

CONSISTENT CHRISTIANS

Read: James 2:14-17.

Text: *Faith, if it hath not works, is dead, being alone.*
Jas. 2:17.

Judged by our fruits. "Conviction, were it never so excellent, is useless till it convert itself into conduct."—Carlyle. But every smothered conviction atrophies into weakness and sin.

The Greek word for character, *ethos*, means literally *action*—we have it in *ethics*. It was their way of saying that the only good impulse you can call truly yours is the impulse on which you are willing to act. You must prove your character and make it your own by action as the homesteader used to prove his land by working it. If you are deeply stirred by a missionary talk and do nothing about it, you lose something fine from your own nature.

You remember the boy who watched the minister nailing up a vine and admitted he was "just waiting to see what a minister says when he hammers his thumb"? Some boy is watching you, and listening.

If you are living to please God, you may not please everybody else, but you will influence people toward God. "If more Christians were Christians like you, more sinners like me would be Christian." (This from a sinner to a Christian who was a "sample copy of the gospel he preached.")

They say that during World War I for some unexplainable cause the sweet-smelling musk lost its fragrance. Once it was known and loved everywhere; now it is rarely seen. Sadder by far the tragedy that many Christians have lost from their lives the fragrance of Christ. Men look to them because of their profession, but find nothing. They are a disappointment to others, to themselves, and to Christ. The fragrance is kept by simple obedience.

> *I'd rather see a sermon*
> *Than hear one any day.*

CONSISTENT CHRISTIANS

Read: Jas. 4: 13-17.

Text: *To him that knoweth to do good, and doeth it not, to him it is sin.* Jas. 4:17.

Act today for eternity. "If there is any good that I can do to any living being, let me do it today. Let me not neglect or defer it; for I shall not pass this way again."— George Fox.

We cannot build a character with good intentions. Yet a surprising number of us think we do so. We judge ourselves in terms of the good we mean to do, and forget that we never actually find time for it.

Procrastination is so natural and so human—can it be sin? But it is God's Holy Spirit that prompts. How long can we shove Him aside?

It is our omissions that form the cloud which gradually shuts God out of our lives.

We can live too hard in the *things* of today and tomorrow with their fluctuations and their ups-and-downs. The business of life has a way of swallowing up its soul.

Guard well your conscience. The goal of the Christian life is character; character is based on conscience; conscience lives as convictions are obeyed. "All of us must be careful lest our religion spoil our morals. Many people accept religion as a system of indulgences to shield them from the rigorous demands of moral law. Every moral lapse loosens character."—H. E. Rosenberger.

Walk whole-heartedly in all the light you have. It is a slow and difficult process to replace moral fiber.

> *Take time to be holy;*
> *Speak oft with thy Lord.*

CONSISTENT CHRISTIANS

Read: Jas. 1: 26, 27; 3: 1-10; 5: 12.

Text: *If any man seem to be religious, and bridleth not his tongue, ... this man's religion is vain. Jas. 1: 26.*

Honor your word as if it were your God's.

> *Of the unspoken word thou art master—*
> *The spoken word is master of thee.*
> —Arabian Proverb

The tongue is the danger point. Most of us could be pretty good Christians if we had only our hands and feet and ears, and even our eyes, to worry about. Better include in our consecration a special article giving our tongue to God for His use only, and review that article every day, with prayer. For man cannot tame it.

They used to give us a good rule to govern our speech. Before retelling a bit of news ask yourself three questions: "Is it true?" "Is it kind?" "Is it necessary?" The result is less talk, but more prayer.

"In the multitude of words there wanteth not sin"— and foolishness and emptiness. How many of us have gone to our rooms after a social gathering and told the Lord we wished we had talked less, and asked Him to let no harm come of any heedless remark! Better, perhaps, if we prayed beforehand to be kept from those heedless words.

The most solemn word you ever utter is the one by which you profess yourself a Christian. Guard well that word, and profane it no more than you would profane the marriage vow. It associates you henceforth with God Himself.

> *All for Jesus! all for Jesus!*
> *Let my lips speak forth His praise.*

KING OF KINGS AND LORD OF LORDS

Read: Mark 11:1-11.

Text: *Blessing, and honour, and glory, and power be unto him.* Rev. 5:13.

King of Kings. The kingdoms of this earth are rocking and reeling—more than that, they are disappearing. We long for a kingdom that cannot be moved; we would have a king that we know will not be dethroned tomorrow. Here He is! When the things we have counted on as sure have slipped from our grasp, when the government we have counted on to protect us crumbles and falls, Christ our King will remain unconquered and unconquerable. His kingdom is forever.

The past centers in Him; it was foretold that He should ride on the "colt, the foal of an ass." The present obeys Him; the owner yields his property unquestioningly. The future fulfils His word: Jerusalem has fallen, but His kingdom grows.

Past, present, and future—He is Lord of all time. Other dictators have their period of rising and then of falling. He continues ever; there is no risk in casting your lot with His fortunes, for He is not subject to fortune.

He is King forever. He is a King who knows. For prophecy and near execution, the long view and the short range, the glorious plan and the nettling details— all are clear to Him; there is neither guessing nor fumbling. I can trust Him in general and in particular.

Power and dominion to Him that shall reign!
Glory and praise to the Lamb that was slain!

KING OF KINGS AND LORD OF LORDS

Read: Luke 19:28-40.

Text: *Prince of Peace. Of the increase of his government and peace there shall be no end.* Isa. 9:6, 7.

He is a King of peace. He rides a peaceful animal; His triumphal procession is made up of those who give freely of what they have. The Caesars filled their triumphs of war with chained enemies whose failures they paraded openly; Cleopatra let the asp kill her rather than be dragged in such a train. But there is no compulsion in Christ's service; I am freest when I yield my will to Him.

He is a King of love. A famous painting pictures war as a great chariot set with gems and drawn by proud horses, on which earth's conquerors (Alexander, Caesar, Napoleon, Genghis Khan) ride over a field of naked corpses. Christ's sway does not ruin His subjects; rather, He takes the palm branch of everyone who honors Him and makes it a royal carpet. "In the King's hands poor gifts wax infinite."

He is a King who demands unquestioning, even blind obedience. "The Lord hath need of him" (of you, of your possessions) is enough.

He is a King who accepts public, extravagant, universal praise. When our testimony is halting or reluctant it may well be that behind the scenes Jesus is saying, "If these keep silent, the stones will cry out."

Jesus is more than example; He is King. If Palm Sunday has any message, it is the deity of Jesus Christ. Let us realize it more fully; evangelical Christians can become Unitarianized practically by forgetting its implications.

> *Blessings abound where'er He reigns;*
> *The prisoner leaps to loose his chains;*
> *The weary find eternal rest,*
> *And all the sons of want are blest.*

KING OF KINGS AND LORD OF LORDS

Read: Matt. 21:4, 5; Zech. 9:9, 10.

Text: *And he hath on his vesture and on his thigh a name written, KING OF KINGS, AND LORD OF LORDS.* Rev. 19:16.

Prophet, Priest and King. Jesus has three sides to His nature. (Unconsciously the people acknowledged this when they sang "Hosanna"—for the Priest; "in the name of the Lord"—for the Prophet; "Son of David"—for the King.) He cannot be taken partially. If you will not have Him as Prophet and Priest, you cannot have Him as King. You cannot look for Him to save politically if you will not have Him to save spiritually. His theocracy is based on spiritual rightness.

Prophet, to tell us God's will for our lives, and so dictate our standards of right and wrong; Priest, to mediate between God and us, and so do away with our sins; King, to claim our personal loyalty and faithful service, and so give purpose and meaning to our lives— all this Christ is to us. He will be "all and in all"—and "if He is not 'all,' He cannot be 'in all'."

Prince of Peace. Conferences and plans to guarantee permanent world peace are uncertain. Earthly heralds of peace are limited in their outlook and their power. Thank God, our hope is fixed in the Prince of Peace. In the right time, in the right way—He will not fail.

Peace without righteousness is unsound. At its heart are smoldering fires of discord that will flare up into a flame of war. So peace can come only as individual hearts are freed from the seeds of hatred.

He is our Prince of Peace in the midst of war.

Jesus, Saviour, reigneth forever and ever:
Crown Him! Crown Him! Prophet and Priest and King!

KING OF KINGS AND LORD OF LORDS

Read: Luke 19:41-44.

Text: *If thou hadst known .... in this thy day, the things which belong unto thy peace!* Luke 19:42.

Not word alone makes Him our King; the shouting crowd fell away in time of testing. There is no complete loyalty until after the cross and through personal faith in the cross. So our nation which prays for peace will find the Prince of Peace through repentance and heart-searching and spiritual revival. The way to lasting peace is through the Cross.

Sooner or later it will happen always to the nation or the individual that will not have Christ's rule: "desolate," abandoned, "Ichabod" written over the door. But all who will have His will may have peace. The song of the angels was, "Peace on earth to men who please Him."

If we only knew, what we really want is what God wills for us. The people's spontaneous choice for king was the same as God's choice. They chose Jesus for His deeds of mercy, of healing, of self-forgetful love; for His words of truth and His pure, shining spirit. To serve Him is to find one's own best good.

"If thou hadst known" all God's good thoughts for thee! But you can know only by taking Jesus for better or worse. Obey today's humble, unpalatable command, and you are headed for blessedness.

Life is activity. Not singing about Christ tells the story of what He means in my life, but the sort of things I invest my energies in, and the spirit I show in day-by-day living. He is an everyday Saviour.

In your hearts enthrone Him,
Lord and Master own Him—
Crown the blessed Saviour King of kings.

THE LAST WEEK

Read: Matt. 21:1-11; 33-46.

Text: *Behold, thy King cometh unto thee.* Matt. 21:5.

As we approach the end with Jesus, reality stands out clear-cut before our eyes. It is the reality of our day too. Every day men are dealing with Jesus. Every day He is being judged—and He is judging. Let us not be deceived; let us not look with idle sight. Those last days were lived for us.

We see men classifying themselves. According to their attitude to Jesus men fall into fixed groups. There their picture is taken; there they are identified forever. We have only a short time to choose our permanent classification. Then "what we have written we have written."

There are *Jesus' helpers.* They get the colt and bring it back as He commands. They serve Him at His need. They do not understand His orders; but they trust His word—and find Him true.

There are the *crowd-followers* who do what "everybody is doing." They are Christian when it is popular to be Christian. Rather dangerous to follow the crowd, for you don't know where it will lead you. It will make you a Christian today and a crucifier tomorrow.

There are the *nominal Christians*: the husbandmen who reject their Lord; the servants who are false to their trust; the church members who would not know Christ if He came to church. They have the form of godliness; in the name of Christ they are running a human enterprise. To run it His way would be too expensive.

> *Hark! What meaneth the sudden call,*
> *"What will you do with Jesus?"*

THE LAST WEEK

Read: Matt. 22:1-10; 26:6-16; 69-75.

Text: *Wheresoever this gospel shall be preached in the whole world, there shall also this, that this woman hath done, be told for a memorial of her.* Matt. 26:13.

We realize the omnipotence of free choice. There are the *excusers*: the indifferent many whose lives are too full to have room for Christ and His blessing. They hear the gospel call, but they ask to be excused. Excused from what? From eternal life and everlasting joy.

There is the *traitor*, who deliberately sold his Lord. Impossible! Yet a habit of compromise, a self-deception that tries to serve God and Mammon, will blind the eyes and callous the heart until men do things they never would have dreamed of. Lucifer was once an angel.

There are the *loyal few.* They do not understand; they are bewildered by the storm. But they know they love their Lord and trust His love. They fail and falter, sometimes when He needs them most. But they have learned one thing: they cannot live without Him. If they stand by long enough and claim His promise, they will receive the stabilizing gift of the Holy Spirit.

Out of the groups stand *individuals.* Jesus knows me by my name. I can be Mary, forgiven much and loving much; or I can be Judas, unappreciative of all He has done for me and all the opportunities He has given me. I can be openhearted Peter, weeping bitterly and repenting sincerely of my sin; or I can be weak Pilate, choosing deliberately to please the crowd rather than Christ, and risking the consequences. No one gives me my name; I choose it myself. But the name I choose here is the name I must be remembered by.

My Jesus, I love Thee, I know Thou art mine;
For Thee all the follies of sin I resign.

THE LAST WEEK

Read: Matt. 26:17-68.

Text: *Then said he, Lo, I come to do thy will, O God.*
Heb. 10:9.

We see Jesus the Son of man, and realize what manner of
men we should be as we follow in His steps. Watch Jesus
as He goes His way those last days, quietly independent
of praise or blame. Can I follow Him? He gets His orders from above. He obeys the word of God to the letter,
pleasant or unpleasant; He does His duty, easy or difficult. He carries out the divine will, even to the cross. He
walks alone in the midst of the crowd, keeps His God-
appointed course, holds to that unseen line known only to
God and Himself.

In His obedience He does not become hard, self-absorbed, fanatical, rigid. He cares for His friends, He
provides for His loved ones; He touches God. His life
is fed from hidden sources; He has strength for His own
needs and strength to give to others. He fights His battles
behind the scenes, and He loves to the end.

He meets injustice, strong in the will of God. Calm,
unwavering, unresisting, he submits to treachery, humiliation, shame. Undeserved, but accepted once for all as
part of God's will for Him. Shame is honor, and injustice is glory if part of His plan for us.

Can we follow Him? If so, we shall see on the other
side that God used it all. He will not waste our consecration.

> Let the beauty of Jesus be seen in me,
> All His wonderful passion and purity;
> O Thou Spirit Divine, all my nature refine,
> Till the beauty of Jesus be seen in me.

THE SEVEN WORDS OF THE GARDEN

Read: Matt. 26:36; Matt. 14:23; Mk. 6:46; Luke 6:12; 9:28.

Text: *I go and pray.* Matt. 26:36.

"I go and pray"—Jesus' Prayer Habit. Jesus' first, natural resource in crisis was prayer—natural then because it was His daily habit. Many would pray in trouble —in today's bitter sorrow—but they do not know how to come in the emergency because they have not practiced in the usual.

Jesus' habit of prayer was not the fulfillment of routine duty; not a good practice recommended to Him by some older saint. It was real conversation with a real Person who understood Him and loved Him, and just as spontaneous, practical, and helpful as that kind of conversation would be to you and me. Prayer is just that sort of privilege for us. Let us not shrink it into something less.

Need we be reminded again that if Jesus prayed in His crisis, we are a bit over-confident if we assume that because we are "saved and sanctified" everything will run along smoothly, and our "sanctified judgment" will work spontaneously? Every sanctified human faculty needs frequent oiling from above to function in a superhuman way in the crisis.

"Don't fit prayer into your life; build your life around prayer."

> *From every stormy wind that blows,*
> *From every swelling tide of woes,*
> *There is a calm, a sure retreat;*
> *It is the blood-bought mercy-seat.*

THE SEVEN WORDS OF THE GARDEN

Read: Matt. 26:37-39; Luke 22:44, 45.

Text: *My soul is exceeding sorrowful, ... if it be possible*— Matt. 26:38, 39.

"My soul is sorrowful"—Jesus' Burden. If you are a mother or a father, you know the sin of one child can break your heart. Multiply that sorrow by uncountable millions, and you will have some faint idea of the burden that weighed down Jesus' soul—even unto death. Remember that His agony measures His recoil from the horror of sin; it measures the Father's eternal refusal to look upon sin. Can we play with sin? take chances with it? think it "cute"?

It was His burden for sinners that made the joyful, joy-giving Jesus also the Man of Sorrows. We should know both His type of joy and His type of sorrow; both are signs of a deep Christian. Usually the one whose joy is only surface gaiety is the one whose sorrow is only surface selfishness.

To have a general negative yieldedness to the will of God is not enough; you must rise to learn His will in specific positive acts of obedience. You can escape the supreme issue of the cross if you never have "set your face to go to Jerusalem." But if you have loved His will in the drive of your life, you will come to the place where He can ask of you your all.

When the supreme test comes do not draw back, evade, and make excuses; draw close to God and make certain it is His will. Then you can go through with a steady heart. Here Jesus says, "If it be possible, let the cup pass." A few moments later He says, "The cup that my Father gives, shall I not drink it?" There is love in that declaration, and victory.

> *Love in that story so tender*
> *Clearer than ever I see.*

THE SEVEN WORDS OF THE GARDEN

Read: Matt. 26:39, 42.

Text: *Nevertheless, not my will, but thine be done.* Luke 22:42.

"If it be possible—nevertheless, thy will be done"—Jesus' Submission. In Jesus' prayer the struggle and the yielding came in the same breath; the personal request and the choice of the Father's will. It should always be so. Never risk asking God for anything without quickly adding, "If it be Thy will."

The will of God was Jesus' passion; He came to earth to do it. And the will of God is the ruling principle of every sanctified man's life.

This word of submission does not mean that heart and flesh may not be torn with unspeakable anguish at the cost of our "yes." Jesus was human as well as divine, and we are human. The devil will taunt us for our weakness; Jesus will understand.

The steps of praying through a personal problem: (1) Love the will of God. (2) Make sure of the will of God. (3) Rest in the will of God. (4) Do the will of God. And remember, "The love of God is always wise."

How glad I am that Jesus did not choose selfishly in Gethsemane; there would have been no hope for my soul. And today perhaps some soul is depending on me not to choose selfishly. I can be sure of it, for God does not waste sacrifice. He will use what I give.

> *My Jesus, as Thou wilt;*
> *O may Thy will be mine!*
> *Into Thy hand of love*
> *I would my all resign.*

THE SEVEN WORDS OF THE GARDEN

Read: Matt. 26:40; Luke 18:1; Col. 1:24-29.

Text: *Watch with me.* Matt. 26:40.

"Watch with me"—Jesus' Need and Ours. Yes, Jesus could struggle through without human fellowship; He did. And His saints can struggle through without our sympathy and understanding today; they are doing it. But they are human, and they feel. Your missionaries giving up all to go, forgotten by many while there, coming back homeless and healthless—watch with them. One missionary said, "After we've been gone about so long, the letters stop. They forget."

To stand by Jesus in Gethsemane is to learn to pray the prayer of intercession. If you decide early in your Christian life that you will always be found at the prayer meetings; if you learn early not to limit your prayers to yourself, but have a definite prayer list and pray your friends through; if you make prayer for missions a part of your Christian program—you will not backslide; you will not even be an "up-and-down Christian."

Jesus has won the victory of grace over sin in the sense that the final outcome is certain. But the battles are going on; there is one in the place where you live. We still can "stand by Jesus." If you will pray and believe and seek the Father's will, He will know and be grateful yet.

> *O watch and fight and pray,*
> *The battle ne'er give o'er;*
> *Renew it boldly every day,*
> *And strength divine implore.*

THE SEVEN WORDS OF THE GARDEN

Read. Matt. 26:41, 43, 44; Eph. 3:13-21.

Text: *The spirit indeed is willing, but the flesh is weak.*
Matt. 26:41.

"The spirit is willing; the flesh is weak"—Jesus' Understanding. It was time to sleep—as natural human beings. But it was time to wake—as friends of Jesus. A pastor said at the beginning of an altar service, "My only dependence (outside of God) is on the people of God and their standing by." Jesus may excuse you, but He'll miss you.

I know that "Jesus understands" and will forgive me if I fail. But I'd rather have His faith in me than His excuses for me; I'd rather have Him depend upon me than apologize for me.

Shall we impose upon His understanding sympathy? Here are two statements; both are true if we are real Christians with ordinary human bodies. But the order in which we put them can make all the difference in the world in our Christian service.

"The spirit is willing, but the flesh is weak"—read it so, if you want to use your poor health as an excuse from prayer meetings and prayer jobs.

"The flesh is weak, but the spirit is willing"—read it that way, and you will find your spirit reaching up to God to strengthen you for tasks to which you feel unequal, and if you are not well enough to pray and fast and attend public services as you used to do, to show you new and blessed ways in which you can stand by.

> *He gave Himself to save His own;*
> *He suffered, bled and died,*
> *Alone, alone.*

103

THE SEVEN WORDS OF THE GARDEN

Read: Matt. 26:45-57; John 18:10-12.

Text: *Sleep on now, and take your rest. The hour is come. Matt. 26:45. Put up thy sword. John 18:11.*

"Sleep on now and take your rest. The hour is come"—Jesus' Disappointment. If only I had prayed! How many times have we said it—afterward. Let us rouse ourselves while there is yet time to pray for the things we know His heart is burdened for, in our environment. We shall not be sorry.

If they had stayed awake, they would have seen Jesus' agony; if they had seen, they would themselves have prayed.

If they had prayed, they might not have followed afar off; if they had not followed afar off, they might not have fallen.

If they could have seen ahead, would they not have beaten sleep from their eyes? If we could see ahead—He can. He would keep us close to Him, and out of danger; but He cannot if we will not.

"Put up thy sword"—Jesus' Method. Our ways of helping the cause are not His. The Crusades seemed childish to God—so do some modern flurries of energy for the church. Jesus' way is to work through prayer. If we have not prayed, then feverish activity may be all waste motion—and quite unchristian in spirit. And if in utter physical exhaustion you are too weak even to reach out your hand of faith to Him, your very leaning hard on the Everlasting Arms can be an act of service and praise.

> *In the hour of trial,*
> *Jesus, plead for me;*
> *Lest by base denial*
> *I depart from Thee.*

THE MEASURE OF CALVARY

Read: Mark 15:22-34; Luke 23:34-38.

Text: *He saved others; himself he cannot save.* Mark 15:31.

Calvary—no one can know its depth of meaning, but all must reckon with it; for it has meaning, meaning for every soul who has lived or will live. It is history's focus. Let me try to understand as I listen to Jesus' own utterances, wrung from His inmost spirit; they are its reality. And let me not forget what I see and hear there; I shall be a better Christian as I live with Calvary.

What do Jesus' words tell of the meaning of Calvary? Numbered with sinners, sharing their fellowship, their pollution, their reputation; forgotten by God, cut off from the smile that was life to Him—this was hell for Jesus. He went there that I might never have to go. Calvary is the measure of the *hell* from which I have been redeemed. (Mark 15:34.)

Holy and harmless—while yet in the power of His enemies, while they were doing their worst, then He forgave His enemies. Most of us find it possible to forgive after it is all over, after they have repented and apologized. Calvary is the measure of *Christian forgiveness.* (Luke 23:34.)

> *Lest I forget Gethsemane,*
> *Lest I forget Thine agony,*
> *Lest I forget Thy love for me—*
> *Lead me to Calvary.*

April 1

THE MEASURE OF CALVARY

Read: Luke 23:39-46; John 19:26-30.

Text: *It is finished.* John 19:30.

How do Jesus' words define Calvary? Supreme audacity for a dying criminal to promise another criminal Paradise through faith in Himself! Supreme shamelessness for a Leader who had betrayed the confidence of His followers, to turn His mother over to the closest of those followers for support! He knew He could and would make good every claim. Calvary is the measure of the Christian's *confidence in Christ* in the darkest hour. He cannot fail. (Luke 23:43; John 19:26, 27.)

Jesus suffered with very human reactions. But even when He said, "I thirst," He was fulfilling prophecy and glorifying God. That teaches me that God does not expect me to be a stoic or an angel, but that my very human self can be used to His glory—if I will give my will wholly to Him. Jesus was a greater help to humanity because He was human—but yielded. So we can be. Calvary is the measure of a *perfect humanity.* (John 19:28.)

Every conceivable human temptation met, the depth of human sin plumbed, the weight of God's condemnation of sin borne, love's utmost done—"it is finished." What does it mean for me? It means everything. Calvary is the measure of *available grace.* (John 19:30.)

"Commit thy way unto the Lord; and he shall bring it to pass." "Committing" is "letting go"; we must let go before God can do anything about it. The greatest victory in all the world was won when Jesus let go and committed His spirit to God. Calvary is the measure of a *committing trust in God.* (Luke 23:46.)

> *Grace there is my every debt to pay,*
> *Blood to wash my every sin away,*
> *Power to keep me sinless day by day—*
> *For me, for me.*

THE MEASURE OF CALVARY

Read: Matt. 27:34-44.

Text: *If any man will come after me, let him . . . . take up his cross and follow me.* Matt. 16:24.

Calvary gives the pattern for our Christian service. Reverse that careless jeer, and it tells the secret of Calvary: "Himself he could not save; he saved others." Forsaken by God, He died for men; abused by His enemies, He forgave them; taunted by a thief, He offered a thief Paradise; misunderstood by His friends, He cared for their welfare. *Self-forgetfulness* is the principle of service—and that is Calvary.

Jesus could not explain Himself fully even to those who loved Him best. What must have been the disappointment—and the disapproval perhaps—of those who loved Him truly and had trusted His claims. That misunderstanding was part of the price He paid to be true to God. Calvary is the measure of *unquestioning obedience.*

Stripped of every earthly possession, mocked by those He would save, misconstrued maliciously by His enemies, not understood by His own friends, not answered by God Himself—still He kept on His saving way. Can I follow Him—as far as God's plan for me demands? Calvary is the measure of the Christian's *endurance.*

In Gethsemane Jesus said, "Yes"; on Calvary He lived out that "Yes." Brave, true, unfaltering—He is my perfect Pattern. If my consecration is sincere, I am not cherishing the secret hope that I shall never have to carry it out, nor evading and rationalizing when the test comes. Calvary is the measure of my *sincerity.*

> *His divine will is sweet to me;*
> *For I remember Calvary.*

THE MEASURE OF CALVARY

Read: II Cor. 5:14-21.

Text: *God was in Christ, reconciling the world unto himself.* II Cor. 5:19.

Calvary shows us the heart of God. Read again that poem of Clarence Edwin Flynn called "Revelation":

> *Men wondered if God wore an ermined gown,*
> *And if His were a jeweled diadem.*
> *He stood before them in a thorn-decked crown,*
> *And dragged a cross-tree up a hill for them.*

Calvary is the measure of *God Himself.* "Having loved his own, he loved them unto the end." How often we almost go through, but give out just too soon, and lose the victory. Praise be to our Christ, He drained the last drop of the cup. Calvary is the measure of the *love* that has promised to see me through.

Calvary is the measure of the love of God for sinful man. And so it is now the measure of our *responsibility.* It is the measure of our guilt if we reject that love or treat it lightly.

He asks me to give up completely my right to myself. Others will take advantage of my consecration to advance themselves, and think me "foolish," "simple." Jesus did it: His body helpless in their hands, His spirit exposed to their scorn—for He trusted God to exalt Him. And God was faithful. Can I fear or grudge a complete consecration while I look at Calvary? Calvary is the measure of a *consecration that believes God.*

> *I found Him in the forest,*
> *I found Him by the sea;*
> *But I never really knew Him*
> *Till I saw Him on Calvary.*—SELECTED.

108

THE RISEN LORD

Read: John 20:1-3; Isa. 53:9-12.

Text: *And they found the stone rolled away from the sepulchre. Luke 24:2.*

God does not stop working when things look hopeless. The Stone Rolled Away. Our enemies are not so powerful, after all. Not when God takes hold for us. Our case seems hopeless—but God is not dead.

Someone has tampered with death—that Someone is God! Death is not final. No longer need we feel when we lay our loved ones in the grave that the last word has been spoken. There is One whose finger will roll away the stone, as a very little thing.

The Empty Tomb. God's Son has died under a cloud; He will not leave His name smirched as an impostor and a deceiver. All the world can know, if they will. Satan still is clouding His name, and casting doubts on His faithfulness. But God is the same. One day the justification will be full and complete. All shall see Him exalted. We shall be there.

The Jesus who called back Lazarus, the Christ who promised eternal life—what is He doing in the tomb? Get your share of His eternal life, and you too will be out of place in the grave.

> *Let me, like Mary, through the gloom*
> *Come with a gift to Thee;*
> *Speak to me from the empty tomb,*
> *Lead me to Calvary.*

THE RISEN LORD

Read: John 20: 4-10.

Text: *Why seek ye the living among the dead?* Luke 24: 5.

The Body Gone. Even the material house that had held His Son God will not leave in the hands of His enemies. An end has come to sport and mockery. "So far, and no farther" is God's law for the persecutor.

Nor will God leave that body in the hands of Jesus' friends. They might come to worship at His grave as at a holy shrine and forget to look up. No material thing must share the glory. He had a better use for it: to show them what resurrection would mean for their own bodies.

The Graveclothes Left. For they do not matter. It does not really matter where we die, how grand the funeral nor how obscure, whether locked in bronze vault or blown to bits by cannon, or "missing in action." The thing that matters is the soul, and that has escaped its fetters.

The Lord Taken? It was wonderful to have Jesus with them in flesh and blood; and when they lost that presence, they thought they had lost Him. But they were to learn that though the body they had loved was gone, a far more glorious Christ was theirs forever. They were to learn that the spiritual always excels the material, that when God takes away one blessing He always gives a better. Have we learned these things?

> *Death cannot keep his prey—*
> *He tore the bars away—*
> *Jesus my Lord!*

THE RISEN LORD

Read: John 20:11-20.

Text: *Then were the disciples glad, when they saw the Lord.* John 20:20.

The Lord Not Gone. He never will leave us if we have chosen to follow Him for good. Our relationship with Him is permanent. "Nothing shall separate us from the love of Christ." "No, never alone." No one can take away our Lord—for He cares.

The Disciples Comforted—because they were disciples. If we love Christ enough to mourn when His enemies triumph, He will see that we are comforted, in a way we did not expect.

If we are concerned enough to stay awake when everyone else has gone to sleep, God can show us the truth and use us to show others.

If we are eager enough to press on in the dark, hope will outrun despair and we shall soon see light.

If we are brave enough to believe, we shall have proofs sufficient. But faith must come first, to interpret fact aright.

If we care enough to look for Him, He will come again. He will not leave us orphans.

If we know Him well enough to call Him truly, "My Lord," He knows us well enough to call us by our name.

If we have trusted any promise of His, He keeps His word. He had promised He would rise; they forgot, but He remembered.

> *Steps unseen before me,*
> *Hidden dangers near;*
> *Nearer still my Saviour,*
> *Whispering, "Be of cheer."*

THE RISEN LORD

Read: I Cor. 15:19-23; Isa. 26:19; Job 19:25-27.

Text: *But now is Christ risen from the dead, and become the firstfruits of them that slept.* I Cor. 15:20.

There is always something more for those who love Jesus. A Way Out. Death is not a dead end. There is an opening on the other side. "He was crucified, dead, and buried"—but He arose.

Wicked men cannot triumph over the righteous. God has a way out. He has planned the deliverance before the trial.

The First Glimpse of Immortality. One great human hunger is for immortality. Man cannot conceive passing into nothing. "He thinks he was not made to die." But he has only a hope; Jesus is the First Fruits. With His resurrection comes the first assurance. "Because He lives, I know, I know I too shall live."

What is beyond the veil? Darkness? Uncertainty? Gloom? So the heathen have felt it, even the best of their philosophers. Jesus' resurrection shows us the Christian's future as shining brightness, peopled with angels of light.

Jesus did not slink back into heaven. The echoes are still reverberating down the centuries of the mighty chorus of welcome to the Victor over sin and death:

> *Unfold, ye portals everlasting!*
> *For, lo, the King comes nigh!*

So for us immortality is triumph. Our songs will be of victory. Death cheated of his prey, the guards of their prisoner, the enemies of their victim, and we escaped forever from the snares of Satan.

> *'Tis finished, all is finished,*
> *Their fight with death and sin;*
> *Fling open wide the golden gates,*
> *And let the victors in!*

BECAUSE HE LIVES

Read: Luke 24: 13-27.

Text: *What is the exceeding greatness of his power to us-ward who believe, according to the working of his mighty power, which he wrought in Christ, when he raised him from the dead.* Eph. 1: 19, 20.

Faith. Because Christ is living I can have unwavering faith. It often seems that evil has won out: apostasy, vice, crime, economic bewilderment, political slavery. Is God dead? they say. But we never can know the black despair of Cleopas and his friend. For we know that Jesus still lives and will ultimately triumph.

Faith can die; it died that pitch-black weekend. Even the hope that "springs eternal in the human breast" must yield to stubborn facts. But the Christian's hope faces every ugly fact and still is triumphant. It is founded on the Resurrection.

If I have to meet life alone, the pessimistic philosophers are perhaps right. For life is full of disappointment, chance, evil, sorrow, perplexity—I am a helpless pawn. But Christ lives, my Advocate and Friend. And His eye is on me.

I have a "creed" when it comes to Jesus. I believe He "was born of the Virgin Mary, suffered under Pontius Pilate, was crucified, dead and buried; the third day He rose again from the dead; He ascended into Heaven and sitteth at the right hand of God, the Father Almighty; from thence He shall come to judge the quick and the dead." That is the perfect Saviour. Anything less or different is counterfeit or deformed, for it lacks either the love or the triumph.

> *Lifted up was He to die;*
> *"It is finished," was His cry;*
> *Now in heaven exalted high—*
> *Hallelujah! what a Saviour!*

BECAUSE HE LIVES

Read: Luke 24: 28-43.

Text: *Their eyes were opened, and they knew him.* Luke 24: 31.

Knowledge. Because Christ is living I can have certain knowledge. It doesn't take deep intellect and profound philosophy to grasp the fact of the Resurrection—only a loving heart. The women saw first, and told. And love has been seeing Him ever since.

Many will call our testimony an "idle tale," "emotionalism," "wishful thinking," "superstition," "visionary," "medieval"—though Christ be risen a thousand times, if He be not risen in your heart He is as good as dead to you. You must see for yourself in things divine. Atheist coming back to meet the pilgrims declaring that he had never seen any Celestial City doesn't prove anything—nor a thousand atheists.

You don't understand the how of the Resurrection. But you can know it is so. Jesus reads the heart, and He will satisfy those hearts where He reads love and interest and the will to obey. Perplexed? Stupid in religious matters? Never could understand spiritual things? Only want Jesus badly enough. Tell Him you don't understand it all, but you have to have Him, you can't live your life without Him—and He will come to you and reveal Himself.

Take Jesus out of your life, and what have you? Emptiness. But you never need lose Him now. It was better that He went, because He rose with all power and He sent the Spirit with omnipresence. A walk with Jesus—what a privilege. But it had to end. My privilege is rarer: He abides with me, goes out with me when I must go, returns when I return.

Jesus will walk with me, guarding me ever,
Giving me victory through storm and through strife;
He is my Comforter, Counsellor, Leader,
Over the uneven journey of life.

BECAUSE HE LIVES

Read: Luke 24:44-48.

Text: *Then opened he their understanding, that they might understand the scriptures.* Luke 24:45.

The Bible. Because Christ is living I can have a living Bible. From sinking sand to solid rock, from raging tempest to infinite calm, from bottomless despair to topless hope; no contrast is too great to picture the change in the outlook of a converted soul. What makes the difference? Just Jesus. And if we lose Him, the light goes out of life again. No backslider is happy.

Our faith in Christ has a strong foundation. It has its visions and revelations, but they are supported by the Bible and by the character of the Godhead. Christ being Who He is must live forever. The Bible becomes a new book to the Christian, for it shows him his Saviour. The New Birth will make you more at home with the Scriptures than will a theological course without it.

"Emotion in religion"—genuine Christian emotion— is not a vague good feeling. It is joy based on God's dealings with us. Its surest spring is meditation on the Word of God. If Jesus lives for you, He draws near when you read the Bible and shows you Himself there. If your Bible reading seems dry, clear away the barriers and invite Him to be your Interpreter. He is waiting for the invitation.

What has the Bible to say about Jesus? "Rose of Sharon, Bright and Morning Star, Wonderful, Counsellor, Prince of Peace, Bread of Life, Water of Life, King of Kings and Lord of Lords, Alpha and Omega"—my heart too burns, and I shout with the small boy, "Hurrah for Jesus!"

Wonderful, wonderful, Jesus is to me;
Counsellor, Prince of Peace, Mighty God is He;
Saving me, keeping me from my sin and shame,
Wonderful is my Redeemer, praise His name!

JESUS WITH US

Read: John 20: 19, 20; John 21: 4-13.

Text: *Came Jesus and stood in the midst.* John 20: 19.

"Jesus in the midst" of our gatherings, social as well as definitely sacred—would our words, our acts, our feelings even, have a different color or a gentler tone? He is there so long as we are truly Christian. Let us recognize His presence and do Him the kind of honor He seeks.

One of our great essayists writes that if Shakespeare should come into the room where a group of literary men were assembled, they would all rise to honor him. But if Jesus Christ were to enter, they would all kneel and kiss the hem of His garment. Do you feel that way? Is He greater than all the great to you? Cultivate the passionate homage of your soul to Jesus. He is worthy.

Jesus is not dead. He is not a Name only, not a historic Fact only, not a beautiful Life only, not a removed, distant Atonement only. He is living: He is Person; High Priest, and, through the Spirit, Companion, Friend, Counsellor, Great Lover. I can talk with Him—I do. He can talk with me—He does. That living fellowship has implications which I must realize—or He is as good as dead to me.

> *Then I saw at once that Jesus*
> *Could be better far than all:*
> *He could lighten up the pathway,*
> *Could surround me like a wall;*
> *He could take the place of loved ones,*
> *Wipe the falling tears away,*
> *Turn my sorrow into laughter,*
> *Change my night-time into day.*

JESUS WITH US

Read: John 20:21-28.

Text: *Peace be unto you: as my Father hath sent me, even so send I you.* John 20:21.

Jesus with us as a Person means peace. The moment before, I may have been fearful of the present and anxious for the future. But when I become conscious that He is with me, a quiet confidence steals through my whole being. Past, present, and future are safe in His strong hands.

Jesus with us as a Person means *power.* Through the abiding Holy Spirit His presence is made real, and we are made positive Christians. An offensive is always stronger than a defensive. In the war against sin the Spirit gives power to witness and to intercede; and that conquering Presence carries the fight into the enemy's territory.

Jesus with us as a Person makes us *know.* He will reveal Himself. We do not have to go through life taking the word of other Christians or following the Christian code only. We can meet Christ for ourselves and find the fullness of a life with Him. Do not try to satisfy yourself with the second-hand or the second-best.

It is thrilling to see a young man who you admit has "no religious tendency," "no spiritual sense," kneel at a mourner's bench, groan and pray his way through, then rise with shining, tear-stained face, saying, "I didn't know it would be like this, but I know I have met Christ." Something real has happened. A contact has been made. In a moment he has gained a knowledge that the philosophers lack. Christ is doing that every day.

> *I know a Name that can drive away all sorrow,*
> *I know a Name that is sweeter than them all—*
> *That wonderful Name is Jesus.*

JESUS WITH US

Read: John 20:29-31; Mk. 16:11-14.

Text: *Blessed are they that have not seen, and yet have believed.* John 20:29.

We know because we trust and obey a Person. You cannot reason your way into faith, you cannot seek your way into faith; you can obey your way into faith. You cannot force your way into light, you cannot think your way into light; you can obey your way into light. And you are safe in obeying, for the word you obey is the word of Jesus and the voice you follow is the voice of Jesus.

After you have obeyed, hold steady if you still do not see, and the way will begin to lighten. Christ's honor is at stake; He will not let you down. "If you do what you know, you'll know what to do." And His face is behind the cloud.

Christ will eventually satisfy every seeking soul, Thomas as well as John. But the doubter will lose many blessings that come to the prompt believer; for he takes the long way around. Better not play with the doubting habit: it makes you slow and stupid and self-centered; it makes the Lord waste time on you that He could use to help others through you; it will grow on you and choke your soul. Form the habit of simple faith; it is the short-cut to knowledge.

Grasp a promise of God and cling to it with all your might. It will not give way. For it is signed with the name of His Son, written in blood.

Peace, perfect peace, the future all unknown?
Jesus we know, and He is on the throne.

JESUS WITH US

Read: John 21:15-19.

Text: *Lovest thou me more than these?* John 21:15.

Jesus with us as a Person makes us love. Find—and keep—Jesus real; love Him truly—this is the Great Commandment. If you have missed that, you have missed everything. You are working hard for His cause. How is your love?

Jesus' one concern is whether our attachment to Him is deep enough. If we love Him enough and keep on loving Him, He knows we will make it through. So He probes.

Jesus will question us as long as we question ourselves. If we are uncertain, He knows it. But the remedy for our question mark is not to crawl off in the dark alone. The remedy is to go straight to Jesus and listen to His questions. Answering His questions honestly will bring the answer to our own question.

We do not love Jesus enough until we love Him "more than these"—and "these" are everything: friends, business, life itself. But if He is Who He is, it is mockery to offer Him a love that is less than that. We deceive ourselves if we think He will share first place. "Lovest thou me?" Then inevitably, "Lovest thou me more than these?"

We do not love Jesus enough until we accept His job for us regardless of every one else's assignment. Otherwise we should get to comparing notes and swapping jobs. Then how about His blueprints?

We do not love Jesus enough until we recognize our love for Him to be our motive for service. Then we shall forget our own hurts in binding up the hurts of others. Then we shall not be offended if we are not noticed and paid for our services. He has done for us far more than ever we can do for Him.

> *Fade, fade each earthly joy;*
> *Jesus is mine;*
> *Break every tender tie;*
> *Jesus is mine.*

FRIENDS OF JESUS

Read: Matt. 9:37, 38; 10:1; Phil. 3:8-10.

Text: *Henceforth I call you not servants; for the servant knoweth not what his lord doeth: but I have called you friends.* John 15:15.

The cause of Christ is carried on by His friends. He does not use forced labor; He has no slaves—but love-slaves. The friends of Christ have been chosen by Him and called to Him. At the outset of every Christian career stands a personal contact; at its heart, a personal relationship. He gives an uncertain invitation who never has met Jesus Himself—yet many are trying to work for Christ who do not know Christ.

A Christ whom we trust absolutely, follow implicitly, obey unquestioningly is the heart of Christianity. Just doing the best we know may be religion; it is not Christianity.

How often I need to hear Him repeat to me, "Ye have not chosen me (only), but I have chosen you and ordained you." Life has a way of knocking the props from under me. I need His sure word to keep me going. But that is enough.

Jesus' special friends during His earthly ministry were few in number—only twelve; but those twelve were representative of all those whom He will choose because they choose Him. Of every "tribe," every religious group, some will be wholly yielded to Christ to "follow Him whithersoever He goeth." Comparatively few; but if they are utterly loyal, He has enough to do His work. I would qualify to be one of these.

> *I'll be a friend to Jesus,*
> *My life for Him I'll spend;*
> *And while on earth I'm living,*
> *My Lord shall have a friend.*

FRIENDS OF JESUS

Read: Matt. 10:5-8; Acts 26:12-18.

Text: *Ye are my friends, if ye do whatsoever I command you.* John 15:14.

Jesus gives His friends, every one, a job—a share in His own enterprise. He commissions them for work. There is no weak sentimentality in this friend relationship. Closest fellowship comes always from working, sacrificing, suffering, and triumphing together in a common cause.

Jesus' friends are empowered—to heal. The limit of that power, who can tell? They are sent to heal all manner of diseases; even the devils are subject. I wonder if we pray too limply, "Thy will be done," pray it in resignation only. Should we not pray it in commanding victory? Should we not insist in faith that devils be routed and captive souls delivered? *His will be done.*

Jesus' friends are authorized—to preach and teach. They are to take His part always, to spread His standards, to show men their need of Him—everywhere, actively to be reminding men of God. It is a heroic task. If you are not to faint, if your strength is not to fail, you need frequent contact with Jesus, to remind you that you have divine authority. All heaven is backing you and is interested in the sermon you preach today, and the class you teach.

Jesus' friends are commanded—to give. They cannot keep to themselves the riches they possess in the secret of Jesus. If ever they cease giving they will cease having. It is so today. Stop testifying, and soon you will find you have nothing to testify to.

> *Give, and to you shall be given;*
> *God His beloved Son gave.*

April 17

FRIENDS OF JESUS

Read: Matt. 10:9-25.

Text: *And he that taketh not his cross, and followeth after me, is not worthy of me.* Matt. 10:38.

Jesus' friends are not promised exemptions here. If you are a Bible friend of His you are not assured an easy berth, a good salary, all the comforts of life, popularity and promotions. These are good, but they seem not to be the marks of His favor. His friends are not protected (apparently); they are sheep among wolves. They are not provided for (apparently); they carry neither purse nor scrip. They are not secure (apparently); they "do not see where their next meal is coming from"; they "cannot see a step ahead of them." His word is their only guaranty. I suppose it is good?

Jesus' friends are sent to persecution and sometimes to death; He did not rescue John the Baptist—nor Himself. They are sent to hostile criticism; John and Jesus both were criticized. They are sent to rejection and to cold unconcern; Jesus knew both. They are sent to perplexity and to naked faith; John faced a blank wall of aloneness, and Jesus on the cross felt God-forsaken. Can I claim exemption and be a true friend?

"Follow, follow, I will follow Jesus." It is a lovely song and we sing it sometimes in a light-hearted mood:

He will lead me safely in the path that He has trod
Up to where they gather on the hills of God.

The path that He has trod is blood-stained. And on the hills of God they will look to see our scars.

> *O Jesus, I have promised*
> *To serve Thee to the end;*
> *Be Thou forever near me,*
> *My Master and my Friend.*

FRIENDS OF JESUS

Read: Matt. 10: 26-38; 11: 28-30.

Text: *Take my yoke upon you, and learn of me . . . . ; for my yoke is easy, and my burden is light.* Matt. 11: 29, 30.

But Jesus' friends are well provided for. His "Fear not" is backed by His faithfulness. They are *rich* here. They have the gospel of Jesus, the only absolute, secure wealth in the world. They always have something to give; giving is their job. For always they can get men in touch with the God who has all sufficiency. Their own needs are taken care of without their anxiety. So long as a minister of the gospel is doing God's business, God has pledged Himself that he shall be fed by God's people.

They are *safe* here. They are identified with Jesus; God will not lose sight of His own Son—nor of those who bear that Son's name. Their hairs are numbered; through every peril they have a heavenly escort.

They have the comfort of the *far look.* Trials can be gloried in if there is victory ahead.

> *Just a few more days to be filled with praise,*
> *And to tell the old, old story.*

Then fulness of life and a sure reward from His hand. Do we use it as an incentive? Jesus did.

They have the *rest* of an easy yoke. No amount of work or hardship chafes if our hearts are rested and at peace. Jesus' friends have learned to love His will because they love Him. The one happy place in life is "the center of the will of God." If you are complaining or fretting or irritable over the circumstances in which God has placed you, perhaps you need to have the yoke adjusted.

> *Heaven's eternal day's before thee;*
> *God's own hand shall guide thee there.*

FRIENDS OF JESUS

Read: Matt. 10:39-42; John 15:11-16.

Text: *Ye have not chosen me, but I have chosen you, and ordained you, that ye should go and bring forth fruit, and that your fruit should remain.* John 15:16.

The friends of Jesus have utmost satisfaction in this life. They have joy in their work. Others looking on will think it monotonous, unrewarding, hard. But they see it from the inside, and know there is nothing like it in all the world for genuine, lasting satisfaction. If you are losing the romance and the delight, and finding only drudgery and routine in your Christian work, perhaps you have lost step with Jesus. Walking with Him gives the exhilaration of the marching step.

The friends of Jesus are sent with a *gospel* too simple for the philosophers to discover by reasoning, but so simple that all can grasp it with the heart. They are sent with a good news that is exhaustless; for it centers in Jesus. Infinite Personality, He has a word for every situation that ever will face mankind, a power for every emergency, a personal response for every individual. Jesus never fails.

They are sent with a *way of life* that is unique—different from any program man has tried, but that works where man's programs have failed. Love conquers; the lowly are exalted; the meek inherit the earth; the poor in spirit are the children of God. Ask the missionaries of the gospel who have seen it work on raw heathendom if their job is tame!

> *Anywhere with Jesus, over land or sea,*
> *Telling souls in darkness of salvation free—*
> *Though His hand may lead me over dreary ways,*
> *Anywhere with Jesus is a house of praise.*

THE BIG BROTHER

Read: Gen. 44:18-29.

Text: *A friend loveth at all times, and a brother is born for adversity.* Prov. 17:17.

Close, strong family relationships cost, but they pay large dividends. If we try to live an isolated life, we shrink our souls. "Edith was a little country," a recent novelist wrote of one of her characters, "bounded on north and east and south and west by Edith." Everyone should be a part of some group that demands loyalty and sacrifice.

You read of the church member who did not come to church because he "belonged to" the Masons? You can be a member of a family, a church, a world, and not "belong" to it. You belong only when you share right family attitudes.

Together for a few years, then scattered to their own firesides, brothers and sisters and fathers and mothers have those few short years in which to build a perfect thing that will be cherished in memory by each child, rebuilt in each new home, and in turn rebuilt in their children's homes to the end of time. What an opportunity to let slip!

Read the legend of two brothers. Each night the married brother carried secretly a bag of grain to his unmarried brother's barn because the latter would have no child to care for him in his old age. Each night the single brother carried secretly a bag of grain to his married brother's barn, for he had children and would need it more than would an unmarried man. This they did night after night. One night they met half-way; and there they built a temple.

Every brother gives. If he has nothing else, he gives that priceless thing, himself.

When the Saviour shall gather His loved ones home,
Will the circle be unbroken over there?

125

THE BIG BROTHER

Read: Gen. 44:30-34.

Text: *How shall I go up to my father, and the lad be not with me?* Gen. 44:34.

Judah, the "big brother," has his place in God's plan. The Judahs always will have their place, for they embody the spirit of responsibility for the weak. It is the essentially Christian spirit.

Noblesse oblige: rank involves responsibility; privilege implies duty. The older are responsible for the younger, the rich for the poor, the educated for the ignorant, the strong for the weak. It is a law that holds good in every social group: in the home family, the church family, or the world family.

The spirit of concern for the weak starts with God. "He is a little one." "His father loveth him." "His life is bound up in the lad's life." From Father to Great Elder Brother—then naturally to us. God has loved every lost soul—loved with a broken heart; Christ has loved every lost soul—loved to the death. We who have been saved by such love, can we dam up the flow?

"Thy servant became surety for the lad." We cannot compel the younger generation to take the right attitudes, but in a sense we can make their covenant for them. We can claim them for God and for the church. We can refuse them to the devil. We can prevail in prayer; we can make Christ supremely real and attractive in our own lives. We can sacrifice our ease and pleasure to show them we care what becomes of them.

"I shall bear the blame to my father forever." We have been trusted greatly; no more than could Cain can we use the alibi, "Am I my brother's keeper?"

He was not willing that any should perish.—
Master, forgive and inspire us anew.

126

WHERE ARE YOU LOOKING?

Read: II Cor. 4:1-6.

Text: *The god of this world hath blinded the minds of them which believe not . . . . God hath shined in our hearts.* II Cor. 4:4, 6.

It makes all the difference where you look. You can see what you choose. But what you see makes you. "We look not at the things which are seen."

The Christian isn't looking at life's hard circumstances. There are plenty of them; but he sees through them, beyond them, above them—and discounts them accordingly. This bitter disappointment—what have you done with it? Best remember it is only temporary—and look away from it to the *real* things you have that will last. Let your hold be loosened on those things you may lose tomorrow.

And the real Christian isn't looking too much at life's supposed good things: wealth, honor, ease. He is a servant here. He looks beyond today, and like Bunyan's Patience, he is "willing to wait," though Passion insists on having his good things now.

"Seekest thou great things for thyself? Seek them not." So we are not living for what we get. We are living to serve—Christ, and others for His sake. Trials and losses make for good serving. For they make us sympathetic and understanding.

> *Whatever goes, whatever stays,*
> *Lo, I am with thee all the days.**
> —A. J. FLINT

WHERE ARE YOU LOOKING?

Read: II Cor. 4: 7-15.

Text: *We look not at the things which are seen, but at the things which are not seen.* II Cor. 4: 18.

The Christian looks beyond the seen to things that others cannot see. Looking within—he has joy. For he has Jesus. I too have a Treasure that war, upheaval, bereavement, all life's confusions cannot rob me of. It is Jesus: Jesus my Friend, my Saviour, my King. This is the secret of contentment, without which millionaires are poor.

A Chinese Christian found his home completely destroyed by the enemy, even his Bible and hymnbook burned up—all but one charred leaf of the hymnbook. He picked it up, and read, "Joy to the world! The Lord is come." The incident is symbolic; and it sings in my soul. Amid the ruins of all we have known and loved, we still can declare, "Joy to the world! The Lord is come"—and know we are rich.

The knowledge of Christ is *Light* in my heart. Plenty of darkness outside, but it doesn't have to get inside. The prospects are gloomy. All over the world lights have gone out and have not been relighted. But this Light never will go out, unless I quench it. It will shine more and more.

Thank God for the Christian's "but nots" (II Cor. 4: 8, 9). They chant a triumphal refrain. The circumstances of life almost have us swamped—"but not"! The enemy says we are driven to the wall—"but not"! The Christian's head always is above water; there is always another moment in the battle, another round in the fight, that brings victory; there is always a way through. There always is a positive Plus; it is the Resurrection *Life* of Jesus—try to keep that down!

> *When all around my soul gives way,*
> *He then is all my hope and stay.*

WHERE ARE YOU LOOKING?

Read: II Cor. 4:16-18; II Cor. 5:1-16.

Text: *The things which are seen are temporal; but the things which are not seen are eternal.* II Cor. 4:18.

Looking at the Cross—the Christian has love. He sees Jesus loving and dying for men, and that love lays hold of him. Calvary and the spirit of Calvary are to him the only life worth living. When everything else seems cheap in comparison, it is no sacrifice to follow Him.

The finest use any person can make of his life is to invest it somewhere in the service of Christ. That is investing in real values. The world is yet to be brought to His feet. You can have your share in the biggest of all enterprises—the basic "reconstruction project." But you have to look behind the scenes to realize its bigness.

Looking up—the Christian gains the morale of a citizen of heaven. He sees his native country. And he walks with a fine dignity; he is a King's son. He lives with a beautiful independence of the crowd; he regulates his conduct by the standards of a better country.

"If a man does not keep pace with his companions, perhaps it is because he hears a different Drummer." —Thoreau.

He feels the upward pull (the "weight of glory"). Weight is attraction. Life's afflictions cause the tug of gravity to be upward. Why grudge any sorrow or heartache that will increase the upward pull of glory?

> *A tent or a cottage, why should I care?*
> *They're building a palace for me over there.*

WHERE ARE YOU LOOKING?

Read: II Cor. 5:17-21.

Text: *We are ambassadors for Christ.* II Cor. 5:20.

Looking about him, after the upward look, the Christian sees his assignment—he has a responsibility. His vision puts him to work. A heavenly citizen? Then an earthly ambassador. Here not to sink to the level of earth; here to lift others to the level of heaven. Here not to take on earthly ways; here to teach others the ways of heaven.

All that patriotism to your country involves, loyalty to heaven involves. Count it up. Glad you are an American? Proud of her name and her opportunities and her protection? Willing to shed life's blood and give heart's dearest for her welfare? Then so much more for your eternal Country.

Looking ahead—the Christian has eternity. He catches gleams from an ever brightening, ever broadening vista: "The path . . . . shineth more and more to perfect day"; "Eye hath not seen, nor ear heard, the things that God hath prepared"; "Now we see through a glass darkly, then face to face"; "Our hope enters within the veil." We have seen but "the dawn of redeeming grace." "The day-star hath risen in our hearts." Our "sun shall no more go down." Is it all true? How then can we ever be disheartened, ever be lazy, ever forget to look at "the things that are eternal"?

> *Ambassador to be of realms beyond the sea.*
> *I'm here on business for my King.**

*© E. O. Excell

GOD'S GOLD STANDARD

Read: I Cor. 13:1-3.

Text: *Though I give my body to be burned, and have not charity, it profiteth me nothing.* I Cor. 13:3.

God's Official Standard of Value—Love. Some Americans used to say, "Of course Hitler is dictatorial, but see what big things he has done for Germany." *Big things, but wrong spirit* is the devil's formula. With God it is always quality first, not quantity; spirit, not achievement; motive, not deed.

The rule is true on the small scale as well as on the large. All through one busy, active day, what counts with God is not what you get done or do not get done, but how much you have loved your Lord and others while at it.

The preacher's moving eloquence, the teacher's keen power, the rich man's large gifts to missions, the altar worker's effective prayers even are perhaps not pleasing Christ so much as the warm love of some quiet saint. (Remember Mary's ointment and the widow's mite.) Or can it be that our aim is something else than simply pleasing Him?

"Eradication of the old man"? "a unified personality"? "a wrong twist of the emotions straightened out"? "a new center of gravity in the soul"? Words all come a little short. Certain it is that before, self was center, or near-center, of our life; now, Christ is Center. Love for Him controls all actions, and love for others for His sake.

> *Here's my heart, O take and seal it;*
> *Seal it for Thy courts above.*

GOD'S GOLD STANDARD

Read: John 13:34, 35; Deut. 6:4, 5; Matt. 22:35-38.

Text: *For God so loved the world, that he gave his only begotten Son, that whosoever believeth in him should not perish, but have everlasting life.* John 3:16.

God's Preference for the Practical. Christ's "new commandment" is still so new and strange that we hardly dare believe it enough to act on it. Really love those who hurt us? Really try to push others ahead instead of shoving them back? Yet it always works, and it always brings conviction.

What God is looking for is men and women, boys and girls, who are willing to be like Him in a world that has forgotten Him. And He is Love.

Love issues in action. How do you love "with all your strength" when you do nothing for the Lord but sit in a pew an hour on Sunday morning? How do you love "with all your mind" when you never read and never think and never study?

Love was a practical matter with God Himself. He could not love the world without doing something about it. His love expressed itself—in Jesus. Love is the strongest of all working forces. There is nothing more practical.

"The Golden Rule must become an accepted rule of life rather than a variable to be applied under some circumstances and disregarded under others." So the best thinkers are saying today. We know that this is gloriously possible through the epochal inward work of the Holy Spirit that removes carnality—and in no other way.

> *And can I yet delay*
> *My little all to give?*
> *To tear my soul from earth away*
> *For Jesus to receive?*

GOD'S GOLD STANDARD

Read: I Cor. 13: 4-8.

Text: *Love . . . . seeketh not her own.* I Cor. 13: 5.

God's Chemical Analysis of Love. There seem to be three main constituents in Christian love: (1) A strange *un-self-centeredness* that is quite unnatural to man; (2) A positive *good-will*—harmless, kind—that insists on "overcoming evil with good"; (3) A *steadfastness,* poise, serenity, that is based on utter confidence in God. Who would not submit to the divine operation necessary to obtain a heart like this?

Selflessness. Love does not crave power over others. A good old part-definition of a holy heart is "the disposition not to have your own way."

Love is good-natured. The sensitive, "touchy" person who makes you watch your step for fear of "offending" or "displeasing" or "hurting his feelings"—does this photograph look like love?

But how about "righteous indignation"? A good principle to remember is that love never resents; it never hits back; it never is angry over anything personal.

Selfishness is discord and inner conflict; it does not know its own best good. Perfect love filling the heart means that a Great Hand has been laid on all the tangled cables of the soul and made them pull together, has touched all the discordant strings and brought them into harmony.

> *I take, O Cross, thy shadow*
> *For my abiding-place;*
> *I ask no other sunshine than*
> *The sunshine of His face.*

133

GOD'S GOLD STANDARD

Read: I Cor. 13: 4-8.

Text: *Love . . . . is kind.* I Cor. 13: 4.

Kindness. There is not much simple kindness in the world today. The sophisticated new psychology is hard on weakness: "He just wants attention," or, "Just a defense mechanism." Love is simple, spontaneous; it believes in you—or if it analyzes your weakness, it does so to help and not to scorn.

Love really enables you to pray for your enemies with no mental reservation. "The acid test of entire sanctification is how much love you have for those who do not love you."—Holland London.

No truly sanctified man is a cynic—or a professional critic. Love finds the one strong thing in a man to build upon it, rather than the weak place to enlarge, and so pull down all the rest about it. I would rather be a builder than a wrecker any day.

Love knows no partiality. The Israelites were to love "the stranger." God loved "the world" and gave His Son for "whosoever." Am I to choose who shall stand in my good graces, and who shall be made to feel a little inferior? The spirit of exclusiveness is not the spirit of love.

Not in vain were we told to "overcome evil with good"; good always will overcome evil if it is given a chance, for it is a living force. To invest your all in love is self-preservation.

Beneath the Cross of Jesus
I fain would take my stand.

GOD'S GOLD STANDARD

Read: I Cor. 13:4-8.

Text: *Love beareth all things, believeth all things, hopeth all things, endureth all things. Love never faileth.* I Cor. 13:7, 8.

Poise. "The grace that meets the emergencies with victory," that is holiness and that is perfect love. And that is what every Christian needs. It is the failures in the unexpected crises that ruin Christian influence.

Love is good for the long pull. Most of us can "take it" for a few days; but to bear the grind for years—God must pour oil on continually. So Bunyan caught a glimpse of the man behind the wall with the oil-can renewing the fire as Satan poured on water. Love is of God.

We all can suffer long—we have to. But when we see a person suffer long and stay kind, we look at him twice and wonder how he does it. The sanctified life shines out in a sinful world and convicts others of their need.

Every child wants to "show off." Every child wants the big thing instead of the valuable thing. Every child would rather have one thing today than ten tomorrow. But love is grown-up.

God's Long-Range Perspective. Love Lasts. There is no problem, national or private, to which love does not hold the key. It laughs at difference of race or class; it draws people together. It believes the word of others; it does not advance self at the expense of another; it makes approaches with no axe to grind. It is crystal-clear as the sunlight or the dew. And it wins.

> *Wonderful love, yes, wonderful love;*
> *Boundless as God's great mighty ocean,*
> *Lasting as His throne above.*

HE LEADETH ME

Read: Ex. 16: 1-8; 19-30.

Text: *Your murmurings are not against us, but against the Lord.* Ex. 16: 8.

Our Way. It is human to look at circumstances and worry when we can't see the way through. But that is counting God out. Once more—what we have been told so often: "If you trust, you do not worry; if you worry, you do not trust."

It is human to grumble when things go wrong. But murmuring against circumstances is murmuring against God; for He has permitted your circumstances. God is hearing your complaints.

It is human to blame somebody else for our hard luck. Human, but not Christian. We have learned a good lesson when we have learned that we never have to fix blame. That is God's job.

It is human to try to look out for oneself. God gave us the instinct of self-preservation. And physical needs are insistent. "We have to eat today and tomorrow." Do we have to? "We have to do something about it." Only the best that God shows us. Who said a man must live? We never have to do wrong in order to live.

It is human to "do it anyway." "If I don't look out for myself, who else will?" So we hoard, take more than our share, break God's living laws to "make a living" for ourselves—only to find we've made a mess of our lives. Selfishness, greed, distrust always "stink" in the end.

It is human to forget. After the Red Sea, worried about bread? After salvation from sin, anxious about starvation? The burden of our guilt carried, but not the burden of our budget? The God who provided the greater, unequal to the less? No, we are just forgetful.

> *While His eye is on the sparrow,*
> *I shall not forgotten be.*

HE LEADETH ME

Read: Ex. 16: 11-18.

Text: *Give us this day our daily bread.* Matt. 6: 11.

God's Way. When God adopted us, He took on the burden of our support. "Moses and Aaron" are not responsible. Nor are we. "My God shall supply all your need."

We don't have to break God's laws to get enough to eat. It is possible to be a Christian in business—the kind of business God expects you to be in. If you have to lose money by your honesty and devotion to principle, He has a way of stretching what is left. Test His faithfulness.

"But this is an emergency." A new thing to us is not a new thing to God. The unknown that so terrifies us is not unknown to God. His resources—and His principles—have anticipated this very situation.

No crisis has ever taken God by surprise—not even this crisis of yours! George Mueller said, "Crises permit critical delivery," and he had tried God often.

When we get into the habit of depending on God for temporal provision, we know the meaning of "manna": mysterious, tasty, daily. There is a delight in the ever-renewed miracle of special supply for special need, fresh from the hand of a God who remembers.

Manna for daily strength; water for daily refreshment. With God new needs spell new means.

> *Who can faint while such a river*
> *Ever flows their thirst to assuage?*
> *Grace which, like the Lord, the Giver,*
> *Never fails from age to age.*

HE LEADETH ME

Read: Ex. 17:1-6.

Text: *He clave the rocks in the wilderness, and gave them drink as out of the great depths.* Ps. 78:15.

The Better Way. The Israelites were children—cannot God expect better things of us? Human means are not causal; only instrumental. Are you depending on a husband, or a son, or your health, to see you through? Rather poor security.

Always we have the choice between the "clay-given mandate," the call of the flesh, and the "God-given mandate," the call of the Spirit. But "seek ye first the kingdom . . . . , and all these things shall be added." It is said with authority.

Even in suffering or hardship, God is providing for our needs—needs that are deeper than food or clothing. He has the long view. He will not pet us today to make us helpless tomorrow.

He does provide refreshment for the spirit, and the joy that energizes soul and body—better than wealth or food. That day when He asks you to make a choice that seems to snatch away every earthly satisfaction, you still can sing, and know the words are true—for He will make them true:

> *All the way my Saviour leads me—*
> *Feeds me with the living Bread.*
> *Though my weary steps may falter*
> *And my soul athirst may be,*
> *Gushing from the rock before me,*
> *Lo! a spring of joy I see.*

I SHOULD BE MY BEST

Read: Gen. 2: 4-17.

Text: *God created man in his own image.* Gen. 1: 27.

Because of what I am: my possibilities. Made in God's image, I was made to commune with Him. I should not let my program get so full that time for prayer is crowded out. Then my likeness to God is only potential; my soul is stunted.

Made in God's image, I have the faculty of reason, of planning and purposing. I should allow myself no indulgences that cloud my reason and make me reckless of my choices and my future. Alcohol is one such indulgence; but there are others: pleasure, ambition, money-making, human love. I would not "just grow"; I would grow in His image.

Made in God's image, I have the privilege of developing that image in me. God is love; He expresses Himself by blessing. I would be that sort of person; I would bring blessing to those I touch. It doesn't come by vaguely wishing.

Because of what I am: my responsibilities. God made man responsible for the earth on which he was placed. Each of us has a plot to till. Each of us has a contribution to make to his generation before he passes on. I have only one life. When I come to the end there will be nothing that I can do about it if the impact of my life has been below par. Today is the time to be my best.

> *Thou of life the fountain art,*
> *Freely let me take of Thee;*
> *Spring Thou up within my heart,*
> *Rise to all eternity.*

I SHOULD BE MY BEST

Read: Matt. 12:9-13.

Text: *How much then is a man better than a sheep?*
Matt. 12:12.

Because of what my brother is: a human personality.
"Better than a sheep"—how so? Made to live forever, made
with a soul worth saving—my brother is more than flesh
and blood. Governments may think of men as human
ants shoving the tanks along. God sees them as souls
for whom Jesus died. We must see them so. We must
treat them so.

If we see others as immortal personalities, we must
see ourselves that way. We must cater to our immortal
part; we must make time serve eternity; we must put
first things first.

How do you look at the human beings you sit with in
the street cars? Those you jostle in the streets? Some
of them are repulsive; some are worried and hard. But
you can see them as hungry, helpless, lost—and turn
your bored moments into a service of prayer. God will
hear prayers for men you do not know—and your own
life will be richer for it.

Invest in personalities. Try to bring out the best in
every one you have dealings with. Take your own trials
to God so that you will be free to bear the burdens of
others. You will be a rich man at the end of your days:
rich in satisfaction, in love, in heavenly securities.

I would have no share in the liquor traffic: it deals in
human souls, tearing down, defacing God's image, de-
stroying. I would invest largely in the church; all its de-
partments too deal with human souls, but to deliver and
build up and save. I would have my money at its best.

> *All for Jesus! all for Jesus!*
> *All my being's ransomed powers.*

I SHOULD BE MY BEST

Read: Rom. 14:19-21; I Cor. 6:19, 20.

Text: *For ye are bought with a price: therefore glorify God in your body, and in your spirit, which are God's.* I Cor. 6:20.

Because of those who have invested so heavily in me: the Holy Trinity. I am the handiwork of God. I will not deface it nor destroy it in myself, and I will consider it in others. I will not knowingly make it harder for anyone else to be victorious over evil habits. I will remember that as I help my brother to be his best I bring honor and satisfaction to the One who made us both. I will remember the feelings of our heavenly Father. (Rom. 14: 19-21.)

I am bought by Jesus Christ; I must be usable, a good investment. My spirit is His; He would live through it. My body is His; He would work through it. And my body often conditions my spirit. Overeating, overdoing, frayed nerves make my spirit a poor tool. (I Cor. 6:20.)

I am the temple of the Holy Ghost. I shall reach maximum efficiency as a Christian only as I recognize my Royal Guest and give Him full control of my personality. I must hear His voice; I must be quick to obey. He will reorganize my thinking and living. He will help me keep my body in trim; He will help me build up Christian habits of living. No act or thought is trivial. I am His. (I Cor. 6:19).

> *Our God is never so far off*
> *As ever to be near:*
> *He is within; our spirit is*
> *The home He holds most dear.*
>
> *So all the while I thought myself*
> *Homeless, forlorn and weary,*
> *Missing my joy, I walked the earth*
> *Myself God's sanctuary.*
> —F. W. FABER

NO FALSEHOOD

Read: John 8:42-45.

Text: *Wherefore putting away lying, speak every man truth with his neighbour: for we are members one of another.* Eph. 4:25.

Trust the truth. It will not let you down. You may seem slow and stupid; you may be misunderstood for a time. Hold steady; the tide will turn. "There is an inherent power in truth to overcome the lie at last." For Christ, the Truth, has eternally overcome Satan, the father of lies.

Love the truth. Love it in the depths of your nature. Recoil from any trace of insincerity; it is the devil's slime and will defile every "good" deed. Cultivate a sensitiveness to Satan's attempts to infect your spirit with deceit.

Only the fiery purging of the Holy Spirit will rid us of "unconscious insincerity." The human heart is "deceitful above all things." We are not proof against deceit until we have been sanctified wholly—and then we must be on our guard.

Lies begin with thoughts. Those suspicions of your fellow Christians that burst out in words of distrust and slander, that you learned too late were false and unfounded—where did they come from? From the father of lies. He loves to sow discord among the brethren.

When you put the worst construction on someone's action, you are following the lead of the devil. When you put the best construction on an action, you are following Christ's Golden Rule: you want to be given the benefit of the doubt yourself. And the better construction is usually nearer the truth.

> *My soul, be on thy guard;*
> *Ten thousand foes arise.*

NO FALSEHOOD

Read: Matt. 5:33-37.

Text: *Let your yea be yea; and your nay, nay; lest ye fall into condemnation.* Jas. 5:12.

"Your Yea, Yea." "What you are is more important than what you do." Better than to "tell the truth" is to be a "truth-teller": to be known as a person whose word is to be trusted.

Habitually to treat the truth so carefully that you need no extra caution for affairs of special moment; to speak the truth, great or small, without private reservation or ulterior motive, because you are a truthful person—this is in some measure to have a word like God's. He needs no oath because He Himself is true.

It is an easy thing, and a dangerous habit, to shade the truth to fit the company you are talking to. Truth has a center and a periphery; stand on one edge, and you are quite far from the other. Stress one aspect to one person, the other aspect to another—your words are true, but the slant of your emphasis makes you double. It isn't quite safe then to ease your conscience by saying you are within the limits of truth.

Just talking. We don't play bridge or go to the movies; we don't believe in worldly amusements. What *do* we do then? "Just talk." And talking can be more devastating than some pastimes that sound worse, if it is just talking for talking's sake. Was it John Wesley who said it is scarcely possible to talk aimlessly more than twenty minutes without sinning? Pope said, "At every word a reputation dies."

> *Set Thou a seal upon my lips*
> *Through all today.*

143

NO FALSEHOOD

Read: Jas. 3:1-13.

Text: *Thou shalt not raise a false report.* Ex. 23:1.

False Reports. "Did you know such-and-such about So-and-So?" News retailed for the sake of telling is liable to be a "false report"; for it is not tempered by love.

There is a subtle fascination in gossip. It is flattering to be "in the know." "Good people" who wouldn't for the world indulge in any other sin will let themselves talk lightly about their neighbors and never give a second thought. Weaknesses are thrown into relief, peculiarities are laughed at, actions are judged—good-naturedly enough, perhaps. But a total false impression is given—and the Golden Rule is broken.

How grateful everyone is to the person who speaks well of him behind his back, who takes his part when he isn't there to speak for himself. Our friends are defenseless in our hands—rather, at the mercy of our tongues. Let us be true friends.

Gossip is usually false witness. It starts—perhaps—with a bit of truth, but that is exaggerated and recolored as it passes from mouth to mouth until at the end it is quite a different story. Once you have let the rumor go, you are helpless to recall the lie. Better check it before it passes your lips.

Gossip at best is only half-truth. It sees only one side of a situation; it judges from externals. Even though we may think we have all the facts, we never can recapture the tissue of motive and feeling, provocation and reaction, that surrounds and conditions the facts.

> When Thou seest me waver,
>   With a look recall,
> Nor for fear or favor,
>   Suffer me to fall.

NO FALSEHOOD

Read: Eph. 4: 17-32.

Text: *Thou shalt not bear false witness against thy neighbour.* Ex. 20: 16.

False Witness. Spreading rumor is bearing false witness. For it is repeating what you do not know to be true. You cannot make things right by explaining that your story is only hearsay; for your caution is forgotten, your spicy bit of news is remembered.

"Explanations" are often false witness. When you have had a misunderstanding, get next the other person, and you'll find "his side" is amazingly right, too. The truth is halfway between. So when you are so busy explaining "your side" to everybody, you can be sure you are leaving out part of "his side," and so giving a faulty picture of the whole. Better keep still. You are never sorry for what you don't say.

Hints can be false witness. You don't have to use words. You can say as much by the lift of an eyebrow, the shrug of a shoulder; an incredulous smile, a questioning inflection; a hesitation in your approbation, a shade less warmth in your tone. You can

> *Damn with faint praise . . . .*
> *Just hint a fault, and hesitate dislike.*

"Love covers." Not to blazon the "whole truth" about a man may sometimes come nearer the real truth than to retail all the known facts. For the unseen longings, prayers, struggles, are as much part of his action as is the seen failure. God has given us perfect love to use without measure; He has not yet made us perfect judges of our fellow men.

> *What's done we partly can compute,*
> *But know not what's resisted.*
> —BURNS

THE ETERNAL GOD

Read: Rev. 4: 1-11.

Text: *Holy, holy, holy, Lord God Almighty, which was, and is, and is to come.* Rev. 4: 8.

The God of Power. "God is still on the throne"—seated —King eternally. Tomorrow I shall see Him in His glory, but today He is just as surely there behind the clouds, the same. I have nothing to fear if I am on good terms with Him.

The servants of God are "owned men." They are sealed as God's peculiar property, and so they are sealed from harm. Anything that belongs to God is safe in His universe.

Queen Victoria said, "We are not interested in the possibilities of defeat. They do not exist!" We can say this with confidence of our God.

God's power is a match for Satan's worst. He doesn't have to have the handicaps given Him. He will often let the situation reach its worst without intervening; He did for Jesus. The appearance of things seems not to count for so much with God. His greatest victories have sprung from apparent defeat.

The two keywords of heaven are *Hallelujah* and *Amen*: praise and certainty. They are the keynotes of the anthem of salvation here too. Hallelujah for the great *Amen* of final victory!

> *For the Lord God omnipotent reigneth—*
> *Hallelujah!*

THE ETERNAL GOD

Read: Rev. 7:9-12.

Text: *A great multitude, which no man could number, of all nations, and kindreds, and people, and tongues, stood before the throne, and before the Lamb, clothed with white robes, and palms in their hands. Rev. 7:9.*

The God of Dominion. There is a big celebration ahead! The Christians will be gathering in from all corners of the world.

> *There'll be singing, there'll be shouting,*
> *When the saints come marching home,*
> *In the New Jerusalem.*

I do not want to miss that thrill!

"All over the world are members of Prince Emmanuel's army" marching home. They have made many weary marches, but they have won great battles. Many in your own column you know—some are ahead, and have already entered through the gates; millions are in the other columns whose names you never have heard. All are headed for the grand review. A few more days, and the number will be complete. Steady and faithful! It is home we are going.

Did you think you belonged to a poor, despised company? Have you been always in the minority, standing with the faithful few? Do not get an inferiority complex. There will be a multitude of redeemed. God's victory is an overwhelming one.

> *Ten thousand times ten thousand,*
> *In sparkling raiment bright,*
> *The armies of the ransomed saints*
> *Throng up the steeps of light.*

THE ETERNAL GOD

Read: Rev. 7:13-17; Ps. 146.

Text: *These are they which came out of great tribulation, and have washed their robes and made them white in the blood of the Lamb. Rev. 7:14.*

The God of Faithfulness. With all the gathered multitude, God and the Lamb are the center of attention. The joy of heaven is the joy of worship. So it should be in our assemblies. The joy of meeting friends and fellow-laborers is great, but the joy of praising God together for victories won and honoring His name is first. When at last we make it through to heaven, we shall have no thought of self-congratulation—only of praise to God. How about our testimonies here?

No wonder we shall worship! Here we catch glimpses of God's faithfulness and truth; but many questions are still unexplained—we have had to leave them to faith. When we see the *why* of all our trials and understand the Father's purpose fully, there will be reason to shout through all eternity.

God keeps His promises forever. Abraham waited twenty-five years after the promise for Isaac, and four hundred years for the Promised Land. Jeremiah waited seventy years for the return from captivity. Daniel's vision waited five hundred years for the Messiah. But every promise was fulfilled on time. The final deliverance of the saints will be on time. God's word is pledged.

The triumph of God is in the victory of His children. His is the Father heart and He is hurt worst by the infidelity or the alienation of His own. So in one sense we are the center of heaven's attention, and we are the chief cause of God's triumph. May I make it through, to gladden His heart.

> *Great is Thy faithfulness, O God my Father;*
> *There is no shadow of turning with Thee.*

THE ETERNAL GOD

Read: Rev. 5:1-14.

Text: *For thou wast slain, and hast redeemed us to God
by thy blood, out of every kindred, and tongue, and
people, and nation.* Rev. 5:9.

The God of Redemption. God cannot help us except
through the Blood. Almighty as He is, He can do nothing
for us if we reject the atonement of Calvary. Unitarians
and moralists really have no right to hope in His mercy.
White robes are the sign of our relationship.

God and man are victors because of the Atonement.
Love is victor by its own nature; it triumphs by the very
act of loving. God showed us this once concretely when
He gave His Son; He will show it throughout eternity in
His kindness to us.

The God of Love. God has asked us to trust His love
even through tribulation; only so can He deliver us. The
pattern on this side of His web is suffering, on the other
side glory; but if you pull out any threads underneath,
you ruin the pattern above. Clip the emperor moth's
chrysalis to let him out easily and you cripple his wings,
for they grow strong by struggle.

To the group which comes up out of great tribulation
He promises the best of all: His presence, His close contact, His personal supervision and care for their comfort
and needs. He is their Shelter; He dwells among them,
feeds them, leads them, heals them, comforts them. The
black night is short. Beyond shines eternal, never-end-
ing day. This is better than thrones and kingdoms. This
is victory.

> *The King of Love my Shepherd is,*
> *Whose goodness faileth never;*
> *I nothing lack if I am His,*
> *And He is mine forever.*

JESUS THE SON OF GOD

Read: John 8: 12-20; John 17: 1-8.

Text: *I and my Father are one.* John 10: 30.

Jesus is God as He claimed—or else He is not even a good man. "A good man," they say. "Greatest of the ages: Socrates, Plato, Buddha, Jesus"—but still one name among the rest. No, if not very God, above all gods, He was a sublime liar; for that was His claim. But His life and His words prove Him true. None but God could have conceived such a life and such words. He is God: the Chief Cornerstone.

Unique, Absolute, Perfect — these infinities Jesus claims; and these make Deity. Nothing here of the "finite God." Let the mind reel, understand it or not, Jesus demands a reckless faith. "Believe Me," He says, "and let every man be a liar."

He claimed a unique oneness with God, a unique Sonship, a unique community of nature; a unique at-home-ness in heaven, a unique understanding of the Father's will. All other men who ever lived have had to climb painfully to God; Jesus brought God down to us. Such oneness with God I cannot have. But Jesus said if I would obey, I should come to know a fellowship with the Father like His own. He would lift me to share their thoughts. Have I despised that honor?

S. D. Gordon says there are three physical things which can be defined only in terms of themselves; they are fundamental, elemental. These three are Light, Life, Power. Add to these Eternity, and you have Jesus' description of His own Being. In Him is everything that is real, fundamental, enduring.

> *All hail the power of Jesus' name!*
> *Let angels prostrate fall.*

JESUS THE SON OF GOD

Read: John 8:33-45.

Text: *And ye shall know the truth, and the truth shall
make you free.* John 8:32.

*If you and I really believe Jesus is divine authority, we
will accept His definitions*—even when they contradict
popular notions. Jesus defines *freedom*: Not "Abraham's
seed," but "knowing the truth." Strange, hard saying,
especially for our day. Hitler's "Aryan blood" thought to
enslave all other races—were not they themselves the
bondmen? We Americans pride ourselves on Jefferson
and "democracy"—but are we prepared spiritually to
lead the nations into freedom? Jesus says, "Not 'a superior nation,' therefore free." Most of us think we are free
when having our own way and dictating to others. But
Jesus says, "No, you are free when you know what is
right and are doing it. You are free when your conscience
is freed to live a holy life."

The man who says, "I can't," is often freer than the
man who says, "I will." The man who says, "I can't lie,"
"I can't stoop to cheat," is freer than the man who says,
"I'll have that if I have to lie and cheat to get it." Obedience to moral laws makes us master of their power; as
our obedience to the laws of electricity will master its
power, while disobedience will only wreck us.

He says, "Freedom is *obedience!*" It sounds contra-
dictory. But not if that obedience is voluntary and to
Christ. When we would have our own way, we found
ourselves shackled with fetters of envy, jealousy, passion, and restlessness. But when of our own choice we
circumscribed our liberties for Christ and others, we
found ourselves free as a bird soaring in the sunshine. He
told the truth! He is the Truth.

*He speaks! and Eternity, filled with His voice,
Re-echoes the praise of the Lord.*

JESUS THE SON OF GOD

Read: John 8:28-32.

Text: *I am the way, the truth, and the life: no man cometh unto the Father, but by me.* John 14:6.

Listen to His claims, and remember they are true. What does it mean to you that this Jesus is your Jesus? Light: the All-Wise Teacher. Jesus defines *Truth*: Himself, His sayings, His life, His nature, His mission. How far afield the philosophers have gone in their search for truth. Yet here stood Jesus. How many expedients the economists and legislators have tried, to build the right sort of world. Yet here was the Sermon on the Mount. How many schemes the psychologists and sociologists have proposed, to make the right sort of man. Yet here was the Cross. We shall yet come back to Him: "the Truth by which the nations live."

He claimed to be All-Wise, not in that He had learned the truth, but in that He is the Truth. Authority—no wonder, because truth originates in His nature. Truth is truth because it is like Him. I may misunderstand Him, I may disobey Him, I may fail to consult Him, and so go wrong; but to the extent that I act according to His counsel I act right. Why, then, so many blunders?

He claimed to be the perfect Pattern. He claimed that He lived a blameless life, that always He pleased God. Gross egotism this, if only a man. But being God manifest in flesh, He spoke truth. He is my perfect Example; and He reminds me that to please God should be the aim of my life also. Can I evade the cross and the girded towel?

> *Thou art the Truth—thy word alone*
> *True wisdom can impart.*

JESUS THE SON OF GOD

Read: John 8: 21-27.

Text: *He that believeth not the Son shall not see life.*
John 3: 36.

Life: The only Saviour. He claimed to be the Only
Source of spiritual life. Those who have not met Him
have no hope of heaven, no vital religious life; without
Him people will die in their sins. Is it really true that
those good neighbors of mine—those good brothers and
sisters of mine—who have heard Christ preached all
their lives but felt good enough without Him—true that
they are eternally dead and cannot make heaven? True
that I with all my faults, but trusting His grace, have
yet the life eternal that can never die? Let me love Him
humbly and recommend Him more urgently.

He claimed to be the one Giver of eternal life, and
that by freeing us from sin. The philosophers talk wisely
and eagerly of immortality; but the only immortality that
has joy in it is that which begins now with eternal life
in the soul. It is a quality, not a duration; it is purity, not
years.

He claimed power over life and death: the power that
was in the Voice that spoke at Creation and that will
speak when worlds are dissolved; the power that speaks
in the thundering waves and the power that speaks,
"Peace be still"; power to make alive and power to destroy; the power I would rather have as friend than enemy. Best of all, power to break the fetters Satan has
forged about me, power to destroy every work of his in
me—authority finally to cast him out and cleanse the
earth.

> *Thou art the Life: the rending tomb*
> *Proclaims Thy conquering arm.*

JESUS THE SON OF GOD

Read: John 8: 46-59; Matt. 26: 57-64.

Text: *I am Alpha and Omega, the beginning and the ending.* Rev. 1: 8.

Power: equal with God. He claimed to be the Only Authorized Spokesman of God. Do not play around with Confucius or Buddha or Tagore. They were only feeling their way; better go straight to headquarters, for you will hear Jesus' voice again when you close your eyes to earth and go out on your last lonely journey. He is Spokesman now in invitation; then, in judgment.

He claimed to be the final Judge of all men. He claimed to hold in His hands the destinies of good and bad. Future Judge because present Judge. Those who rate now in His sight as children of the devil will, unless they repent, still rate so when they stand before Him on the Last Day. Sooner or later I must meet His keen eye and let Him measure my life. I can do it now, and I will.

He claimed to be Eternal: the God of Abraham and all the fathers—the Alpha and Omega. All of God's revelation is full of Jesus Christ. The song of the Lamb will be not a solo, but a chorus; not of a generation, but of the centuries. I am in the biggest thing of all the ages—and the only real thing—when I trust in Jesus. Let me not be a castaway by losing my grip on Him!

He claimed to be the One Thing Needful—in this life and the next. "All that I want is in Jesus." Far below truth to say you would lose everything rather than lose Him. Rather say, "Lose Him and you lose all."

> *Thou art the Way, to Thee alone*
> *From sin and death we flee.*

May 20

THE FATHER'S PROMISE GIVEN

Read: Acts 1:1-8.

Text: *Behold, I send the promise of my Father upon you: but tarry ye in the city of Jerusalem until ye be endued with power from on high.* Luke 24:49.

The Promise. Is the Holy Spirit's baptism a privilege or an obligation? Jesus' work is unfinished until it is completed. In each succeeding generation it must be taken up anew—by whom? Men never could do it; it is a task for God. His work is to be completed by the Third Person of the Trinity in human hearts. The risen Lord did not leave His part of the task incomplete. He did not go away until He had made arrangements for the reception of the Holy Spirit. When the Spirit came, He came *as Jesus had said.* His coming was not an accident, not an interesting phenomenon; it was to be identified with Christ's promise and Christ's command. Acceptance of the Holy Spirit in the relationship Christ defined is binding upon all Christians. This is the Spirit's day.

The command to receive the Holy Ghost is as binding as any other of Christ's commands. We should take it seriously. Or do we take any of His commands seriously? Purchasing salvation for us was a tremendously serious matter with Jesus.

The baptism with the Holy Spirit was important enough to occupy Jesus' last thoughts and words on earth. It was important enough to be the Forerunner's introduction of Him, and His own farewell. It was more important than water baptism, or prophecy, or the signs of the times. It was more important than temporal success or prestige. It was more important than Christian work—without it. How important is it to me?

He who was promised, Gift of the Father,
Have ye received the Holy Ghost?

155

THE FATHER'S PROMISE GIVEN

Read: Acts 2:1-18.

Text: *Ye shall receive power, after that the Holy Ghost is come upon you.* Acts 1:8.

The Power. Why live a failing Christian life when success is possible, and expected of us? Colonel Brengle's big little book *When the Holy Ghost Is Come* has for the text of each of its twenty-three chapters the promise, "Ye shall receive power after that the Holy Ghost is come upon you." So many aspects of the promised power are there. Flowing through the life as the electric current through the wire, He is present in every activity, to purify, to energize, to vitalize, to direct.

What are the enemies I must meet? The world, the flesh, the devil. Against each one the Spirit furnishes power. Every one wishes victory, but not every one realizes the process that makes a victor. The "power over all the power of the enemy" comes not by legions of angels or magic formula; it is given not to you but through you; it works by what you let be done in a yielded heart. It is "power to do the will of God patiently, with naturalness and ease, or to suffer the will of God with patience and good cheer, that comes with this blessed baptism."—Col. Brengle.

How much of wear and tear on our spirits and strain on our nerves because we lack the oil of the Spirit. How much "trial and error," how many failures in our work for God because we have not the guidance of the Spirit. How much reproach on the name of God because we lack the perfect love which is the work of the Spirit.

> *I worship Thee, O Holy Ghost,*
> *I love to worship Thee;*
> *With Thee each day is Pentecost,*
> *Each night Nativity.*

May 22

THE FATHER'S PROMISE GIVEN

Read: John 14:25, 26; 16:16-22.

Text: *When the Comforter is come .... he shall testify of me.* John 15:26.

The Promiser. Would you have Jesus real in your life? The Holy Spirit speaks of Him. Jesus is living—and it is "to Him" that we are to witness by the Spirit. As He lives in us we are to reproduce Him to the world. Did any one ever say of you, as the small boy said of Phillips Brooks, "I saw Jesus this morning"?

Jesus is in Heaven. When He arrived there He sent back the Spirit—the best proof; as Nansen the explorer sent home the dove when he reached the Arctic. We do more to prove His deity if we have His Spirit than if we fight for "fundamentals."

Jesus is coming again—till then let us be faithful. And we shall show our loyalty not by pining for His return, but by obeying and witnessing. We are better Christians when doing missionary work than when arguing the manner of the Second Coming.

Power to believe, power to hope; power to preach, power to pray; power to serve, power to suffer; power to testify, power to hold your tongue—which is your great need today? If you have received Him, let Him work through you in the way you need. He is not some vague, mystical influence, but waits to make Christ live again in your trying situation this day, if you will keep the connection clear. Jesus began and ended His ministry with the promise of the Holy Ghost baptism. It was His great gift. I wonder what He thinks of me, and of my attitude toward it.

> I worship Thee, O Holy Ghost,
> I love to worship Thee;
> My risen Lord for aye were lost
> But for Thy company.

GOD'S BETTER THINGS

Read: Heb: 8: 6-11.

Text: *This is the covenant that I will make with them after those days, saith the Lord; I will put my laws into their hearts, and in their minds will I write them.* Heb. 10: 16.

The Better Covenant. Always brighter, always fuller, always forward—God always leads on to "something better." The key word of the new covenant and of the whole book of Hebrews is *better.* When I walk with God, my face is to the light and my best days are ahead.

Better, because the promises of the New Covenant are better. In the Old Testament God promised to multiply flocks and herds to the obedient; in the New Testament He promised to multiply grace. In the Old He promised remission of past sins; in the New He promised deliverance from the power of all sin. Have I a New Covenant faith?

Better, because it promises to deliver you from compulsion in your service to God. It changes law to love, "I ought" to "I want to," bondage to freedom, duty to pleasure. So it guarantees success and rules out failure. For what a man really wants to do he can always find a way to do.

Better, because the New Covenant is a very personal matter. Everyone who has been sanctified wholly has made an eternal covenant with God, and God has sealed it. For the covenant-makers the "sun no more goes down"—no matter how black their circumstances. If no personal covenant, then no entire sanctification.

> *O glorious hope of perfect love,*
> *It lifts me up to things above,*
> *It bears on eagle's wings.*

GOD'S BETTER THINGS

Read: Heb. 9:1-14.

Text: *How much more shall the blood of Christ . . . .
purge your conscience from dead works to serve the
living God?* Heb. 9:14.

The Better Worship. Better, because my worship is not
limited in place. Now I need not journey to the tabernacle
whenever I meet with God—not even to the church altar.
I can make an altar in my room and build a sanctuary in
my heart; I can drop the curtains of my soul around me on
the crowded street, and talk with God.

Better, because there are no external things between
me and God. My tabernacle is not made with hands;
my sacrifice is not of animals; my worship is not with
golden candlestick and loaves of bread. But let me not
lose their spiritual meaning: consecration and cleansing
and prayer and praise.

Better, because now there is no priest between my
soul and God. I can come to Him direct as person to
Person, as child to Father.

Better, because the sacrifice is not "once a year."
Once for all Christ's blood has been shed and I am redeemed; once for all I have appropriated the Blood and
found salvation; and every day I may enter the Holy of
Holies to hold communion with my Lord.

Better, because it is inward, not outward. It makes
a change in the man himself. If your religion is just going to church and coming home, with nothing happening
inside you, it is not New Testament grace.

Better, because it puts away sin utterly. A religion
that plans for confessing sin every day has little conscience of sin. Do we loathe sin and seek to be holy as
God is holy, or are we living in the dispensation of "bulls
and goats"?

*Called unto holiness, Church of our God,
Purchase of Jesus, redeemed by His blood.*

GOD'S BETTER THINGS

Read: Heb. 9: 15-28.

Text: *And for this cause he is the mediator of the New Testament.* Heb. 9: 15.

The Better Sacrifice—the Better Mediator. Better, because the blood shed is the blood of the Eternal Son of God. That divine sacrifice meant something — enough to convulse all nature. Does it mean nothing to me? Power is there—the power of an infinite dynamite. And power to all eternity—"the Blood will never lose its power." Is it enough for my little self?

Better, because it cost so much. Bargains usually show up for their price. A salvation that cost the death of the Son of God has worth incalculable, infinite. I will prize it above all else. No other treasure is to be put in a class with it.

Better, because the Mediator is one who has unbounded, unquestioned influence. I can be confident of pardon and cleansing if I come in the name of Jesus.

Better, because it is the will and testament of God. By the death of Christ it was sealed. Now we can enter into our inheritance. No one can break the will—not even Satan. I can be sanctified wholly if I will.

Better, because our Intercessor lives in heaven. If we sin we have an Advocate there. Christ did not bear my sins and then forget me when He entered His glory. My name is written on His hand now. And if I slip, mercy waits for me, not judgment. He prays for me.

> *The Father hears him pray,*
> *His own Anointed One;*
> *He cannot turn away*
> *The presence of His Son.*

GOD'S BETTER THINGS

Read: Heb. 10:1-18.

Text: *Wherefore Jesus also, that he might sanctify the people with his own blood, suffered without the gate.* Heb. 13:12.

God's Best. Better, because it deals with the substance rather than the shadow. When shall we learn that the things we see are only the pictures; the unseen things (God, Christ's sacrifice, the heavenly city, the temple of our spirits)—these are the realities. The real beauty is the beauty of holiness in my heart, not the beauty of the church I worship in.

Better, because it provides for our entire sanctification as a definite crisis. Once for all we are to be cleansed from sin and identified with Jesus Christ. Keeping down the sin in our nature is a weary life; here is full deliverance and victory.

Better, because it gives assurance. The witness of the Holy Ghost rings a bell of certainty. The Jews still wail; the Christian shouts. He knows what is his relation to God, he knows where he is going, he knows he has access to God.

Better, because it is God's best. It met the worst that Satan could do with the best that love could do—and it was enough. It transforms a child of hell into the image of God. It makes a sinner's soul fit for a holy heaven. Human mind could not conceive it. But I can have it.

God's vision and provision for us in this new dispensation is "better"—infinitely better. I must not abuse His generosity. Better—not less— than theirs of the Old Covenant must be my sacrifice, my earnestness, my hatred of sin, my appreciation of God, my deliverance from bondage.

O boundless love divine, how shall this tongue of mine
To wondering mortals tell the matchless grace divine,
That I, a child of hell, should in His image shine!
The Comforter has come.

ABIDING IN CHRIST

Read: John 14:15-23; John 17:21-23.

Text: *Your life is hid with Christ in God.* Col. 3:3.

Union with Christ is the Bible pattern for a complete Christian. Does anyone wish to be an unfinished half-Christian?

The real Christian life is an unseen, super-natural thing. It moves among men, but has its springs deep out of sight. Let us not become superficial or standardized Christians. Our hope is in our fellowship with "the Friend inside." "Don't listen to friends when the Friend inside you says, 'Do this.'"—Gandhi to Kagawa.

Does God seem unreal and far away? Get Jesus in your heart by the baptism with the Holy Ghost, and God will be a living reality. You don't find those who have been sanctified wholly troubled with doubts about God and His ways in the world. You know people to whom God is real. They talk of Him naturally; they talk to Him freely. Do you really want to be like them? If that is the kind of Christian you want to be, you can be. *You* determine the amount of God you have in your life.

Oneness with Christ means oneness with other Christians. The genuine church unity doesn't come by legislating union; it doesn't come by preaching co-operation only. It comes by the personal union of each member with Christ. Is your love for your fellow Christians wearing thin? Make a fresh contact with Christ. And the conviction for sin we are longing to see on the sinners of the congregation we shall see when the Christians are fused together by fresh visions of Jesus.

> *He hideth my soul in the cleft of the rock*
> *That shadows a dry, thirsty land;*
> *He hideth my soul in the depths of His love,*
> *And covers me there with His hand.*

ABIDING IN CHRIST

Read: I Cor. 6: 15-20; Eph. 5: 25-30.

Text: *The temple of God is holy, which temple ye are.*
  I Cor. 3: 17.

The nature of union with Christ: He is the Vine, we the
branches; He the Head, we the body; He the Bridegroom, we the bride; He the Shekinah, we the temple—
no comparison is too intimate to express the relation
Christ wishes to have with His own. He expects to be
closer to us than any thing or any person, vitally close.
We were vital to Him on Calvary.

The Shekinah in the temple. What was the "glory" Jesus
had as He walked the dusty ways of Galilee and faced the
hostile churchmen of Judea? It was the God-consciousness that never left Him. What was the "glory" Jesus
Christ knew in heaven with the Father? His own radiant
Deity and the light of the Father's face. What was the
"glory" of the temple of the Old Covenant? The manifest
presence of God in the Shekinah. What is the "glory"
He promises us? That certainty of His inwrought presence which we may have here and the assurance of an
unveiled Presence hereafter.

We can always be *confident* of His presence; we
cannot always be *conscious* of His presence—a good rule
to remember as we are called to go through the tunnels
by faith. Yet that God-consciousness increases in our
lives as we practice looking into the face of Jesus.

Every act will be an act of worship if your body is a
temple. Your thoughts, set free, will turn to prayers;
your words will be said for Him.

The Bridegroom and the bride. "This is the will of God,
even your sanctification, that you should stop flirting
with the world."

He has come to abide, and holy must be
The place where my Lord deigns to banquet with me.

163

ABIDING IN CHRIST

Read: John 15: 1-10; Eph. 4: 11-16; Eph. 2: 20-22.

Text: *I am the vine; ye are the branches.* John 15: 5.

The Vine and the branches. It does not take a big branch to bear big fruit; only a sturdy vine, well pruned. It does not take a big church to do a big work, nor a big person to accomplish big things; only a vital connection with Christ.

We wonder at the faith of George Mueller, who repeatedly gave away his last shilling and trusted God to supply more. But are we not all called upon to do the same in the spiritual realm? Give our last ounce of strength and not know where the next is coming from, give our last precious revelation from God to a small prayer-meeting handful and trust God for a fresh message for the Sunday crowd, open our mouths to testify when we seem to have no words. That is real fruit, for it is trust in His doing, not our own.

Community of interests with Christ is the price of real prayer. Short of that we cannot be trusted with our own desires.

The Head and the body. Christ has no body except His church. He needs our hands, our feet, our voices to get His work done. And the Head must have control.

He is the great Head; how safe I am. For if I let my actions be dictated by Him, He will care for me as a man protects the apple of his eye.

The Foundation and the building. A building loses its essential nature when it loses its foundation. Supposed to be a refuge, it degenerates into a heap of decaying timbers. So of a Christian who tries to live apart from Christ.

> *Just as the branch is in the vine,*
> *I'm joined to Christ,*
> *I know He's mine.*

ABIDING IN CHRIST

Read: Rom. 8: 5-13; John 15: 2, 10.

Text: *I am crucified with Christ; nevertheless I live.* Gal. 2: 20.

The price of union: "Crucified with Christ." Test your relationship with Christ by the quality of your spirit and the principles that dominate your life. Love or hate? Humility or pride? What you can give people or what you can get out of them? Love marks Christ's men.

Life is beautiful; death is ugly. A beautiful Christ-like character is attractive; the agony of self-crucifixion that precedes it is not so pleasant. But this is the only way to reach that.

A close relationship with Christ is not a luxury; it is a necessity. Too many have calculated that they did not need to go on to a second work of grace by consecration and complete yielding. Jesus Himself says if we do not "abide" we shall be destroyed.

How long can a person delay the utter abandonment of himself to Christ that brings union with Him? Until he sees clearly that it is the will of God and that he will become disobedient by refusing. For Jesus says that commandment-keeping is the one condition of abiding.

Guard jealously your lifeline of connection with Jesus Christ. Disobedience, cooling of love, self-will, prayerlessness will cut you off from the supply of grace and you will find yourself powerless in your time of sudden need. Be watchful to detect any barrier between yourself and headquarters.

The most beautiful union with Christ can be broken. For as long as I live I shall be choosing. It will steadily be harder to choose against the will of Christ; but to the very end it will be possible.

> *So dead that no desire shall rise*
> *To pass for good, or great, or wise*
> *In any but my Saviour's eyes—*
> *Let me die!*

EVEN AS YOUR FATHER

Read: Matt. 5:43-48.

Text: *Be ye therefore perfect, even as your Father which is in heaven is perfect.* Matt. 5:48.

God expects us to be Godlike. Homer, in his epic poems, when he speaks of a great hero, designates him regularly as "godlike." He has that something in his nature that cannot be explained in terms of ordinary human nature; it raises him above the normal; he is superhuman. So of God's men. We can't excuse ourselves by saying, "It's only human to do thus and so." We are expected to live a life that is stamped with God.

The dealings of God with man are based in *moral responsibility.* God is holy. He has limited Himself to moral rightness. There are evil things He cannot do because He is Himself. That sense of personal accountability to do the highest good we know is the core of personality, the image of God in the soul. I do not want to deface it. I want no wider liberty. The soul is damned that loses it or casts it off.

God has limited Himself by *specific responsibilities*: to every part of the universe He has made, to every creature of His hand. He is Love. So we are bound by responsibilities in every one of life's relationships. For every new situation in life there is a new set of relationships, and so a new set of responsibilities. This is what "adjustment" means for Christians. Shifted suddenly from one environment to another? Find your responsibilities: as a man to men, as a Christian to needy souls.

Stamp Thine own image deep on my heart.

EVEN AS YOUR FATHER

Read: Lev. 19:1-4.

Text: *Thou shalt have no other gods before me.* Ex. 20:3.

God expects us to be like our Father. Christian ethics center in a *Person* and in personal values. The Ten Commandments and all the Old Testament regulations are not merely moral precepts, noble and uplifting though they are. They are God's attempts to get to His people, to show them what He is; and to show them that the human beings He has created are persons too, fit to become children of Himself. All His commands are alive with meaning for a world in which the only real values are personal.

All true religion begins with *humility.* It is not "the superior man" making himself noble; it is the child of God trying to be like his Father. The best moral man is still of this world; each of us must enter the kingdom of God as "a little child."

No idols. Why? Because of Who our God is. Not that He is jealous, petty and demanding as men are petty and demanding. Rather, that he is *perfect;* He proves Himself as the best, the only Real in all the universe. He knows that if we worship any other person or thing, we are getting the cheap, the counterfeit, the harmful. He knows that when we set our hearts on the material or the human, we are shutting out the only Living Source of help. Because He knows we need Him above all else, He demands that we hold Him above all else.

> *What have we to do with idols*
> *Who have companied with Him?*
> —J. STUART HOLDEN

EVEN AS YOUR FATHER

Read: Lev. 19:11-13; 15-18; 35-37.

Text: *Be ye holy, for I the Lord your God am holy.* Lev. 19:2.

God's own nature is the basis and the beginning of His demands. God is holy; His child must bear the family likeness. Break up His holiness into its spectrum colors. Remember His love shown to you, His justice; remember His kindness, His truth; remember His impartiality, His fairness. You are called by His name—would you lack any quality?

Our God is transparent, perfect *sincerity,* crystal clear. In His presence no shadow of a lie can hold up its head. When we swear falsely by His Name we profane that Holy Name; we pollute it. So when we call ourselves Christian and juggle with the truth. We want to be sincere, transparent in our dealings with men: free from reservations, quibbling, double meanings, ulterior motives —trustworthy as our Father.

Our God is *honest;* He always gives value received, and more. He respects every man's property. He does not lie nor steal to get His way. He does not even steal a reputation or a man's personal freedom in order to make His own plans work well. He counts on the power of simple honesty and truth to win out. So can we. So must we.

> *Gladly I'll forfeit all of earth's treasures,*
> *Jesus, Thy perfect likeness to wear.*

EVEN AS YOUR FATHER

Read: Lev. 19:14; 32-34; Matt. 7:12.

Text: *Thou shalt love him as thyself.* Lev. 19:34.

Our God is impartial; He treats us all alike—and the weak most gently and thoughtfully because they cannot help themselves. So do we if we are like Him.

How do you treat the person who is in your power? They say it is the acid test of character. Your very ordinary neighbor who has no influence; your servant who is at your mercy; the deaf man who cannot hear the joke at his expense; the blind man who cannot see your clever wink. If you are like God, you treat them as you would be treated in their place.

Our God *forgets no one.* The weaker and more helpless, the better the Father's memory. You know this from the way He thinks of the old and the stranger. We can be more like Him in paying special attention to the ones nobody else thinks of: the bore; the unpopular girl; the tiresome old woman. There are plenty of them!

Our God's name and His nature are *Love.* Out from Him goes only blessing. (Men may refuse to accept it, and choose the curse. But that is their fault.) He has given us a principle to live by if we would mirror His likeness in our lives: His Golden Rule. Whose image, then, is that of the talebearer, separating friends? Of the man who nurses a grudge into hatred? To call ourselves Christian is as much as to call ourselves "Golden Rulers," if we accept the implications.

> *Oh to be like Thee, full of compassion,*
> *Loving, forgiving, tender and kind;*
> *Helping the helpless, cheering the fainting,*
> *Seeking the wandering sinner to find.*

IN HEAVENLY LOVE ABIDING

Read: Gen. 45:1-5; Ps. 105:9-24.

Text: *It was not you that sent me, but God.* Gen. 45:8.

The only city that excels the City of Brotherly Love for a home is the city of Providence. It is rest to mind and heart to take up one's abode inside the love and care of God. It is blessedly possible. And that is the only safe place to live—secure in the midst of all life's ups and downs.

The best, happiest, truest way to interpret life is in terms of God's doing. Instead of being vexed by annoyances, irritated by interruptions, cast down by delays, hurt by injustice, overwhelmed by apparent contradictions, we shall then say, "Not you, but God." To interpret every event as of God's sending takes out all the sting and the smart.

Not circumstances, but "the Word of the Lord" had "tried" Joseph. He had been submissive in the dark to a plan he could not understand, and at the end he found he had sowed better than he knew. So of the missionaries who sacrificed in the early days to spread the gospel in the South Sea Islands; they prepared the way for some of their own nation to be spared. "God did send them before to preserve life."

Strange that God has chosen suffering to develop our souls to their full capacity. Even His Son must learn obedience by the things which He suffered. There is no other way.

Looking backward, every child of God has only words of praise for His goodness. Trials, sorrows, failures, successes, tests, achievements, all are seen to take their place in the pattern of His good purposes. The characteristic note:

> *All the way my Saviour leads me,*
> *Oh, the fullness of His love!*

June 5

IN HEAVENLY LOVE ABIDING

Read: Gen. 45:9-15; Ps. 105:1-8; 42-45.

Text: *Seek the Lord, and his strength: seek his face evermore.* Ps. 105:4.

Only our confession of dependence on God makes it possible for God to continue to use us. There are more and harder tests ahead. Our present grows out of our past; our future is determined by our present. And all life is proving-ground for eternity.

Have you ever reached a sudden climax when many prayers of years were granted, and unexplained questions were answered, all in a single moment of fulfilment? Have you ever come spiritually upon a moment that seemed to you the summit of a long, long climb in the dark, when a glorious sunrise revelation of God's purposes burst upon you? Such moments are a foretaste of the resurrection morning when every dark thing will be made plain. We are headed for that morning.

In view of this faith the only possible attitudes for the child of God are *gratitude* toward his Heavenly Father and *magnanimity* toward his brother man. Our all-embracing debt to God obligates us to forgive men, who in wronging us have hurt only themselves. God has turned their injury into blessing for us.

Magnanimity—greatness of soul—how is it they say it is measured? "The greatness of a man is measured by the size of the thing he will argue over." "The greatness of a man is measured by the size of the thing that offends him." "The greatness of a man is measured by the size of the wrong he can forgive."

Forgiveness pays. "All that we send into the lives of others comes back into our own"—with interest added.

> *He knows the way He taketh,*
> *And I will walk with Him.*

CHRISTIAN ESSENTIALS

Read: I Tim. 6: 11-21.

Text: *Lay hold on eternal life, whereunto thou art also called, and hast professed a good profession before many witnesses.* I Tim. 6: 12.

"The Meridian Test of the Minister," an article in a well known religious journal, points out that at middle age there tends to be a "slackening of effort in the momentum of service," a "tendency to live on past experience." "We do not feel keenly the wonder of eternal things." "There is no more deadly and insidious condition of soul than the dread ease with which we proceed to our tasks, unmoved." The church too has its "meridian test."

The problem does not seem so simple today as it used to, the problem of living a holy life and "spreading scriptural holiness." Then the issues were clear-cut and evident; we "gave up the world" and took the "way of holiness." Now society is more complex, temptations take on unfamiliar forms; worldliness comes in a new guise. How about it? Are we supposed to change our gospel with the changes about us? Does the church need "a new message for a new age"? Or is the way of holiness essentially the same if we will search and find it?

We do not all see things alike. But more and more as we "walk in the light"—that is, follow the illumination of the Spirit upon the Word of God—we shall approximate unity of judgment in the things of God. The Spirit of truth is guiding us all to harmony in the great essentials. Holy people come to see the fundamentals pretty much alike, after all.

> *Jesus calls us o'er the tumult*
> *Of our life's wild restless sea;*
> *Day by day His sweet voice soundeth,*
> *Saying, "Christian, follow Me."*

CHRISTIAN ESSENTIALS

Read: I Pet. 5:1-10; I Tim. 6:1-10.

Text: *Be clothed with humility.* I Peter 5:5.

Some attitudes are incumbent upon the church of Christ if it is to conquer the world—incumbent, therefore, upon individual members of the Church.

We must understand the *social aspects* of our gospel. Christians are not to live in a vacuum, not in a monastery safe from contact with evil, not even in a retreat expecting the immediate return of their Lord. They have to mingle with people and live among them. What of their attitudes?

The church is done with *social ambition*. Christianity tears down all barriers of money, caste or clique. All Christians are brothers; the church stands for brotherhood. There can be no snobbishness within the church. Her Master made Himself of no reputation and became a servant. The elite can be saved; but they become humble first.

The church is done with *financial ambition*. Rich men can be saved, but increasing luxury and love of ease are not truly Christian. The spirit of contentment with little, the spirit of giving, not getting—this is the glory of the church whose Lord emptied Himself and had not where to lay His head.

The church is done with *compromise*. She must not be overconcerned with conciliating good opinions. She does not expect to make it through without opposition and persecution. She accepts these as the trial and testing that will prove her loyalty, and is concerned only that she be blameless—for so she is safe.

Remember our "week of probation" is to be followed by an eternity of reward.

> *How can I make a lesser sacrifice,*
> *When Jesus gave His all?*

CHRISTIAN ESSENTIALS

Read: I Pet. 4: 7-19.

Text: *Be sober, and watch unto prayer.* I Pet. 4: 7.

To the very end of time *the Christian church is committed to some positive Christian principles.* The church has the long view, and so lives by a different scale of values from the world. Its *summum bonum* is not anything that can be realized in time: not money, not social prestige, but eternal life.

The Christian's *wealth?* Good works here and eternal values laid up in heaven. Are those the investments I am concentrating on?

The Christian's *conduct?* Soberness, prayerfulness, charity (love)—the Bible has not a word to say about brilliance or cleverness or "leadership qualities" or "tact" or "social adaptability." Am I majoring in the right things?

The Christian's *life?* A fight. The world will never be a friend to grace. I am deceived if I think all is going smoothly; that is my moment of greatest danger. Am I looking for an "easy way"?

The Christian's *attitude to money?* Stewardship. Do I dole out my tithe to the Lord, then lavish the rest on "keeping up with the Joneses"—or leading them? Or do I spend every dime as for the Lord?

The Christian's *ambition?* To make heaven and take as many with him as he can. Am I more interested in anything than I am in saving souls and helping them on their way to heaven?

The Christian's *secret of success?* Faith. Not popular favor, not pull with the great, not his own efforts or his own winsomeness, not favorable circumstances. Just his confidence in the God of battles who cannot be defeated. Do I live as if I believed God?

> *If every member were just like me,*
> *What kind of church would my church be?*

June 9

SPIRITUAL MATHEMATICS

Read: II Pet. 1:1-4.

Text: *Grace and peace be multiplied unto you, through the knowledge of our Lord. . . . Whereby are given unto us exceeding great and precious promises.* II Pet. 1:2, 4.

We add; God multiplies. This is the Christian mathematics. Our human best is sadly inadequate; but if we do that best, God adds the touch of infinity that makes it enough. All we really accomplish in the spiritual realm we do by laying hold with all our little might of the mighty promises of God.

"Crisis" and "process"—through the promises. One clear thinker said there are two essential promises. *The* promise of the Old Testament is the promise of a coming Saviour; *the* promise of the New Testament is the promise of an outpoured Holy Spirit—both promises made good by the finished work of Christ. The New Birth and the Spirit's fullness—let me claim both; I need both.

We are saved and sanctified as we lay hold on the two essential promises; we grow in grace as we lay hold on the thousands of promises that meet our thousand and one human needs with the infinite resources of an infinite Father. But we must match our needs to the promises. We are not meant to be self-sufficient—not even for one day.

Limitless assets for every Christian—for you today, though the job you have to do seems more than you can swing. You are certain it is His assignment for you and not some notion of your own? Then get out your checkbook and fill in the amount you need. You deposited your little all; your heavenly Banker has multiplied it by infinity—with grace ready for you.

Standing on the promises, I now can see
Perfect, present cleansing in the Blood for me.

SPIRITUAL MATHEMATICS

Read: II Pet. 1:5-8.

Text: *Giving all diligence, add to your faith.* II Pet. 1:5.

Growth in grace—through the promises. Our Christian growth is just a process of getting acquainted with God. He doesn't change; He is always Himself: infinite in power, love, and wisdom. But every test makes us know Him better. What are you going to let this trial of yours teach you about Him? It all depends on you. The promises are there.

Not enough courage? You will not add courage by whistling louder; not by gritting your teeth and saying, "I will be brave." You add courage by remembering that He said, "I will never leave thee nor forsake thee." "Courage is fear that has said its prayers."

"Stupid" in spiritual things? You will learn best by claiming the promise, "If any man lack wisdom, . . . it shall be given." Will to take the counsel of God rather than of the crowd, and you can prove, "If any man will to do, . . . he shall know."

Like things easy? Lacking in self-control? Quick on the trigger? Will to be different—yes. But also remember that "the fruit of the Spirit is temperance (self-control)," and yield yourself consciously and completely to His control. Better than self-mastery, and surer, is mastery by Christ.

Tempted to give up easily? Prone to discouragement? You can't become patient by willing, but you can look through the "upper window" and "see Him standing by." You can hear His words, "He that endureth to the end shall be saved"; "To him that overcometh, . . . the crown of life."

> *All so freely given,*
> *Wooing us to heaven—*
> *Wonderful words of life.*

SPIRITUAL MATHEMATICS

Read: John 14:13-16.

Text: *Partakers of the divine nature . . . . Neither barren nor unfruitful in the knowledge of our Lord Jesus Christ.* II Pet. 1:4, 8.

Christlike character—through the promises. If we really wish to become Christlike, we can. The reason the human sticks out so prominently in our lives is that we are not working to make the "honor roll" in our spiritual mathematics. For the grace will be multiplied if we furnish the desire.

Jesus is our Great Example; but we do not become like Him merely by imitating His deeds as recorded in the Gospels. We become like Him by living inside the promises: that if we keep His commandments He will live in us and manifest Himself to us; that if we obey, the Spirit will teach us of Jesus' ways; that if we walk in the light we shall have fellowship with Him. It is a living relationship with Jesus that will make our Pattern real.

We do not become like Jesus by working hard at the job. Life under strain is not the normal Christian picture; the person who is all "endeavor" is often very disagreeable. "Out of the abundance of the heart," is the formula. We receive the mind of Christ; then it is easy to act like Christ. So strain is gone, and peace is multiplied.

We are made fruitful—through the promises. The "second blessing" does not make me independently holy; it does give me an eagerness to have God "will and do of His good pleasure" in me. It gives me the disposition to love, the disposition to believe the promises, the disposition to let the Spirit have His way. It makes my heart good soil; as I keep that soil improved, the heavenly Gardener will grow the fruit.

> *Trust, and thy trusting soul shall prove*
> *Christ is thy life, and Christ thy love.*

SPIRITUAL MATHEMATICS

Read: II Pet. 1: 9-11.

Text: *If ye do these things, ye shall never fall.* II Pet. 1: 10.

We are kept steadfast—through the promises. We keep ourselves in the love of God by obedience and trust, but we do not keep ourselves from falling. We count on His word: "Able to keep you from falling." We stay on the foundation; and "the foundation of God standeth sure."

Young Christians fear they "can't hold out"; some hesitate to start for fear they "can't make it." God gives the rule; if we follow it we "shall never fall." It is ours to watch our spiritual arithmetic. If we keep busy for God, many temptations to turn aside we shall not even see.

Backsliding often comes gradually and imperceptibly. It comes by not "adding" faithfully and steadily. Some morning you wake up to find your blessing gone and your heart cold, and you are tempted to wonder if you "ever had any experience anyway." It was because you planned to have just enough religion to "get by." Those who make it through are those who are "all out" for Christ.

Eternal Security—If. God's Word says we "shall never fall"; yes, but God's "eternal security" has a big "if"—an essential "if." We shall be saved finally, surely and without question—eternally secure in heaven—*if* through faith we have been born again and sanctified wholly, and *if* we continue to grow in grace.

Plan to go through. Plan to make heaven. Instead of arguing too much against eternal security as a doctrine, make up your mind to gain eternal security as an experience. Sad if with a right doctrine you be found at last with a faulty experience.

> *Standing on the promises I cannot fall,*
> *Listening every moment to the Spirit's call,*
> *Resting in my Saviour as my All in all—*
> *Standing on the promises of God.*

SIGHT OUT OF BLINDNESS

Read: John 9:1-7; 13-15.

Text: *He went his way therefore, and washed, and came seeing.* John 9:7.

The blind man learned that blind eyes do not have to stay shut—not when Jesus comes our way. Many of us have learned that too. We were blind to the horror of sin, blind to the vistas of God's grace, blind to the beauty of Jesus, blind to the need of a lost world. But one touch of Jesus changed it all. A real experience of salvation makes one "wiser than all his teachers." For in one moment he knows the reality of the things that count most.

He learned that it pays to obey Jesus in the dark. The darkness will surely turn to light if we take the steps of obedience. He learned that he was not good for much himself when it came to solving life's problems. He learned to sing,

> *Just as I am, without one plea,*
> *O Lamb of God, I come.*

He learned to sing,

> *Transformed by grace divine,*
> *The glory shall be Thine.*

The God-touched man is humble.

He learned that the people who profess the most are not always the most Christlike. And the sooner we recognize it—and then stop worrying about it—the better for us all. For we don't have to let "the hypocrites in the church" separate us from Jesus.

> *So blind was I, but now I see,*
> *And that's enough for me.*

June 14

SIGHT OUT OF BLINDNESS

Read: John 9:8-12; 35-38.

Text: *The Lord is my light and my salvation; whom shall I fear?* Ps. 27:1.

The man whose eyes are opened learns something about Jesus. Jesus understands. Others may blame or wonder. But Jesus knows the facts of your case even better than you do. His insight is unfailing; and He is always fair.

Jesus cares. Others are usually too busy or self-centered to worry much about your case. But He never looks at you with a careless, impersonal eye. You are not a fly under the microscope to Him, nor a guinea pig for an interesting experiment. He wants to help you more than you want to be helped. His name is Love.

Jesus can. Others will pity or sympathize and "wish there were something they could do." His is the power to fit your very need. Trust Him—and try Him.

Jesus is the best of all friends. Better than father or mother, better than fellow church members. Others will help you as far as they can go comfortably and conveniently; He never counts the cost to Himself. Others will help as long as they can remember; He never forgets. Others will stand by you so long as it is the popular thing to do so; He is thinking first of you. Some will help to the limit of their strength, but that gives out. There are no limits with Him.

Jesus never fails. If you have really been saved and have learned to know Jesus, you have a secret that makes you a match for all and everything life can bring you.

> *What a friend we have in Jesus,*
> *All our sins and griefs to bear!*

SIGHT OUT OF BLINDNESS

Read: John 9: 24-34.

Text: *One thing I know, that, whereas I was blind, now I see.* John 9: 25.

The man with opened eyes learns something about witnessing. We must testify. Eyes are on us. It is not enough to "live the Christian life and say nothing about it." We must give glory to Christ. Others must know that He is "the Man who opens eyes." The world knows that he is a coward and an ingrate who does not acknowledge a benefactor.

It is better to witness than to argue. "A man convinced against his will is of the same opinion still." People who argue about religion really don't want to know; they only want to upset you. And there is no answer to a genuine testimony.

You do not have to be a philosopher or an orator—just a witness. The testimonies that count for most are those that tell simply what Jesus has done and is doing for ordinary people like you. It isn't the "how" that counts in testimony—only the "now."

Your testimony will bring you most blessing when it costs you something. When Jesus knows that you have suffered for His sake He is sure to hunt you up and give you a special blessing.

And it is not always the testimonies that come "bubbling up" that ring the truest; sometimes the words you have to force yourself to say from sheer conviction count the most. *Testify to your "facts," not your "feelings."*

> *I love to tell the story;*
> *It did so much for me.*

181

SIGHT OUT OF BLINDNESS

Read: John 9: 16-23.

Text: *We ought to obey God rather than men.* Acts 5: 29.

The man with opened eyes sees—or should see—Jesus larger than people. One of the strongest desires of man is to stand well in the sight of his fellows. He wants to be good; he wants his neighbors to think of him as good. "Saving face" is a powerful motive of action; a powerful deterrent from evil—and sometimes from good. Watch it. For your neighbor's standards sometimes conflict with God's.

Ostracized? Unpopular because you are a Christian? For Jesus' sake you have lost what men hold dearest? Hard to bear, yes. But Jesus will find you in your loneliness, and your heart will sing for joy as you worship. He will stand by you.

Let us never ostracize from our fellowship a person who knows Jesus, even if he seems to upset our program or fails to fall in line with our ways. For kindness is better than a smoothly working system; and we may find ourselves on the opposite side from Jesus.

What a contrast! Men timid, cowering, fearful of place and power, refusing to own the truth if it cuts across their interests, forgetful of others' need in their absorption with self—but Jesus direct, fearless, kind, strong; seeing with keen insight, acting of Himself from conviction and love, going straight to the goal without shifting. He taught us what human freedom is—shall we give up our birthright?

> *Foes may hate, and friends may shun me;*
> *Show Thy face, and all is bright.*

SIGHT OUT OF BLINDNESS

Read: John 9:39-41.

Text: *Lord, open his eyes, that he may see.* II Kings 6:17.

Blind Spots. The self-righteous man never can see himself as he is; for his vision is filled with one big image—himself.

The hardest man for the gospel to reach and move is the man who "thinks he is all right."

The conceited man will never learn; for he cannot think anyone knows more than he does.

The prejudiced man is always illogical; for he has his mind made up already and must make his logic fit his theory if he has to tear it to bits.

The man who always wants to argue religion betrays his dishonesty. If he were willing to walk in the light, he could soon know the truth.

The man who would reduce everything to the natural plane will never see the glory of God. For he has no room for a supernatural Christ.

The man who would rather prove himself to be in the right than learn the truth is in for a tragic loss. For he misses connections with Jesus and truth. He refuses, perhaps, to seek God one night for fear of "what people will think." After that he "sees things differently." He has blinded himself.

Lord, show me my blind spot, and touch it. I would not be deceived, nor fail to stand by Thee, nor lack in kindness to one that Thou dost own.

> *Open my eyes, that I may see*
> *Glimpses of truth Thou hast for me.**

THE LORD'S DAY

Read: Isa. 58:13, 14; Ex. 31:12-18.

Text: *The sabbath of rest, holy to the Lord. Ex. 31:15.*

We should form the Sunday habit. One of the most terrifying symptoms of our day is the Christians' careless Sundays. It used to be that a Christian would not even continue a necessary journey on Sunday; now some who make loud profession start sightseeing trips on Sunday without a qualm. Careless treatment of the Lord's Day is symptomatic of disease; it betrays a callousness to Bible standards, to our Lord's example, to God's command, to the needs of the Kingdom, to the welfare of our own souls.

Sunday is "the Lord's day." All its activities belong to Him. It is not the day to catch up with all our piled-up correspondence or social duties. Our hearts and minds should be free from pressure on Sunday to do the Lord's business and to cultivate His society. He demands this relaxation of spirit because He knows we need it if we are not to wear out.

The letter may be written, the call may be made; but it should be done as a special service to God or to man for His sake. The hours of the day are not mine, but His.

Rule a line around Sunday—keep it safe. Build a wall around Sunday—do not let the claims of the week intrude. You will have to fight for it—do not yield to temptation. Keep the day open for the Master's use. Never let yourself be so busy on Sunday that He cannot have as much time as He asks.

> *O day of rest and gladness,*
> *O day of joy and light!*

THE LORD'S DAY

Read: Matt. 12:1-13.

Text: *For the Son of man is Lord even of the sabbath day.*
Matt. 12:8.

We should use Sunday to let our Lord bless us. The Lord's
day is a day of privilege as well as debt. How many good
gifts of our Lord we shall miss completely if we rob Him
of His day.

Sunday is the Lord's day: in it Jesus will show His
authority over our *minds.* Sunday is a good day to increase my store of truth. Let me go to His house expecting to receive a new revelation of truth direct from
Him through His minister. He has it for me; He knows
that no second-hand human theorizing will serve my need.

Sunday is the Lord's day: in it Jesus shows His
authority over our *spirits.* Sunday is a good day to seek
deliverance from sin. If the demons of selfishness or pride
or envy or worldly ambition have got a grip on my soul
anywhere, let me use His day to seek the holiness He
offers. He concentrates on setting captive souls at liberty;
He is looking my way.

Sunday is the Lord's day: in it Jesus would show His
authority over our *bodies.* The best way to keep in good
health is to rest one day a week. In the sanctuary, in quiet
meditation, you will find poise and refreshment. And if
you will give God time to talk to you, you may find Him
willing to do some temporal things for you—healing, supply of financial needs, practical guidance—you never
could have found in the week's rush.

> *Day of all the week the best,*
> *Emblem of eternal rest.*

THE LORD'S DAY

Read: Acts 16: 13-18.

Text: *I was in the Spirit on the Lord's day.* Rev. 1: 10.

We should use Sunday to be a blessing to others. "Sunday is such a long day. If I do not study, do not work my garden, do not go to ball games, do not go pleasure-riding, do not read secular literature, what can I do?" First have your heart changed, and then you will enjoy doing the kind of things Jesus did on the Sabbath, and find the day all too short. Everybody should show respect for Sunday; only Christians can fully keep it.

Certainly some part of Sunday should be used for prayer for God's work. Have we even begun to realize the potency of prayer? Have we tested it? When we consider John Knox's prayer for Scotland and then hear that down to today "Scotland is the only nation that has not subscribed to the Roman legend," we may begin to catch a glimpse of the beneficent influence of prayer.

We say we have not time for much prayer: we live in a rush; so many things press. Here is the need of the hour—prayer. And Sunday surely holds a few hours that can be used for intercession and communion.

And what if you are a busy mother or a hospital nurse, and Sunday is like every other day in its duties, or worse? Build the sanctuary in your heart to your Lord, sing the special hymns of praise in your heart to Him, do your work as a special sacrament—He will give you the Lord's day blessing and put in your hands the touch of healing for someone you work with.

> *Speak to my soul, dear Jesus—*
> *Lead me to glorify Thee,*
> *Help me to show Thy praise.*

THE LORD'S DAY

Read: Mark 1:21-34.

Text: *As his custom was, he went into the synagogue on the sabbath day.* Luke 4:16.

Jesus is our Example for the use of the Sabbath—or is He? Did you ever try actually to build your Sunday schedule by what you imagine Jesus would do if He lived in your home under just your circumstances? It would help you to settle many a debatable issue.

Jesus at church. Jesus went to church Sunday morning and He took an active part. Every layman should be a positive force in the service through singing, praying, testifying if the opportunity is given, listening well—in short, by lifting, not dragging.

Expect to think when you go to the house of God; do not ask always to be entertained. You can make your preacher a better preacher by thinking with him.

When Jesus is in church, souls are being delivered from Satan's bondage. Your prayers must help to free them.

Jesus after church. Jesus' rule was not, "Go to church in the morning and have a good time the rest of the day." His Sabbath day was more than one hour long. Jesus in the home was a Healer always, never an added burden or a vexation. He more than paid His way by the blessing He brought.

Even for the man who "works hard all the week and has only Sunday for recreation," true recreation can be got in Jesus' way better than by a "modern Sunday." And how can we Christians in our complex life carry on His work of relieving human need if we do not keep one day free to give specifically to the needs of others?

> *We own Thy sway, we hear Thy call,*
> *We test our lives by Thine.*

187

THE LORD'S DAY

Read: Heb. 4:1-11.

Text: *Ye are the salt of the earth.* Matt. 5:13.

We should carry the spirit of Sunday through the week.
Jesus would spend every day doing good: (1) teaching
right belief, freeing men's minds from error, upholding
Bible standards of thought and life, showing what it is
to be a Bible Christian; (2) casting out evil spirits, freeing men's souls from sin, proving the Gospel's power,
making Christians; (3) healing the sick, freeing men's
bodies from disease, making life wholesome for those
around Him, making it easier for them to be Christians.
So we are the salt of the earth: wherever and however
we touch men, we should bring blessing.

Jesus was always active, always giving out, always
strong. You fail sometimes; you want sometimes to be
petted, to have someone bear your burdens; you have
not the strength He had. Is it strength you lack, or in-
clination? Are you willing to be poured out? willing to
be God's fuel and burn? willing never to call a day your
own? "As he is, so we" are to be.

Would you not want to be known as a helper? I
would. So that when people saw me coming, they would
not expect a flood of complaints, but would feel free to
tell me their cares and know that I would help them
find relief. Only the heart that has entered into His
Sabbath rest is a heart at leisure from itself and its own
worries.

Are you making any impression for good on the
world you live in? If you were taken today, what would
the world lose? The world is hungry for the strong man
or woman, the helper. Unbroken contact with Jesus
will make you one.

> *To me the rest of faith impart,*
> *The Sabbath of Thy love.*

THE FAITH THAT SAVES

Read: Rom. 3:21-31.

Text: *Christ Jesus; whom God hath set forth to be a propitiation through faith in his blood.* Rom. 3:25.

My faith has a solid basis—Calvary. "I can trust the Man who died for me." Faith is efficient because it takes my eyes off my weak self and fixes them on my mighty Saviour. I have been bitten by the serpent and there is no help in me. I must look to the brazen serpent, symbol of the Great Deliverer.

The cross of Jesus is something more than the place where a good man laid down his life. It is the place where the Son of God bore the sins of the whole world. Mine were included, if I will claim my deliverance. He identified Himself there with my sin if I will identify myself with Him now.

Faith is not antinomian; faith in God is not an evasion of God's holy law. Because through faith my sins have been nailed to the cross of Christ I do not look lightly on sin; rather, I loathe it more, for it killed my Lord. Faith links me up with power to keep on the rails of the law.

"The best 'moral man' is a Christless man; the weakest Christian is a man plus Christ—and the difference is infinite."—C. W. Butler.

Calvary is enough. If God gave Christ, He will not fail me. Through Calvary life is related rightly with eternity. To Calvary I pin my faith forever.

> *My faith still clings to Calvary,*
> *Where lifted high upon the tree,*
> *The Son of God I see.*

THE FAITH THAT SAVES

Read: Heb. 11:29-40.

Text: *Who through faith subdued kingdoms, wrought righteousness, obtained promises. Heb. 11:33.*

My faith is dynamic. Mustard-seed faith moves mountains, obtains promises, works miracles. The majority of religious people today find the church ritual intensely beautiful. They admire religion. But it is a religion without life; Christ does nothing for them. They are not believers.

The modernist compliments prayer, but he says its worth is that it makes a change in the man who prays: it soothes him, quiets his nerves, adjusts his will to God's. Yes, it does all this, but it does more. It is the hand that lays hold of the will of God, embraces His promises, and obtains results.

You do not see how prayer can "change things"? You "can't believe"? Look at your radio! Then tune in your prayer transmitter and your faith receiver.

"Never turn God's facts into hopes, but simply use them as realities, and you will find them powerful as you believe them."

After all, though it sounds very good to say, "I want to *know,*" I must stretch out the arm of faith and take if I am to receive. I must believe Christ purchased the experience for *me.* I must myself step over the line into Canaan; I must let the heavenly Surgeon perform the operation on my heart; I must endorse the check with my own name. I must appropriate the blessing.

> *Faith is the victory*
> *That overcomes the world.*

THE FAITH THAT SAVES

Read: Eph. 2: 8-22.

Text: *By grace are ye saved through faith.* Eph. 2: 8.

My faith does something in heaven; it changes my record on the books of heaven. "Who is he that condemneth?" The only one who has a right to speak against me now is the "Christ that died," and He has become my Friend. If Satan reminds me of my past sins, I can remind him that the black past is washed away in the blood of Jesus. It can never be found. The page is clean.

My faith brings me into a new relation with God; I am at peace with Him. "I looked to Him, He looked to me, and we are one forever."—Charles Spurgeon's testimony, and the testimony of every truly believing soul. That is conversion.

My faith does something in me; for gloom and fear and despondency it brings me peace and joy and hope. The Christian hope is a rejoicing thing. Only the believing heart dares look clear through to the end of time.

Faith is positive, certain, sure. The moment faith wavers, doubt has entered and faith is no longer faith.

And "the wireless current that God has chosen for the conveying of His power to the world is our faith."—I. Lilias Trotter.

> *Gone is the night with its shadows drear,*
> *Morning hath dawned upon me;*
> *Gone is the burden of anxious fear,*
> *Freedom my portion shall be.*

THE FAITH THAT SAVES

Read: Rom. 5:1, 2.

Text: *The just shall live by faith.* Rom. 1:17.

Through faith I am sanctified wholly. Sanctification is an establishing grace; but it is maintained as well as obtained by faith. I am sanctified while I believe. The promises of God are living seed that will bear fruit in our lives—but only if they are planted and watered by our faith. Try it with the promise you need most. Perhaps it is this one: "The very God of peace sanctify you wholly. . . . Faithful is he that calleth you, who also will do it."

The proof of your faith that a man can be wheeled across Niagara on a tightrope is, "Get into the wheelbarrow." Perhaps it seems as impossible to be sanctified wholly. But God says, "If you believe me, get into the wheelbarrow of entire consecration!" "Let go—and let God."

By faith I live the Christian life. "Christ dislikes to have His people make a show thing of Him and not use Him." It is as if His promises were "life belts made to exhibit in a shop, but of no use for swimming."—C. Spurgeon.

Strange, how even good Christians seem to resent using the wings of faith. When the ground is cut from under their feet and they can do nothing to help themselves, they will dodge and twist and take every way but simple faith; they will fuss and worry and try to do things in some human way rather than believe God and rest. It is not natural to live by faith every day; it is super-natural.

> *My faith looks up to Thee,*
> *Thou Lamb of Calvary, Saviour divine.*

THE GLORY OF CHRIST

Read: John 1:14-18.

Text: *No man hath seen God at any time; the only-be-gotten Son . . . . he hath declared him.* John 1:18.

The Word. The world has not seen God, and—the pity of it!—does not realize the difference. Seventeenth-century Henry Vaughan wrote:

> *I saw Eternity the other night,*
> *Like a great ring of pure and endless light;*
> *And round beneath it Time*
> *Like a vast shadow moved.*

In the midnight fog of Time statesmen burrowed like moles, and misers sat on dark heaps of dust. Only a few "soar up into the ring" to God. I know people—so do you —who have no more idea of the glory of God and heavenly things than a mole has of the sunlight.

"Not really living," we say, of the miners who must spend all their days in darkness underground. "Not really living," of those alley-dwellers who never see the sunshine. And, "Not really living," we say a thousand times more truly of those who never have realized God through Jesus Christ.

Possible for man to see the divine glory? Possible to be freed from uncertainty and insecurity? Possible to find God? Many an intellectual has committed suicide because he did not believe it. But this is our gospel. Is it worth telling?

Blessedly normal and to be expected, for men to find God. For the Son of God came to make the connection. He is our road to God and certainty.

> *He sheds the beams of light divine*
> *O'er this benighted soul of mine.*

THE GLORY OF CHRIST

Read: John 1: 5-14.

Text: *He that hath seen me hath seen the Father.* John 14: 9.

The Light. Gleams of Jehovah shine through the earthly life of Jesus—for those who have eyes. To be a consistent Unitarian it would seem one must be willfully blind.

The Creator knows how to handle and use His own handiwork. Earthly things to Jesus are not for accumulating, in houses and lands. He used the soil to teach men truth, the fish to feed men, the swine to free men from devils. Persons He created not to be oppressed by things, but to be blessed by them.

Jesus the Creator living with His creation showed us the right values to set on things. I have not His divinity, but I do have His humanity; and as He lived on earth, I would do well to live. His emphasis may well be mine.

Rebuking the sea, He is God of nature. Healing the sick, He is Creator and Understander of the human frame. Raising the dead, He is Maker and Preserver of life. Multiplying the loaves and fishes, He is Provider for man. Cleansing the temple, He is Lawgiver and Judge. Teaching with authority, He is Omniscience. Transfigured on the mountaintop, He is Omnipotence unapproachable in shining glory. Risen from the tomb, He is the Eternal I AM. This is the God Whose I am and Whom I serve. Hallelujah!

> *His head with radiant glories crowned,*
> *His lips with grace o'erflow.*

THE GLORY OF CHRIST

Read: Eph. 1: 7-14.

Text: *Jesus . . . . made a little lower than the angels for the suffering of death, crowned with glory and honour; that he by the grace of God should taste death for every man.* Heb. 2: 9.

The Cross. The true glory of God is revealed in the Atonement. To read the Word of God in Jesus you must read His life clear through to the end; there you come to the Cross. And only there do you see the heart of God laid bare. You have a small God if you have no Atonement in your creed.

Let me not view the Cross with idle sight. There I see the real nature of my God; for I read His name as Holy Love: Holy, because He could not overlook sin; Love, because He bore the weight of it Himself for me. And I see that for me, too, spiritual glory is far to be preferred to material; for there my King serves His enemies and my God saves by His shame.

A religion can lift you only as high as its core. At the heart of beautiful Bali, isle of the South Seas, is the dance; and unspeakable lusts grow out of its "lovely" religious rites. At the heart of Confucianism is "the superior man"; and ethics will make an upright, but self-centered character. At the heart of the Roman religion was the state; at the heart of Nazism was force—both made nations of slaves. But at the heart of Christianity is the Cross of holy love. How high should it lift me?

> *Love so amazing, so divine,*
> *Demands my soul, my life, my all.*

THE GLORY OF CHRIST

Read: John 14:22-28.

Text: *The light of the knowledge of the glory of God in the face of Jesus Christ.* II Cor. 4:6.

The Face. The glory of God abides with us in the face of Jesus Christ. For He makes Himself known to us who receive Him, and He has promised to reveal Himself to us constantly through the Comforter. We need not rest satisfied with a historic Christ.

No truly repentant soul ever saw in the face of Jesus anything but kindness.

People who have looked much into that marred face are full of humble reverence. Those who know Christ well are never flippant about Him.

Christ! "In the beginning with God"—and some think "science" can discover newer truth than He taught! "Grace"—yet some are tempted to think the Father who sent Him cruel! "Truth"—yet some say, "Why doesn't God stop war and suffering?" and forget that He who sees that the nations have chosen wrong values suffers with His children, but cannot give peace till the lessons are learned. Without the face of Jesus we might doubt. With it, never.

One of the most beautiful words is *Emmanuel,* "God with us." One of the saddest phrases is, "His own received him not." Men always have returned God evil for good. But we can be different. He will notice if even I appreciate His love. I will not disappoint Him.

Jesus, the very thought of Thee
With sweetness fills the breast,
But sweeter far Thy face to see
And in Thy presence rest.

THE COURAGE OF FAITH

Read: Ex. 3:1-10.

Text: *I can do all things through Christ which strengtheneth me.* Phil. 4:13.

Our errand is too big for us. Almost everyone who has ever had a call from God to a special work for Him has seen it as a sheer *impossibility*. God has let him see it that way. He has told him, "I am sure Pharaoh will not let you go," yet insisted, "Go and deliver Israel." He has let him feel he would be ruined if he accepted the commission and lost if he refused. God's call is not to quick and easy success.

For God cares less about our work for Him than about our relationship to Him. He doesn't plan that we shall ever feel "equal to the job"—alone. So His call is to a life so *dependent on God* that we do not trust ourselves a moment.

It is human nature to want to do. But, "You cannot conquer outside until God has conquered inside."

God's ways commend themselves by their perfect balance. The call to utmost dependence on God is also a call to *utmost human effort*. "To trust as if everything depended on God, then work as if everything depended on us"—how Christians have slipped off on one side or the other through the centuries, because they were so human. But God is still looking for Wesleys and Moodys who can both pray and work.

The call is to superhuman *patience*. The success promised is final and overwhelming, but it may not come for years or generations. We may not see it in our lifetime. It is human nature to faint when it fails to see results; God demands that we faint not, only believe.

> *I must have the Saviour with me,*
> *For I dare not walk alone.*

THE COURAGE OF FAITH

Read: Ex. 3:11; 4:1, 10, 13.

Text: *Who am I, that I should go?* Ex. 3:11. *Thou art my servant; I have chosen thee.* Isa. 41:9.

Our excuses come from looking at ourselves. My handicaps are so big to me; they seem real reasons. They are real, very real, while I look at myself. But they are the same old excuses everybody has made from the beginning of time—everybody who looked at himself and not at God. Let me face them squarely and recognize their flimsiness—and be ashamed to admit one of them again.

"People won't believe in me." "Everybody knows I'm not a leader." True, no doubt. But the choice is not people's—not even church people's—but God's. He vouches for you, if you are doing His work.

"The enemy is too powerful for me." "Evil is too strongly entrenched in our town." True again. Sin and Satan are too strong for you; and you'll never find the devil friendly to the work of God. But you forget the death of the First-Born. There is power in the Blood— yours while you look to the Cross.

"I have no talents." "Anybody else could do the job better." "I haven't a magnetic personality." "I can't." True enough perhaps, but what of it? You can't, but God can.

It is false humility to keep looking at your weaknesses when God says you'll do. He knew what you were like when He picked you out. For after all, the job is not to be done by your great talents and winning personality. It is to be done by His Spirit illuminating your very ordinary personality.

> *So trusting my all to Thy tender care,*
> *And knowing Thou lovest me,*
> *I'll do Thy will with a heart sincere—*
> *I'll be what You want me to be.*

THE COURAGE OF FAITH

Read: Ex. 3:12; 19-22; 4:1-17.

Text: *Certainly I will be with thee. Ex. 3:12.*

Our encouragement comes from looking at God. It is much easier to look at self than to look up. Self is big. Before you can die to your excuses you must die to your self. But once be willing to be authorized by God and misunderstood by people; once be willing to take on a job that is too big for you, depending only upon God—then it is natural to look up. Then God has a chance to encourage you.

"What is that in your hand? Use it and I will make it enough." "Be yourself—blessed." God is encouraging you. And He will give you *signs* that he is using you. Maybe someone will tell you that your stammering testimony was a help to him. Maybe someone will ask you how it is that you can be patient under strain, and so you will have an opportunity to witness for Christ. Step by step you will have evidences that His power is in your life. You will find that a very ordinary man with God becomes a leader—when he stops trying to be someone else.

God encourages by His *promises.* "I will stretch out my hand," He says. That is what counts. He has pledged His word that every time we stretch out our little arm at His command, His great hand is stretched out too—invisible but almighty. All His promises are on my side, once I begin to obey Him. Can I plead poverty or weakness?

He encourages me by His *presence.* "Just a little more faith," He says, "a little more confidence, a little heavier leaning." And suddenly I find myself singing,

> *His yoke is easy, His burden is light;*
> *I've found it so, I've found it so!*

THE COURAGE OF FAITH

Read: Ex. 3:13-18; Matt. 28:16-20.

Text: *Thus shalt thou say . . . . I AM hath sent me.* Ex. 3:14.

And He encourages me by His patience with my stumbling and my slowness. He really makes me feel that He needs me and cannot get along without me. Even when I do not measure fully to His expectations—I know He must be disappointed in me—even then He takes what I will give Him and makes of me the most that I will let Him. He knows I want to please Him; He knows I love His cause. Lord, help me to be reckless in my devotion. The reflection is on Thee, not me, when I fail to trust Thee fully.

God is enough. God is the answer to all our excuses and all our fears. His answer to Moses is His answer to us who would serve Him: the bush that burned but was not consumed, the human life ablaze with God. If our lives have been opened to Him for His indwelling and His glory so that He truly sets them aglow, He will convince the world.

His name I AM—the Eternal—is enough. He sees the end from the beginning; He can direct me safely. He created all things; He can readily supply any small need I have along the way. He will one day speak the word that dissolves into nothing the worlds that we have known; surely He can melt away any obstacle that blocks my path. And He says, "Certainly I will be with thee." Where are my misgivings when I have Him?

> *How firm a foundation, ye saints of the Lord,*
> *Is laid for your faith in His excellent word.*

LONG-TIME CHOICES

Read: Ps. 1; Ps. 97.

Text: *The fear of the Lord is the beginning of wisdom.*
Ps. 111:10.

*Life is full of storms and cross-currents and shifting
winds.* If I am not to be beaten from my course and bat-
tered to pieces, I must have a stability of soul, an inner
fixity that will hold me steady. God's Word, and only
God's Word, shows me where to find this. I dare not
face life on my own resources.

Standards and principles of conduct are a blessing,
not a burden. A man is most a man when he is master
of his choices: when he really makes choices and does
not just drift. Life finds true value only in enlightened
choice—or God would not have shown Adam the tree.
True liberty is in voluntary submission to the highest law.

There are several long-time choices to be made. Decide these definitely; make them governing principles.
You will find your life immensely simplified as you fit
its details into this pattern. This is the true adjustment
that will bring success.

Recognize the absolute authority of God. Wisdom is
practical knowledge—knowledge turned to the uses of
living. The scholar has learned how to think; the wise
man has learned how to live. The first lesson in living
must be learned from God; the first step in living is sub-
mitting the will to God. For living lasts a long time. He
only is Master of Eternity.

> *Guide me, O Thou great Jehovah,*
> *Pilgrim through this barren land;*
> *I am weak, but Thou art mighty;*
> *Hold me with Thy powerful hand.*

LONG-TIME CHOICES

Read: Jer. 35:5-10; Prov. 1:8-10.

Text: *Abstain from all appearance of evil.* I Thess. 5:22.

Recognize the Christian conscience. Thank God for the church and the Christian home. They have been the greatest factors in making sound character, for they have given us our standards. When we break loose from them, or weaken their influence, or dilute their principles, we are cutting ourselves adrift from our own moorings.

Of course you can start fresh and "try it for yourself." Topsy "just growed"; but I doubt if you want to. And suppose we started fresh in science and education. Suppose every new generation had to spend its time inventing an alphabet, and start from scratch rediscovering the laws of physics. Great moral laws do not change. Better count on them and thank God you know them.

I should be slow to run counter to the convictions and practice of mature Christians. Actually you will find that some decisions made in the dark, simply following the Christians you know live closest to God, prove beautifully right when you come to see why. Christian principles are tested principles.

Recognize your responsibility to choose the good when you know it. Commit yourself irrevocably to the right. There is only one way for a man to take: the right way. No one can afford to tamper with his conscience; it might stop working. The upright man doesn't look first to see how an action will affect him. "Let him but see what he must do; let God see what shall follow."

> *Trusting Thee, I cannot stray;*
> *I can never, never lose my way.*

LONG-TIME CHOICES

Read: I Cor. 9:24-27.

Text: *So run that ye may obtain.* I Cor. 9:24.

Recognize spiritual values as superior to material. Fools want their own way and think it the best; wise men know there is a higher way and know it is beautiful. A child will grasp any shining disk; a sane man wants genuine coin—more, he discriminates between coins of different values. We think we are grown up, but it is hard to reject the pressing demands of the present and the seen in favor of the long-time unseen best—hard always to keep our values straight.

To live for time and sense is to be caught in a quicksand. You sink deeper and deeper; every self-indulgence brings on another. The world is not big enough to satisfy one soul. You must call a halt; you must cry to God desperately for a new heart. He can set you on the Rock.

Live for the long run. The law for the man who would be strong is abstinence, sacrifice, restraint. Abstain from the harmful in order to enjoy the good. Sacrifice good in order to have better; restrain impulse in order to achieve control. It is the law of the runner. It is the law of the Christian athlete, who has the longest of all long runs.

"There is in man a higher than love of happiness: he can do without happiness, and instead thereof find blessedness!"—Carlyle. And the wonder of grace is that blessedness brings happiness as its by-product. The negatives that appear so bleak to the man looking on only condition the soul for deeper joy than any worldling can know. Self-control gives way to Christ-control.

> Soon shall close thy earthly mission,
> Swift shall pass thy pilgrim days;
> Hope shall change to glad fruition,
> Faith to sight and prayer to praise.

PRAYER AND THANKSGIVING

Read: Ps. 103.

Text: *Bless the Lord, O my soul; and all that is within me, bless his holy name. Ps. 103:1.*

Prayer and thanksgiving belong together. There is nothing gloomy about the right kind of prayer. It is tied up with joy, for it sees our God. You do not really pray if you do not think of God. And you cannot think of God very long without thanksgiving.

If you do not feel a "spirit of prayer," meditate for a few moments on this topic: "Why should I give thanks?" Why give thanks?

1. Because of the nature of God Himself—loving, understanding, caring, forgiving, healing. (Ps. 103.)

2. Because of God's dealings with your poor soul in past days—how many times you have been brought low and He helped you; how many times you have played the fool and He has delivered. (Ps. 107.)

3. Because of Jesus who died on the cross—for you; who intercedes now—for you. (John 17.)

4. Because of the Holy Spirit, who lives in your heart—and "the fruit of the Spirit is joy." (Eph. 5:18-20) The remembering Christian rejoices easily.

We hear a great deal about "vicious circles." There is a "blessed circle": Praise begets Hope and Hope in turn begets Praise. And Faith is not far away.—E. E. Angell.

Joy is the antiseptic that keeps the germs of sin from lodging and developing in the Christian's heart; it is the vitality that keeps the Christian going and enables him to accomplish without exhaustion work that would wear out others.

> *O my soul, bless thou Jehovah,*
> *All within me bless His holy name!*

July 9

PRAYER AND THANKSGIVING

Read: Matt. 6:5-15; John 17:13.

Text: *Father, I thank thee.* John 11:41.

If your prayers seem to be all "Give me," try following Jesus' directions for prayer and Jesus' example in prayer. Like every other genuine thing, prayer has its counterfeit. Real prayer is secret: even if hundreds are hearing, the soul is alone in a real, personal audience with God.

The one thing we must remember, and the one thing Satan would have us forget, is that God is our Father: with all the love and all the authority the name implies— the only One who has the right and the wisdom to give us counsel and direction. We come as children when we pray.

Real prayer is optimistic. We must put the Kingdom first; but it will pay us to do so—the kingdom and the power are sure. We must be submissive to God's will; but we have also the privilege of dependence upon His provision. We must be willing to stay out of temptation; but we have the guaranty of deliverance if we should fail. We must forgive; but we shall also be forgiven. Prayer as our Lord taught it has the poise of perfect balance.

There is a deeper joy in prayer than the mere getting of things. There is the joy of maintaining right relations with God and men. There is the joy of forgetting self in bringing blessing to others. Jesus in the shadow of the cross prayed that His disciples might know His joy.

> *There is a place where Jesus sheds*
> *The oil of gladness on our heads—*
> *It is the blood-bought mercy seat.*

205

PRAYER AND THANKSGIVING

Read: Phil. 4: 6, 7; I Thess. 5: 16-18.

Text: *Pray without ceasing. In every thing give thanks.*
I Thess. 5: 17, 18.

If it seems you have no right to be thankful in an evil world, study Paul's recipes for prayer. There is always a "Thanks be to God" included.

There are four steps in every successful prayer: (1) Stop worrying! (2) Share your problem with God. (3) Give thanks before you feel like it. (4) Enjoy the peace that has no human basis—it passes understanding.

There are three life attitudes that combine to make a successful prayer life: (1) the praise habit: keep a song in your heart whatever your circumstances; (2) the prayer habit: count nothing too small to take to God in prayer; (3) the submission habit: take everything that comes to you as from the Lord. With these three habits you are invincible.

True prayer has no whine in it. We can spend hours on our knees rehearsing our worries and feel worse when we get up. We have not prayed a word.

Bishop Quayle tells how he had been pacing the floor in anxiety for hours when suddenly he stopped short, laughed aloud and went upstairs to sleep. He had heard God's voice saying, "It's all right now, bishop. You go to bed, and I'll stay up the rest of the night."

What does it mean to me to know that All-power, All-love, All-wisdom is at the other end of my prayer?

> *I'll drop my burden at His feet,*
> *And bear a song away.*

PRAYER AND THANKSGIVING

Read: John 17; I John 5:14, 15.

Text: *If ye abide in me, and my words abide in you, ye shall ask what ye will, and it shall be done unto you.* John 15:7.

If you pray a good deal but do not see many answers, learn to clinch your prayers. Put your little prayer up beside the great prayer of Jesus. Put your weak faith up beside the mighty "faith of the Son of God." You cannot do it alone; but with Jesus you cannot lose.

Some have felt great assurance in prayer for the healing of a loved one—yet that loved one died. What did it mean? Must faith be wrecked? God blesses you when you "pray through" for one of two reasons: either to assure you of the granting of your request or to strengthen you to endure refusal. In either case, He is telling you He has heard and will send you His very best. He never lets you down. (I John 5:14, 15.)

Jesus Himself when on earth did not have all His prayers answered as He would have wished. But He always delighted in the Father's will—and saw that will fulfilled.

Strange blend of persistence and humility, of boldness and self-effacement, of confidence and acknowledged unworthiness—this is prayer. For we come as children of darkness who have been adopted, as paupers whose Friend has made them rich, as outcasts who have been accepted in the Beloved. If we have lost either the humility or the boldness, we have left only the form of prayer. But if we are living as friends of God, we can have the boldness of friends of God.

There's a blessing in prayer, in believing prayer,
When our Saviour's name to the throne we bear.

THE BREAD OF LIFE

Read: John 6: 22-35.

Text: *Labour not for the meat which perisheth . . . . He that cometh to me shall never hunger.* John 6: 27, 35.

The proof of Jesus Christ is that He satisfies completely. Listen to the testimonies: always "I'm glad." Watch the lives: happy without the latest thrills. Hear the songs that try to tell it. The "scientific" skeptics are not following the scientific method when they shut their eyes to the great fact of Christian experience.

He who has found the Living Bread will not be seeking satisfaction in the world's garbage barrels. Tell people that when they say, "You don't go to shows? Poor thing! What *do* you do for a good time?"

Jesus knows our hungers, varied and complex. But His supply is infinite—can we realize what that infinite means? He multiplies, not adds—things increase fast by geometrical progression—and He always has a reserve. I need not fear that I shall ever unearth a depth in my nature for which He will not have the fullness.

It is sin that hinders satisfaction. Many want the "loaves and fishes": material well-being or emotional satisfaction. These are by-products; let Him give them or not as He will. Seek His deliverance from the weight and power of sin. That is His work. And that is fundamental satisfaction.

If we were in foreign lands we might see more who are hungry for freedom from sin, torturing themselves to obtain release. The sense of sin has been educated out of us. Holiness is the fundamental hunger; and until it is satisfied no other will be.

> *Hallelujah! I have found Him*
> *Whom my soul so long has craved.*

THE BREAD OF LIFE

Read: John 6: 41-51; Num. 11: 4-9; Ex. 16: 11-15.

Text: *Verily, verily, I say unto you, He that believeth on me hath everlasting life. I am that bread of life.* John 6: 47, 48.

Always Jesus must be the Giver and we the receivers. Many people do not know how to receive graciously. But we do not earn this bread; it is a royal gift. Have you been wishing for salvation? Even trying? Stop trying, and take.

Our English language is rather poor at times. It says *believe* when it means to accept the fact that 2 and 2 make 4; and it says *believe* when it means to rest all the weight of the soul for eternal salvation upon an Omnipotent Arm. You say you "can't believe." Is it so hard when you remember that to *believe* is to *trust* the love and power of Jesus? The beauty of New Testament grace is that it is an intelligent relationship with the Person of Jesus Christ.

The Israelites were filled; but they said "Manna" ("What is it?"). Praise be to our Christ, my spirit can grasp Him. I can bring to Him my every emptiness and have it filled from His own hand. I can know Him whom I have believed and love Him whom I have not seen.

Bread is everyday food—necessary to life. From the beginning to the end of my spiritual life—and it shall never end—I must feed on Jesus. Have I made contact and got my supply for today?

> *Bread of heaven,*
> *Feed me till I want no more.*

July 14

THE BREAD OF LIFE

Read: John 6: 52-59; Ps. 107: 1-9.

Text: *The words that I speak unto you, they are spirit, and they are life.* John 6: 63.

How does He feed you? Remember your own past experience. The gracious provision was His, but by definite acts of will again and again you came and ate. And each time you felt you had been in your anxieties like Spurgeon's little mouse nibbling in the granaries of Egypt, who feared the supply would not be enough for his needs. It will always be enough. "Feed on Him by faith in thine heart."

A sinner, you heard Him say, "Come unto me, all ye that labour, and I will give you rest"—you came and fed. His death was made life to you.

Poor in temporal things, you heard Him say, "Seek ye first My kingdom, and all these things shall be added." You trusted, and His promise was made bread to you.

Needing friends, you heard, "Bless them that persecute you." You obeyed, and His command was made your bread.

Needing direction for your life, you heard, "He that would be greatest, let him be servant." You followed His example, and it became bread to you.

Needing wisdom above your own, you heard His legacy, "I will send the Comforter—He shall guide you into all truth." You claimed your inheritance.

It is by literally turning His words into life that we make them bread. Beside how many of them in your Bible can you write "T and P" ("Tried and Proved")?

> 'Tis true, oh yes, 'tis true,
> God's wonderful promise is true;
> For I've trusted and tested and tried it,
> And I know God's promise is true.

210

THE BREAD OF LIFE

Read: John 6:60-69; Isa. 55:1-3.

Text: *Lord, to whom shall we go? Thou hast the words of eternal life.* John 6:68.

The deceived heart feedeth on ashes. What is taking place in our poor old world today shows what happens when people refuse the Bread of Life and feed on their own notions. Hitler tried to feed his "have-not" nation with false nationalistic pride. Germany, groping her way to a solution of her problem, turned to violence and hatred, to snatch prosperity. The communists and rebels against society have thought to find satisfaction in equal shares of food for rich and poor, with the key in the hands of the poor. Even our educators have said, Realize the personality by breaking restraints and indulging impulses. We were to feed ourselves. We are hungrier than ever!

Why the world's restlessness? People are hungry and they do not know for what. We know—and Jesus knew. God told Satan (in Goethe's *Faust*) that man would never "eat dust with a relish." He knew man's nature.

Our center is wrong. We were made for God, but we try to live from ourselves. We were made for eternity, but we try to feed our souls with earth. So we shut eternity out of our thoughts and say we will "die when our number is called," "there is nothing we can do about it."

There is something we can do: we can make connection with Jesus. Jesus feeds and ennobles the soul of man. Schemes to "help the masses" can degrade and starve the spiritual nature. He alone nourishes my spirit with fine wheaten bread.

> *Bless Thou the truth, dear Lord,*
> *To me, to me,*
> *As Thou didst bless the bread*
> *By Galilee.*
> *Then shall all bondage cease,*
> *All fetters fall,*
> *And I shall find my peace,*
> *My All-in-all.*

July 16

THOU SHALT NOT STEAL

Read: Lev. 19:11-15.

Text: *Thou shalt not defraud thy neighbour.* Lev. 19:13.

Not all thieves steal money. "Why talk to us about stealing? Talk to the downs-and-outs and the kleptomaniacs!" But when did you steal your neighbor's reputation by a shrug of your shoulder? When did you steal your pastor's influence with your own children by thoughtless criticism at the Sunday dinner table? Those intangibles were worth more to their owners than money.

You can rob another man of the regard due his personality. You do it without realizing what you are doing; it is an insidious thing. You do it by "having men's persons in admiration because of advantage"; by pretending to like a person who you think can be of service to you; by being just a little nicer to the person who has "influence." He feels "sold" when he learns the truth; he is "robbed."

Social tangles. "Defraud not" your social inferiors. You owe certain things to every person you hold any relationship to; pay every man his due. A man's character is measured by the way he treats those from whom he can expect nothing.

You owe those who work for you a fair wage, both of money and of courtesy and consideration. For they are your fellow creatures; you owe them their share of the Golden Rule. Some day the wheel of fortune may turn and put you in their place. Then you will know instinctively how great is the theft of a man's self-respect.

> *Walk in the light! and thou shalt find*
> *Thy heart made truly His*
> *Who dwells in cloudless light enshrined,*
> *In whom no darkness is.*

THOU SHALT NOT STEAL

Read: Luke 19:1-10.

Text: *Owe no man anything, but to love.* Rom. 13:8.

Industrial tangles. We have nice words for our business stealing. "Clever deals," "shrewd methods," even "sharp practices," perhaps—but not sins, not stealing. And we have excuses. "A man must live." We want to "get ahead" (of the other fellow?). The strange thing is that our excuses seem so valid—until we meet the eye of Christ. Then "cleverness" looks more like dishonesty.

"Is there such a thing as an honest tradesman?" "Can a man succeed in business and be a Christian?" Succeed or not, a Christian will be honest. Rich or not, he will have the wealth of a good conscience. And Christ will stay at his house. The business men who have dared carry on by Christian principles have been powerful forces for righteousness.

Conscience is a stronger power than men reckon on. After men have oppressed others and crushed them, they are not going to lie down and sleep comfortably. Conscience will raise its head, and awakened, it is ruthless.

"Owe no man anything but love." How much? I want to be honest; I want to settle my debts. One debt I never can pay in full; for I owe it to everyone to love him as Christ loved me, and that was an infinite love. I never can pay it in full, but I am not dishonest so long as I am paying as much as I can. If ever I stop doing my best, I shall be stealing. As long as I live, that debt will keep me busy—humbly and gratefully.

> *When on the cross those cruel nails*
> *Gave me a Christ that never fails—*
> *How much I owe!*

THOU SHALT NOT STEAL

Read: Prov. 11:1-8; I Sam. 12:1-5.

Text: *Ye shall do no unrighteousness in judgment.* Lev. 19:35.

Inner integrity comes high, but it pays. We don't get bargains in the moral realm. If we try to get by cheap, we have to pay more in the end. Honesty comes high sometimes, but it is still—and always will be—the best policy.

Your conscience is not an appendage you can discard when you please, and never miss it. Your conscience is you. Conscience is the whole man at work deciding moral issues. Play with your conscience, and you tamper with the inner springs of your own nature. Weaken its hold, and you weaken yourself—irreparably.

"There is but one rule of conduct for a man—to do the right thing. The cost may be dear in money, in friends, in influence; in labor, in a prolonged and painful sacrifice; but the cost not to do right is far more dear: you pay in the integrity of your manhood, in honor, in truth, in character. You forfeit your soul's content, and for a timely gain you barter the infinities."—Archer C. Jones.

"The honest man," said John Earle three hundred years ago, "doesn't accept a bribe and call it a gift." In other words, he doesn't accept favors that he must pay for with sacrificed convictions. It is a fine thing to have your friends know that, much as you value their kindness and their good will, your soul is not for sale. You want nothing that is not rightfully yours—no favors with strings attached.

And are you one of those "friends" who want to rob others of their freedom?

> *Men heed thee, love thee, praise thee not;*
> *The Master praises—what are men?*

MEETING LIFE'S PROBLEMS

Read: Phil. 3:7-14.

Text: *Get thee behind me, Satan.* Luke 4:8.

The one great problem can be solved first. We hear a great deal about "problems"; we talk a great deal about "problems." With Jesus there were not so many perplexing small problems to be solved; there was one all-inclusive problem. He met that and solved it once for all; after that the specific problems life brought fell into place easily. Not that nothing was hard; rather, nothing was cloudy. The one great solution included all the others. It might be so with us. One decision made emphatically might save a deal of confused thinking later.

Jesus' great problem was ours: which voice to follow, God's or Satan's. He settled it once for all. He declared His independence of Satan. He recognized the voice of Satan as temptation: recognized it and resisted it by the Word of God. Many things were settled when that was settled—never to appear again as "problems."

Lord Halifax said regarding the English compromise at Munich, "If you don't defend the principle of right when you can, you may be called upon to defend it when you cannot." Fail to start your Christian life with a positive decision, and you will find yourself entangled later in situations you cannot cope with. Start your Christian service with a clear-cut principle, and you will escape many later temptations that might have overwhelmed you.

"I will bind myself to that which, once being right, will not be less right when I shrink from doing it."

> Strengthen all the ties that bind me
> Closer, closer, Lord, to Thee;
> Every bridge is burned behind me;
> Thine I evermore will be.

MEETING LIFE'S PROBLEMS

Read: Luke 4:1-13.

Text: *Thou shalt worship the Lord thy God, and him only shalt thou serve.* Luke 4:8.

Jesus settled it that He was to live by God's Word, not Satan's. He settled it that He was to act as the Son of God, not by the world's definition but by God's; that is, not Himself to enjoy ease or honor, but to lift men to royal place; not to indulge Himself, but to bless others. He settled it that He was to live for the spiritual, not the material; that He was to work by God's methods, not Satan's; that He was to worship God, not Satan, and worship by obeying.

Jesus decided that He would draw the line clear-cut between evil and good. He would not compromise nor straddle issues. With Him it could not be "good Lord and good devil"; there are two distinct systems—and He chose to live by the heavenly. By that distinction He escaped many thought-muddles.

There is no expanse of "No Man's Land" between sinners and Christians; if I sin wilfully I am a sinner. And the standard is God's plumb line—not even the conduct of good people.

Live by the standards of Kingdom righteousness, and Christ has pledged His honor that you will have what material things you need. Righteousness is the best policy —but not always immediately and apparently. You will have to do right (because you are right and love right) even when it doesn't seem to pay.

Basic to your Christian life must be trust in a Person. That was Job's solution; that is the ultimate solution for us all when we cannot see: "He knoweth the way that I take; when he hath tried me I shall come forth as gold."

> *Lead on, O King Eternal,*
> *Till sin's fierce war shall cease,*
> *And holiness shall whisper*
> *The sweet Amen of peace.*

MEETING LIFE'S PROBLEMS

Read: Acts 26:9-23; Phil. 3:3-7.

Text: *Man shall not live by bread alone, but by every word that proceedeth out of the mouth of God.* Matt. 4:4.

It is safe to trust God's judgment—always. It is safe to trust *God's knowledge* where we cannot understand. The Bible is a Book of Miracles because every human problem, moral and spiritual, is found there, with its solution. No, your name and address are not there, but your case is there. I challenge you to look for it. The Book was written for you.

It is safe to adopt *God's standards of value* as our own. Jesus settled it to take God's definitions and live by them —so may we. To make lives is more important than to make money.

I am serving a greater than Mammon. I am working for more than money or even position. So I cannot be offended or slighted or starved. God pays my wages.

It is safe to carry out *God's commission* at any price. Jesus settled—so may we—to do God's will whatever the cost. The time comes for all of us to carry out the consecration we made at the altar. Well for us then if we actually died to our own will.

Jesus' commission was a fulfilling of prophecy. So is ours, though not announced so publicly. Every one of us is an essential link in God's plan of saving the world. We have a place to fill. He is counting on us.

We need not feel sorry for ourselves if we accept God's commission for our lives. It will not make us popular with a certain group, but it will make us bringers of blessing to shadowed, captive hearts. It is good news we have to tell.

> *Jesus, I my cross have taken,*
> *All to leave and follow Thee.*

217

July 22

ON THE MOUNTAIN TOP

Read: Mark 9: 2; Ex. 33: 18-23; II Cor. 3: 7-18.

Text: *Shew me thy glory.* Ex. 33: 18.

The "glory" of Jesus is His reality. In His flesh He was veiled in suffering humiliation; in His transfiguration He is shown as He really is. The glory of Jesus is a realization of *Who He is,* so keen that forever after we know that dealing with Jesus is dealing with Deity. We still have to walk by faith, but, thank God, the veil is removed often enough to keep us aware of the abiding real beyond the seen.

There are conditions for seeing Christ's glory. We should be more Christ-conscious than we are if we would cultivate His friendship. For the vision was given to those three who kept closest to Him.

We should realize His presence more often if we went more often apart by ourselves—with Him. Too many of us depend on praying on the run. It takes time to "climb the mountain," above the flurry and bustle of everyday affairs, till the atmosphere is clear of dust and smoke— fit place for shining garments.

Heaven's reality would burst upon our consciousness more readily if we were better listeners. We have forgotten to meditate; we think of prayer as a one-way street, or as a radio with transmission facilities but no receiving set; we forget that God has messages to get to us —or are in too great a hurry to wait for them. We have not learned to "be still and know."

> Lord, speak to me, that I may speak
> In living echoes of Thy tone.

ON THE MOUNTAIN TOP

Read: Mark 9: 3, 4, 7, 8; Rev. 1: 9-16.

Text: *We would see Jesus.* John 12: 21.

The genuine heavenly vision has a definite content. Jesus' glory is *whiteness* like nothing on earth. He is absolute holiness. Till you saw His spotless purity you did not realize the sinfulness of your own heart; unless you stay much in His presence you will find yourself excusing "little sins." And if you expect to see Him at last, you will keep pure.

When you have seen Jesus real, you read the Bible with understanding. You see the Law and the Prophets fulfilled in His cross; you see Him as *the culmination of the Old Testament dispensations.* The Bible is a glorious whole, and Calvary is its keystone.

When I see Jesus for myself, I see Him as the great *Head of the Church.* I begin to realize His fellowship with all the saints of all the ages: He knows His people personally and His church numbers among its members Moses and Elijah, Abraham and David. I am little, but I belong to a glorious company.

When I see Jesus, I see Him as *the Father's Word.* I accept His sayings as the truth of God. I am inconsistent and insincere if I profess exalted Christian experience, but pay little attention to the Sermon on the Mount.

The climax of any revelation of Jesus is the sense that He is *mine*: not far away enthroned in splendor, but ever-present Friend, Saviour, Helper. Visions over, His presence abides.

> *Jesus, oh how sweet the name,*
> *Jesus, every day the same;*
> *Jesus, let all saints proclaim*
> *His worthy praise forever.*

ON THE MOUNTAIN TOP

Read: Mark 9:4; I Pet. 1:16-19; Rev. 1:17-20.

Text: *I was not disobedient unto the heavenly vision.* Acts 26:19.

A glimpse of Christ's glory has consequences that abide. Confidence. The world is full of people who are depending for their religion on "fables" and guesses. Thank God if you have been an eye-witness. Even if you should backslide you will know "it's real." But you will not backslide if you keep renewing the vision and walking in its light.

Moses and Elijah saw their confidence fulfilled in His first coming; the prophecy to us of His second coming is just as sure. We are not shaken though worlds totter. If I had been Peter, I believe I should have remembered the "holy mount" when I saw them bring my cross. I should have known there was light ahead.

Conduct. "Living on the mountain, but away from home a good deal?" Yet every child bears the stamp of his home, and his conduct shows up the standards of that home. We should carry about with us something of the mountain atmosphere.

A pastor, burdened for his flock, said, "It seems tragic that they can pass so easily and quickly from the sublime to the ridiculous—and forget the sublime." Our job is to keep the "sacred" so real that it permeates every "secular" act: to live our Mondays and Tuesdays in the light of our Sundays, to build our lives by the "pattern seen in the mount."

> *Shine all around us by day and by night,*
> *Jesus, the Light of the World!*

ON THE MOUNTAIN TOP

Read: Mark 9:5, 6; Ezek. 1:26-28.

Text: *And the Lord spake unto Moses face to face, as a man speaketh unto his friend.* Ex. 33:11.

Communion. Wherever Jesus manifests Himself, there is no boredom. You smile at Peter, but have you never wanted to "build three tabernacles"? In your own secret place, in the fellowship of the communion table, at the altar praying souls through into light—"where Jesus is, 'tis heaven there."

We should like to give God advice. We should like to be rid of temptation and trials; we should like to be rid of unpleasant circumstances and uncongenial environments; we should like to live with sanctified people in the heart of a revival. But He sees we are not ready yet to live in the glory. He says, Live in the world, but train your eyes to the Light and your ears to the Voice.

When Peter and John woke up that morning, they did not realize that the day was to hold an experience of which the world should hear, one of earth's unique events. So it might be with any one of our ordinary days. But if they are made truly great, it will be because of the presence of Christ in them.

The one moment in all their lives when they looked into eternity—in it these simple men had found the perfect touchstone of truth for all their later years. They remembered and they were spoiled for counterfeits. How about your mountain-top experience, when you saw Christ glorious and altogether lovely? Earth will fade out the vision: you must renew it; you must live in the implications of it.

> *Friendship with Jesus, fellowship divine;*
> *Oh, what blessed, sweet communion,*
> *Jesus is a Friend of mine.*

THE CHRISTIAN IN THE WORLD

Read: II Cor. 6:3-10; I Pet. 2:9, 10.

Text: *As poor, yet making many rich; as having nothing, and yet possessing all things.* II Cor. 6:10.

The Paradox of the Christian: poor, yet rich. Abandoned, you feel, when tribulation comes? Forgotten by God when everything has gone wrong and the things you have lived for slip away one by one? You say *abandoned;* God says *chosen* for that very hour and that very test. If you go through right, you will see it as your hour of victory and you will give thanks that you did not miss it.

Refugee, hunted, homeless, goods gone and lives a prey—how many Christians have known that fate. *Refugee*—but God says *royal,* if they hold fast their relation with Him.

Persecuted, distressed, cruelly tortured, just for doing good. *Injustice,* we say; *mercy,* God says. For they are enjoying the smile of God, and their "light affliction" of a moment is piling up the "eternal weight of glory." A rich investment, loyalty to God.

Outcasts, to judge by appearances. *His people,* God says. His as Christ was His Son; and allowed to suffer as He was allowed to suffer, in the will of God.

The Christian life is a paradox only if we limit God by time and space. If we will trust God's perspective, we shall see ashes changed to beauty.

> *I once was an outcast, stranger on earth,*
> *A sinner by choice, an alien by birth,*
> *But I've been adopted, my name's written down—*
> *An heir to a mansion, a robe, and a crown!*

THE CHRISTIAN IN THE WORLD

Read: I Pet. 2: 9-12; I Pet. 1: 13-17.

Text: *Ye are a chosen generation, a royal priesthood, an holy nation, a peculiar people.* I Pet. 2: 9.

The Status of the Christian: a citizen of two worlds. Christians are *holy* people. Their hearts are clean. They have accepted the facts that they must do without anger, jealousy, self-seeking, deceit; that they must work by love, self-denial, kindness, patience. All their distinction is to be in their likeness to Christ. Crucifixion? But the beginning of eternal life.

Christians are *pilgrims.* They are not trying to see how much like the world they can be. They are regulating life and practice by the standards of heaven. They are passing through the world, but they expect to live in heaven and they want to be at home there. Test your soul habits. Are they good fashion for heaven?

Christians are *fighters.* Not against worldly people, but against the worldly spirit. The world will never help you towards God: the current is all the other way; you will have to swim upstream. Note the definition of worldliness: any desire that "wars against the soul"; any practice that hurts your spiritual life. You can tell it.

Christians are *good citizens.* For God is the Author of law and order, and He sponsors it. Laws unjust, rulers arbitrary, but until conscience is violated we owe loyalty and co-operation to those in authority. And He makes it blessedly possible for us to obey even the unreasonable without a servile spirit or a loss of self-respect; for He says that in obeying them we are serving Him. There is always a look beyond.

Though exiled from home, yet still I may sing,
All glory to God, I'm a child of the King!

223

THE CHRISTIAN IN THE WORLD

Read: I Pet. 2:13-19.

Text: *Render therefore to all their dues.* Rom. 13:7.

The Obligations of the Christian: his credit is good. Christians are *debt-payers,* and they live in a world of debts. Every relationship in life involves its peculiar responsibilities; and Christians are to be honest in every one. They are not seeking exemptions; they are seeking to know their duties.

It is almost startling how few people seem to be able to act or even think impersonally. Is it because of a subtle selfishness? If we are delivered from self, should we not be able to see straight and recognize our duty to the office and not to the person? The fact that my father is unkind doesn't mean that I need not be a good son; the fact that the government does not suit my likings in its policies doesn't mean that I may cheat the government.

When God tells us to obey authorities—even the unjust—He has not left us without recourse. He has told us to pray for those in authority. Perhaps we should have less injustice if we prayed more. One woman, at least, was thought to have shaped some government policies by keeping informed of bills that were up in Washington and praying definitely and persistently.

"Souls are not saved in bunches." Christians are individuals first. They are saved alone; they stand before God alone; they meet the world alone. They associate with other Christians for mutual strengthening; but they never lose their identity in the group, nor their responsibility. Monday to Saturday is the test of Sunday.

> *Teach me, my God and King,*
> *In all things Thee to see,*
> *And what I do in anything,*
> *To do it as for Thee.*

THE CHRISTIAN IN THE WORLD

Read: I Pet. 2: 20-25; I Pet. 1: 3-10.

Text: *Christ also suffered for us, leaving us an example.*
  I Pet. 2: 21.

The Pattern of the Christian: Jesus. Through all life's
ups-and-downs and ins-and-outs you don't have to guess
or theorize or act on impulse. Keep your eyes on Jesus
and the way He reacted to situations. Peter remembered
always the judgment-hall and the Cross.

The Christian is expected to suffer unjustly. The
truly Christian attitude begins, not ends, where injustice begins. "If there were no injustice in the world,
there would be no possibility of a moral risk"—and no
possibility of showing the meekness of Jesus.

"We can take it." We Christians can afford to be big-
souled because we have tomorrow. We are not paid off
every Saturday night. We can afford to take injustice because we have the Judge of all the earth on our side. If
we take our case in our own hands now, we repudiate
our Great Avenger.

According to the Bible, Christians often have been
scattered sheep in an unfriendly world. Don't think God
has made a mistake if you find yourself one of these.

And after all, we are His sheep, saved and protected.
His honor is pledged to bring us safely home, if we keep
trusting and following. He is the Good Shepherd, however loud the wolves howl.

> *No danger nor harm can touch one of them,*
> *For I will be with them alway—*
> *My sheep know My voice.*

JESUS SAYS YOU SHOULD FORGIVE

Read: Matt. 18: 1-14.

Text: *The eyes of the Lord run to and fro throughout the whole earth to show himself strong in the behalf of them whose heart is perfect toward him.* II Chron. 16: 9.

Because you are God's child. He'll take care of you if you'll let Him. The moment someone really hurts you, that moment God's eye lights on you and His compassion goes out to you. But the moment you take up the cudgels for yourself, the moment bitterness enters your heart, that moment God's sympathy goes elsewhere. God fights on the side of the weak who trust in Him.

Jesus' pictures are vivid: the stumbling-block placed —or left—in the road, the unkind man dragged under the water by the huge millstone about his neck; the hand cut off, the eye gouged out; the hurt child comforted, the lost sheep found. Which fits your case? Jesus is terribly in earnest about this matter of how we treat one another. Nothing but kindness must go out from us toward another person. However just our cause, we must not risk "offending," hurting, striking back.

Always better to be hurt than to hurt. Carry a grudge and you become the offender. Better cut off your hand! It is Jesus who says it.

Vengeance is God's work. Do not assume it. It is a boomerang. Let it alone.

Stay simple, humble, loving, and no one can really harm you. For you have Heaven on your side, and Heaven always wins.

> *Beneath His wings of love abide;*
> *God will take care of you.*

JESUS SAYS YOU SHOULD FORGIVE

Read: ,Matt. 18:15-17.

Text: *Love as brethren, be pitiful, be courteous.* I Pet.
3:8.

Because he is your brother. Hurts from worldlings do
not cut so deep as hurts from fellow Christians. Yet
grudges held between Christians are ruinous to the work
of God. The devil knows that and encourages them all
he can, and Jesus knows it and warns us particularly
against them. Better side with Jesus.

Breaches between church members are wounds in
the body of Christ. They must not be allowed to fester.

Jesus' directions are specific. Why not follow them as
we would any prescription? They center in principles.

· 1. Don't talk *about* your brother; talk *with* him. Air-
ing a grievance always makes it bigger; and perhaps if
you saw his side you would understand better.

2. Don't wait for him to make the advances; you take
the first step. Grievances always grow with time; and
perhaps he is waiting for you.

3. Mend broken fellowship within the church. Don't
let your personal misunderstandings become a public
dishonor to the cause of Christ. Jesus is always practical.

Sometimes to please God you have to go the second
mile. You have to let the other fellow walk over you
You have to let people take advantage of your consecration. And God lets it happen; He does not say a word
in your defense—not now.

> *He prayed for them that did the wrong:*
> *Who follows in His train?*

JESUS SAYS YOU SHOULD FORGIVE

Read: Matt. 18:18-20; Acts 12:5-17.

Text: *If two of you shall agree on earth as touching any thing that they shall ask, it shall be done for them of my Father which is in heaven.* Matt. 18:19.

Because there is a tremendous power in united fellowship. Your prayer on earth rings a bell in heaven; rather, it pushes a button that releases power from heaven. Something happens every time you pray—unless a barrier between you and your brother blocks the current. Fellowship is just that important. If the circuit is cut, the circuit of *Christ—your brother—you,* better get to work at once on a repair job.

Prayer is a personal contact. It involves a strange three-cornered personal relationship. Jesus is with me if I am with my brother or my sister. When we get together He too is with us in a peculiar sense. Our relationship with Christ cannot be a self-centered, ingrown affair.

How sorely God's cause needs prevailing, united prayer. How foolish, then, for us to let trifling differences separate us and hinder the flow of the Spirit in our prayers. The "agreement" that defeats the devil is no superficial, casual lip-asking; it is the outgoing of the depths of hearts that know only one desire—"as the hart panteth after the water brooks."

There is a scene where spirits blend,
Where friend holds fellowship with friend—
Around the common mercy-seat.

JESUS SAYS YOU SHOULD FORGIVE

Read: Matt. 18:21-35.

Text: *Forgive us our debts, as we forgive our debtors.*
Matt. 6:12.

Because God has forgiven you. "Seventy times seven."
There never can be an end to your forgiving because
there never can be an end to your need of God's forgiveness. Be ungracious to someone—and the next minute you will find yourself having to say, "Pardon me,"
to someone else, and feeling small. Watch the way it
goes. Much more, refuse to forgive someone; very soon
you will find yourself needing God's forgiveness—and
unable to get it.

"Even as I had pity on you." How great His mercy
to us. We cannot compute our debt. If we lived more
in the mood of thankfulness, we should be so conscious
of our canceled ten-thousand-talent debt that we should
delight in forgetting the hundred pence our neighbor
owes us. When our salvation becomes commonplace to
us, our hearts will become hard.

"From our hearts." Every hurt that comes is an opportunity to be like Christ. But the opportunity comes
disguised; all we see, for the pain, is the injustice of it.
Don't use part of the Atonement only. Let Jesus carry
your hurts as well as your sins.

> *Amazing grace, how sweet the sound,*
> *That saved a wretch like me!*

JESUS SAYS YOU SHOULD FORGIVE

Read: Phil. 2:1-11.

Text: *Let this mind be in you, which was also in Christ Jesus.* Phil. 2:5.

Because forgiveness always wins and unforgiveness always loses. Simple common sense should teach us to forgive. Forgiveness is winsome; there is nothing so disarming as kindness. Unforgiveness begets unkindness; most people hurt others because they have been hurt themselves. Unforgiveness is a growing thing; let us stop it when it reaches us.

"She hurt me? Of course. But forget it! I can't be bothered with it." I heard one girl say this and I have always remembered. If we cherish all the hurts that come to us we shall be carrying a heavy load that will weigh us down—and perhaps sink us into hell. We "can't be bothered"!

Because you cannot remain Christian and have an unforgiving spirit. The two don't mix. All the notes of the Christian life vibrate to the chord of kindness: the child's humility and trustfulness, the helpfulness of the servant, the compassion of the healer, the self-sacrifice of the Cross. Resentment strikes a false note; it makes a discord.

Jesus took insults and forgave His enemies. We cannot ask exemption without shame.

The Christian does not bargain for his own wages; he submits to the judgment of God. He knows the Master will give him "whatever is right." If insults and injustices come here, they come as part of the program. In the end justice will be done. "Patience is willing to wait."

> *Earth has no sorrow*
> *That Heaven cannot heal.*

August 4

THE STORY OF DELIVERANCE

Read: Ex. 5.

Text: *Lord, . . . why?* Ex. 5:22.

The Story of Deliverance is always the same. Yesterday, today, forever, our God is the same Mighty Helper. Your case seems different, your bondage more bitter than any other, your sin or sorrow more hopeless. But:

> He is able to deliver thee . . . .
> Though by sin oppressed, go to Him for rest;
> Our God is able to deliver thee.

Extremity. "I've prayed and believed, but things are getting worse and worse. What about God's promise to help?" Almost always after you pray the situation looks blacker. But just before dawn it is darkest, and the crisis comes always at the lowest point. Hold on one moment after it is "impossible"—and relief will come. A practical prescription. It works.

"Why does God ask me to wait until the situation is impossible? Why does He wait?" There is a reason. God is never careless. There is more than one reason: (1) The enemy and the world must know it is God and recognize His power. (2) You must know it is God and give Him praise. (3) You must remember for the future and learn to depend on God.

A great emergency means a great deliverance, and a great deliverance means great glory to God. Is it worth waiting for?

> Keep holding on, just one more hour
> May bring to thee the promised power;
> Keep holding on, thy Lord doth care—
> He'll not forget to answer prayer.

231

THE STORY OF DELIVERANCE

Read: Ex. 6:1-9.

Text: *I am the Lord, and I will bring you out.* Ex. 6:6.

Deliverer. Your only asset in your struggle with Satan is the Word of God. But the value of that Word is measured by the character of that God. And what a God! Measure your resources today by the size of your God. He is big enough.

Perhaps you too were thinking of God as *the Almighty*: the God who can *do.* And you have been impatient and discouraged when He did not "do" as much as you expected. Now you need to know Him as I AM: *Eternal Wisdom.* The God who knows the end from the beginning you can trust. The God whose "time" is Eternity you can wait for. The God of the worlds and the dispensations is God of the nations—resistless.

God our Father is strong. God-with-us is strength: strength for the crisis and strength for the daily grind. There is no other strength for man.

"The only happy man is the man who is wholly dependent on God." And the only strong man is the man who has learned to use God's unfailing strength instead of his own uncertain strength. Self-sufficiency is of the very essence of sin.

God remembers His covenants. Back of the lives of nations are the prayers of godly men and women. We do not know just where or when all these prayers were prayed; but we know they must be answered, for God is faithful. This tissue of prayer is plain to His eye, and He is working out the answers.

> *O God, our Help in ages past,*
>   *Our Hope for years to come,*
> *Our Shelter from the stormy blast,*
>   *And our Eternal Home.*

August 6

THE STORY OF DELIVERANCE

Read: Ex. 6:10-13; 28-30; Ex. 7:1, 2.

Text: *The Lord spake unto Moses, saying, I am the Lord: speak thou unto Pharaoh. Ex. 6:29.*

Co-operation. Only your refusal to co-operate with God can keep you from being saved or sanctified or victorious. God is so eager to help us and the Spirit's ministries are so constant that it takes almost more stubbornness to refuse than will to accept the blessing. Don't make God punish you into yielding; open your life and let His grace flow in.

We all want to be rid of our sin: our uneasy conscience, our fits of temper; the scrapes sin gets us into, the habits that keep us from our best. We want to be rid of sin; but not enough to give up our own way—and that is what it costs. "Lord, make me clean," said Augustine —"but not now."

Larger things than I are at stake when I let God deliver me today. There is a continuity of grace. The prayers of my father and mother are being answered; the future of the kingdom is being assured. I am a link—a necessary link—in the chain of God's plan. I am caught up into the vast sweep of the will of God. He has purposed and has promised; but each separate step He must fulfill through someone. Use me today, Lord, if Thou canst—me, in my generation.

> *Keep holding on; no hand but thine*
> *Can break thy hold on Christ divine.*

THE STORY OF DELIVERANCE

Read: Ex. 12: 31-36; 40-42; 51.

Text: *Call upon me in the day of trouble: I will deliver thee.* Ps. 50: 15.

Freedom. Battled for by two forces, God and Satan, we are not free until we have been freed. We are not God's own until we are delivered from Satan; we do not get His protecting care so long as we stay in Egypt. God must deal first with our heart rebellion. There is no salvation without a separation from sin. At the outset of every Christian experience is a Passover and a Red Sea.

Just how great a deliverance do you want? Deliverance from sin's distress and penalty? Deliverance from the tyranny of evil habits? Or a thorough purging from the virus of sin? deliverance to a life of God-dependence? deliverance to the purposes of God? Real freedom is found under "the easy yoke of the will of God."—J. G. Gould.

The new calendar begins the day we are saved from sin. (Exodus 12: 2) The new order is under way. We are starting fresh. The bitter memories of the past are swept away; its stains are washed clean. We shall not please God by remembering; He has forgotten.

"The Lord did bring them forth." Always that is the last sentence of the chapter, if your faith holds. The story of a Christian never ends in tragedy.

Salvation is an open door to the spacious purposes of God.

> *My hope I cannot measure;*
> *My path to life is free.*

WONDERFUL SAVIOUR

Read: John 3:14, 15; Heb. 7:25; Rev. 22:17.

Text: *He shall save his people from their sins.* Matt. 1:21
He is a personal Saviour. He is Saviour of the world, but
He came with His eye on individuals—on you, on me.
If we are to walk straight through life, facing our facts
with no evasions, the first fact we must meet is that we
have a Saviour provided, to accept or to reject. To
dodge the issue is not to settle it.

James Simpson, when asked what his greatest discovery was, said he had discovered that he was a great
sinner and Jesus the great Saviour; that was greater
than his discovery of chloroform. He saw clearly.

Jesus came to save us from our sins. If you are over-
powered by your besetting sin, He has not done His work
for you. A Christian minister, who for a solid year had
met one tribulation after another with a courageous
smile, said, "If my grace doesn't work under pressure,
it isn't the grace I have preached."

Jesus specializes in hard cases and impossible sinners.
The man who "thinks he is pretty good" does not need
Him—and never will find Him. Wonderful that Jesus
sees us as we can be made by His power. We are worth
something to Him, no matter how worthless we seem to
ourselves. He says in Francis Thompson's poem, "None
but I makes much of naught."

Is Satan whispering that it is no use? You are too
bad, you have delayed too long, you never can make it?
Answer him with "Whosoever." With infinite knowledge
and infinite love Jesus included you in the "Whosoever."
Now you must include yourself by "willing" and "believing."

> I was bruised, but Jesus healed me,
> Faint was I from many a fall;
> Sight was gone, and fears possessed me,
> But He freed me from them all.

235

WONDERFUL SAVIOUR

Read: Matt. 20:25-28; Luke 15:1-7.

Texts: *For the Son of man is come to seek and to save that which was lost.* Luke 19:10.

Christ Jesus came into the world to save sinners; of whom I am chief. I Tim. 1:15.

He is a Saviour for lost men. The first requisite for salvation is a sense of lostness. There is no hope for us until, like Paul, we have seen ourselves as "chief of sinners." Others, looking on, may say, "He's a good fellow," "Not so bad." Our hearts know that our indifference has wounded the heart of God. That knowledge is the beginning of grace.

He is a seeking Saviour. He came not to be honored as earthly Ruler; He came to help, to serve, to meet human need. He came not to build up a dictator's kingdom, raising Himself by climbing on me; He came to give His life for mine. He came to buy me from the power of Satan—and the price was His blood. He came to be the world's Redeemer—and mine.

Jesus should be setter of styles in His own kingdom. It should be popular in Christian circles to sacrifice self to save others.

If we would follow Him, we should be more earnest seekers of the lost. One great missionary tells that when he was a godless lad of eighteen a man invited him seven consecutive Monday mornings to come to Sunday school the next Sunday, before he went once. But see the result!

> *Jesus sought me when a stranger,*
> *Wandering from the fold of God;*
> *He to rescue me from danger*
> *Interposed His precious blood.*

WONDERFUL SAVIOUR

Read: John 6: 66-69; Acts 16: 29-33; Acts 4: 5-12.

Text: *Neither is there salvation in any other: for there is none other name under heaven given among men, whereby we must be saved.* Acts 4: 12.

He is the only Saviour. If it were enough to pay compliments to Jesus, everyone would be saved; for everyone has a good word for Him; He is always named first among the world's great and good men. Jesus must have more than compliments; He claims allegiance as Master, He claims complete dependence as Saviour, He claims worship as God. He must be all, or He is nothing.

The deity of Jesus is the essential doctrine of the Christian faith. Without it the Incarnation is futile and the Atonement meaningless. Let no subtle sophistries rob your Jesus of His Christhood. You will need it.

How many today have turned from simple faith in Jesus Christ for salvation from sin. "I used to believe in the old-fashioned religion, but—." "My mother was an old-time Methodist, but—." But what? What have they substituted? Uncertainties. Vagueness. High-sounding phrases. Reasoning that flatters the intellect, but has nothing to say to the heart. Endless wanderings in a labyrinth instead of the straight road home.

Henry Van Dyke's *"The Lost Word"* pictures the tragedy of those who lose from memory the saving words of life. But what are those words? The saving name: "Jesus." The saving commands: "Come," "Repent," "Believe," "Follow." Hold them precious by obeying them.

On Christ, the Solid Rock, I stand;
All other ground is sinking sand.

WONDERFUL SAVIOUR

Read: Rom. 8:31-39.

Text: *In all these things we are more than conquerors through him that loved us.* Rom. 8:37.

He is a complete Saviour. He saved us from infinite evil; He saves us to infinite, ever-increasing good. Once I cast my lot with Jesus, I never can know real evil any more. He is the Great Blesser; He is touching for me all that men call evil and changing it to good. Day by day let me hold fast to Him, and go singing.

Beyond the veil Jesus is praying for me, and praying for the souls I love and yearn over. Before the throne He stands my representative. Can I fail? Not until I discharge Him as my Advocate, for He has undertaken to see my case through.

Calvary pledges God's love to us—unchanging and sufficient. Calvary pledges to us a sustaining Presence by our side, through every test that life can bring. A friend is worth more than money any day—and what a Friend!

A young man knelt at an altar of prayer, struggling to yield his faith to God. He could not understand the "why" of God's dealings with him. A wise pastor said to him, "I remember the time in my life when all the lights of my soul seemed to go out. Then I was glad I had Jesus." We have to reckon on the time when all the earthly lights of the soul will go out.

> *All in all I ever find Thee:*
> *Saviour, Lover, Brother, Friend.*

August 12

WONDERFUL SAVIOUR

Read: Phil. 2: 5-11.

Text: *That at the name of Jesus every knee should bow.*
Phil. 2: 10.

He is a triumphing Saviour. "In this sign conquer." Constantine saw the cross, put it on his banner, and was invincible. It is as true today; the banner does not count so much, but if you will wear the cross in your heart and trust in the Christ of the cross, a way will open before you always and you cannot know defeat. If you find yourself defeated, look to see what you have done with the cross.

Why not more of triumph in our lives and our Christian work? Have we forgotten that,

> *At the sign of triumph*
> *Satan's host doth flee?*

The cross is no longer badge of the slave; it is mark of the conqueror.

God could take care of Jesus' reputation—can He not look out for yours? Throw yourself into the saving work God has assigned to you, forget what people will think of you, and let God confer the honors. They will come, at the right time.

We have not yet viewed the closing scene of the great drama of Redemption. The central figure, Jesus exalted; the stage, the throne room of the universe; the atmosphere, triumph, adoration. But it is not spectacle only; it is experience. I am not an onlooker; I am a participant. I shall be one of those who bow the knee and confess His Lordship. Am I ready?

> *We'll join the everlasting song,*
> *And crown Him Lord of all.*

FISHERS OF MEN

Read: John 1: 29-39.

Text: *He saith unto them, Come and see.* John 1: 39.

Is every Christian called to be a winner of souls? Meeting with Christ is a personal matter. You have heard Him preached about all your life; you believe all that the Bible says about Him. But one day you realize that you need Him for yourself; and you stand alone before Him, the whole world shut out. Till then you have not begun to be a Christian.

Meeting with Christ is a compelling experience. As the Holy Spirit makes Christ real to you, His clear eye will be fixed upon you, His voice will ring insistently in your ear, you will be forced to say, "I know the Lord has laid His hand on me." Twist, turn, evade, there is no other way for you to go. But do not rebel; it is the compulsion of love.

Meeting with Christ is an unforgettable experience. A person may backslide afterwards and try to satisfy himself with earth; he may even persuade himself he was mistaken—there is "nothing in it." But down in the depths of his nature he knows; he has had a glimpse of Absolute Reality and he cannot forget. There is a memory to appeal to in the backslider—count on it if you are after his soul.

A meeting with Christ changes the course of one's life because it changes one's desires. Before, wealth was calculated in material possessions; now, in spiritual goods. Before, success was measured by earthly goals; now, by the smile on the Saviour's face. Once see His face, other values seem cheap!

> *I had walked life's road with an eager tread,*
> *Had followed where pleasure and comfort led,*
> *Until one day in a quiet place*
> *I met my Master face to face.*

FISHERS OF MEN

Read: John 1:40-42.

Text: *He first findeth his own brother Simon, and saith unto him, We have found the Christ.* John 1:41.

Spontaneously with conversion comes the desire to bring others. Did you ever know a person really to find salvation and not go after his friends to share his blessing? The urge to win souls is almost a hallmark of the genuine Christian experience.

The surest way to confirm and strengthen your own Christian experience is to go after some one else. Jesus was an expert in psychology long before William James drew up his famous laws of habit. He knows human nature; His methods are practical, His commands reasonable and completely workable.

The call to be saved is a double call: to be saved from something and to be saved to something. It offers a deliverance, but also a responsibility; it calls you to drop the burden of sin, but to take on the yoke of Christ. It is a call to the "charge to keep"; a call to a meaningful life. Do not think you can go half way.

Christ deals with us individually and personally. He calls fishermen to be "fishers of men"; he calls farmers to be "sowers of the Word." He will use our individual slant and our individual gifts—but all for the same great end. There is some one—there are some ones—that you can reach, you and no one else, you with your personality and your background of experience. Do not hold back.

> *I hear my risen Saviour say,*
> *"Follow Me!"*

FISHERS OF MEN

Read: Mark 1:16-20.

Text: *Jesus said unto them, Come ye after me.* Mark 1:17.

Let Jesus make His own choices. When they include you, co-operate. If the big jobs pass you over, get His assignment for you. There is one—the right one.

"Straightway" is safest in dealing with a call of God. You will waste your best years by arguing or dallying, or "thinking about it tomorrow." For His call comes at the very best time for your decision; to answer promptly is economy.

God would have our lives run on schedule time. He has measured our possibilities and His grace; He knows how far we should have traveled on our way by today, by tomorrow. If we procrastinate when He speaks or drag our feet in obeying, we shall soon lag behind and miss connections somewhere.

The Christian's call, however special, is also general. He is called not simply to some cause, some institution, some profession; he is called to save men anywhere, everywhere. A veteran missionary home from China, nervously exhausted, weak from Japanese imprisonment, could not think of himself as on vacation; but when forced to wait in a railway station spent the hour in giving out Testaments to service men and found it one of his happiest hours in America. Always on duty and delighted to be so—that is the Christian soldier.

Soul-winning is not a career to be chosen; it is a charge, a devotement—it may be a martyrdom. My life is a sacred trust. I have no right to hand over the guidance of it to anyone else; there is no human being that I can follow blindly without losing my crown of individuality. It is different with Jesus. When I yield myself to follow Him, my personality is fulfilled.

> *His voice is sounding all the day,*
> *"Follow Me! Follow Me! Follow Me!"*

FISHERS OF MEN

Read: Matt. 9:9; Dan. 12:3.

Text: *Faithful is he that calleth you, who also will do it.*
I Thess. 5:24.

The call of God is to a larger life and a bigger catch. You
groan and sigh over God's call; some day you will see
how little you would have amounted to if God had left
you to take your own way. The General Superintendent
of a great church struggled when a youth over giving up
his great ambition. He had wanted to be a veterinary!
It is always safe to stake your all on the faithfulness of
God.

A letter from a young woman trying to choose between two openings asks, "Just how much will the position mean in terms of valuable experience and preparation for the future? I feel a need of purpose and service
in my work." It is a natural question for any young person to ask of a vocation: "Is there a future in it?" The
call of Christ opens the only door to the future. The
"fisher of men" is saved for eternity, partner of Deity,
millionaire of souls—one soul worth more than all the
world.

Peter and Andrew never would have been heard of
if they had refused to answer Christ's call; George Whitefield would have lived and died an unknown brewer,
and David Livingstone an obscure cotton-mill worker.
But they answered. Peter and Andrew turned the world
upside down; Whitefield spread revivals over America;
Livingstone "turned the eyes of the world on Africa and
the eyes of Africa up to God."

And you do not know what may depend upon your answer today. There are world transformations yet to be
wrought, and world evangels yet to be carried. Obedience will make you great.

> *My thought is now for the souls of men;*
> *I have lost my life to find it again.*

243

FISHERS OF MEN

Read: Luke 5:1-11.

Text: *I will make you to become fishers of men.* Mark 1:17.

Jesus Himself is the best soul-winner. I would enroll for a course with Him, a course for the duration of my life. It will cost all I have and am, or else it will be playing school; for winning souls cost Him the cross.

"Follow me, and I will make you." "The Christian's task is not to live by his wits, but to live by grace"—so the Christian worker's. There is no success apart from Christ; there are no rules for soul-winning that can be followed mechanically as a cooking recipe or a chemical formula. There is a personal, guiding, helping Christ at our side.

From the time we set out to follow Christ, our every success is associated with Him. We cannot expect to win men for His kingdom by ways of life other than His. Tricks of psychology and a hail-fellow-well-met manner will win numbers to your side, but not souls to Christ. Only love does that.

I will make you fishers of men. We do not do it; He does—this miracle of catching men. Work in our own strength (with suppers, programs, clubs, psychological adroitness)—what fruitless toil. Co-operate with His orders through His Word and His Spirit—what good success.

And we shall have to adopt Jesus' emphasis in our ministry of saving men: His keen sense of sin, His standards of righteousness, His teachings of repentance and the New Birth and the baptism with the Holy Spirit. We are not winning souls at all unless we are winning them by His definitions.

> *I cry aloud, "Lord, make me meet*
> *To follow the marks of Thy wounded feet."*

FISHERS OF MEN

Read: John 1: 43-51.

Text: *Study to shew thyself approved unto God, a work-man that needeth not to be ashamed, rightly dividing the word of truth.* II Tim. 2: 15.

He will teach us the laws of soul-winning. He knows the path to the hearts of men. He knows where those are whose hearts will respond to my approach; He knows what words of mine will open the locked gates. Let me follow His directions carefully; it is criminal to bungle where immortal souls are at stake.

He knows just what kind of work in His service will suit me best; He knows where I can win most souls. I will follow Him not only in general, but in particular. I will let Him choose my vocation, my place of service, my methods, my program.

A preacher of His gospel? Then surely I do not go as a matter of course to the church that pays the largest salary without asking whether or not my Master is pointing there. Some smaller spot may be the place with most fish for my nets just now.

A good share of success in personal work consists in caring for men's souls: being wide-awake to opportunities in all your everyday contacts. You will find a way if your heart is in it.

A great missionary cited as the qualifications of a good missionary: an experience with God, adaptability to circumstances, training for leadership, good health, a sense of humor. We need and should acquire every possible form of personal development if we are to be effective winners of souls, here or on the other side of the world. What we furnish Him God can use—and only that.

> *All that I am and have,*
> *Thy gifts so free,*
> *In joy, in grief, through life,*
> *Dear Lord, for Thee.*

FISHERS OF MEN

Read: Acts 2:37-41; 5:12-16.

Text: *Fear not; from henceforth thou shalt catch men.*
Luke 5:10.

Christ promises results. It may take time, but the catch
is sure. If He has asked you to preach or to go as a missionary, or just to be a true Christian, you are not called
to be a failure nor to mark time. His word is not, "Do
your best"; not, "Try to catch"; not, "Hold the fishing rod";
but *"Thou shalt catch."*

He makes us fishers of men by His blessing. But we
have to do the fishing. We have to cast the spiritual net
and bait the spiritual hooks and use all the fisherman's
ingenuity and patience for a spiritual catch. Fish do not
come to our hand begging to be taken—nor do souls;
and fishermen fish where they know there are fish. It
does not need an angel from heaven to tell us to do likewise in soul-winning.

The fisherman's heart is more important than his rod
or his flies; the fish do not pay much attention to the
amateur's fine equipment. Some trained psychologists
have very little success in dealing with people because
they do not really love them. All our good rules for
soul-winning will fall flat unless our hearts are aflame
with love for souls.

Christ's voice is not the only one that calls us today.
Ours is a noisy world, full of clamoring, conflicting voices:
voices of pleasure, ambition, home, country, love, duty,
war, death; voices of fear, of worry, of confusion. To
what voice are you listening? Whom are you following?
Is it a better voice than His? a safer guide? a kinder
master? Tune in to the station you really want to hear.

> *Close beside the Shepherd we His joy may share;*
> *He that winneth souls is wise.*

LOVE IS BEST

Read: I Cor. 13; Rom. 13:8-10.

Text: *And now abideth faith, hope, love, these three; but the greatest of these is love.* I Cor. 13:13.

Love is life's best—do we believe it? Better than "winning friends and influencing people" is loving them? Better than having money or popularity or a good time is just loving—invariably, constantly? Try it; you'll find it the hardest thing—impossible without God—but the greatest. You will conquer by love, for you yourself are conquered.

Love is religion's best. The thing that counts, with people and with God, is not what you do, but what you are —first.

So far is the experience of perfect love from being the result of voluntary human endeavor that it actually delivers us from habits, ways, soul twists that we ourselves scarcely realized we possessed. One woman was unduly inquisitive—her friends knew it better than she did; but with the sanctifying blessing that rather offensive curiosity about other people's affairs dropped off. Another was forever justifying herself; the blessing took care of that. Small things, but springing evidently from too much love for self, too little love for others.

Boundless faith in the transforming power of Christ Paul had, to hold this picture up before the wrangling, carnal Corinthians and say, "This is for you." But to this transformation every truly sanctified person can testify: before, an ungovernable temper, now peace under provocation; conceit turned to humility; selfishness lost in sacrificial service. It is the finger of God.

> *A heart in every thought renewed*
> *And full of love divine;*
> *Perfect and right and pure and good,*
> *A copy, Lord, of Thine.*

LOVE IS BEST

Read: James 2: 8-12; Col. 3: 12-14; I Cor. 13: 4-7.

Text: *Put on the new man, which is renewed in knowledge after the image of him that created him.* Col. 3: 10.

Love is God's best. Lives of love will write into our characters lines of beauty and Christlikeness. And character is a value God rates high. Given a new spirit, let us keep busy translating it into specific attitudes. I don't love out into space. That is sentimentality. I love people under specific—and usually trying—conditions. Love will work as I work it.

1. I shall find it beautifully natural and happy to be unretaliative because I am no longer self-centered. I can see the other person's point of view, and I shall learn to look for it.

2. I shall not be eternally suspicious, because I am not worried about my own interests. I have given them to God to take care of. He can track down rumors better than I.

3. I shall not be itching for praise at the expense of others; I shall be glad for others to have their share. I love them as myself.

4. I shall be stirred, excited, thrilled over God's cause because my heart is centered there.

5. I shall look for the best in others, and find it. That is the nature of love.

Not automatic, not always easy; plenty of opportunities always to show some other spirit—but always the sense of fitness and naturalness. To love is normal, satisfying always.

By Thy wonderful power,
By Thy grace every hour,
Help me to love like Thee.

LOVE IS BEST

Read: John 14:19-24; I Cor. 13:8-13.

Text: *Charity never faileth.* I Cor. 13:8.

Love is best because it never will wear out. The earthly things we grasp at will give out. Anything that is of the surface will die with the rest of the physical, material universe. The heart, the spirit, persons and their right relationships, will live forever.

Old, feeble, dying, when we can no longer think or work or give, we still can love. When earth is past and all its knowledge is useless, we still can love. When hope is fulfilled, and faith is lost in sight, we still can love. Sad for us if we never have learned how!

George Fox, the saintly Quaker, tells how God took out of his heart everything that would not be kind, loving, gentle. "And then He shut the door." Perfect love is God-created. We are powerless to be loving: we can only tack on good deeds; God must change our natures. He will, if we will put them into His hand.

They used to tell us we should read I Corinthians 13 once a week, at least. Just as we look in the mirror to see how to dress, just as we study the pattern to make the product perfect, so we were to keep the "love chapter" fresh in our minds to check up on our spiritual condition. Should we resemble the portrait more closely if we looked at it oftener? Are we satisfied with something inferior?

> *Love divine, all loves excelling,*
> *Joy of heaven, to earth come down,*
> *Fix in us Thy humble dwelling,*
> *All Thy faithful mercies crown.*

THE LORD OF LIFE

Read: John 11:1-23.

Text: *Lord, he whom thou lovest is sick.* John 11:3.

Christians are not "exempt." Mary and Martha, close friends of Jesus—theirs a bereaved home? Those who really love Him will learn not to expect immunities from the common lot.

Sometimes Christians—but they are following afar off —grieve as if God had done them wrong when losses come. They forget that Jesus will come to them if they look for Him; and He will certainly have something to say to them. Never allow a sorrow to fester in your life. Take it at once to Jesus and get His word.

No Christian is wholly bereaved. He knows there is healing for his loved one if God sees best. Even if that loved one dies, he will meet him again. In any event, he can commit the case wholly to Jesus. Christians reap their dividends when sorrow comes.

"If only"—it is the language of human regret; and the devil is only too ready to play upon our self-accusations with his, "Too late! Too late!" "Even now"—it is the language of hope; and Jesus is always quick to hear our faltering plea and make a way where there is no way. He is the "God of hope." There is never a dead-end with Him.

When He seems to delay too long, He is not making a mistake. He has planned ahead; He knows what He is doing. If you could see clear through, you would choose this very same program. Lazarus and Mary and Martha would not for worlds have missed their great experience. You are headed for a miracle of grace—if only you can wait.

> *Not so in haste, my heart!*
> *Have faith in God, and wait:*
> *Although He seems to linger long,*
> *He never comes too late.*—SELECTED.

THE LORD OF LIFE

Read: John 11:24-38.

Text: *Behold, how he loved him!* John 11:36.

How will He help? Jesus helps just by being there. Perhaps, if you are grieving overmuch, you have forgotten His presence. Bring your grief to Him.

He is Power, but He is also Love. He is "the God of great compassion." The surgeon cannot operate on his own family; he must not feel deeply, or his hand will shake and his skill is gone. Not so with our Christ. You are not just another impersonal "case"; you are His own. But His hand never shakes.

We find it natural to believe for the "possible." If the possible deliverance has not taken place, it is all up. But Jesus plans to do the "impossible." There is no impossible with Him. He knows how big a miracle you need.

Our faith tends to be limited by our experience. Jesus would have it based on Himself: His power and His love. Better perhaps if we did not compare quite so much with what we have always seen; if we let Him stretch our faith by a closer intimacy with Him.

What will He do? Will He raise my dead? Perhaps, if He needs that kind of miracle performed where I am. He has answered prayer and brought lives back from the jaws of death for a testimony to unbelieving doctors. He has let other just as good Christians shout the victory through their tears, and so convince cynical onlookers of the reality of grace.

> *He is here, to help and cheer,*
> *To lift my load of anxious fear.*
> *His tender voice I now can hear;*
> *He is here, yes, God is here.*

THE LORD OF LIFE

Read: John 11:21, 32; 39-46.

Text: *If thou wouldest believe, thou shouldest see the glory of God.* John 11:40.

There is something He can do about it. Bereavement with Jesus there is different. We have seen it different in so many homes that we know it is not that some people are naturally stronger, but that Jesus' presence makes the whole situation different. There is always something He can do about it.

"If" is the most torturing word we have: the "If" of circumstances. "If things had been different," we say. (Which really means, "If God had done differently.") But God has an "If" too: the "If" of faith. He says, "If you will believe." The circumstances He has allowed He can dominate: it is our trust in Him now that counts. Let us give up our "If" and take His; it puts the emphasis in the right place.

Between the two "Ifs" is the width of the moral universe; your "If" determines your whole philosophy of life. The weak "If" of circumstances marks you a fatalist, helpless in the grip of chance. The strong "If" of faith marks you a responsible free man, mastered by Christ and master of circumstances. I can believe God, and I will.

Not always do we have the opportunity of seeing Jesus in action. For man chose death when he chose his own way, and God is letting him have his choice for a time. The touch of death is on us all, and He does not interfere. But one day He will destroy Death and show us what Life really is. The day He raised Lazarus He gave us a glimpse of Himself: Life unfettered, Power unleashed.

Unanswered yet? Faith cannot be unanswered;
Her feet are firmly planted on the Rock.

THE LORD OF LIFE

Read: Luke 7: 11-16; Mark 5: 35-43.

Text: *Jesus Christ hath abolished death, and hath brought life and immortality to light.* II Tim. 1: 10.

Jesus in Action. When Death confronts Life Eternal it is conquest, not contest; there is only one possible outcome. Life is Master. Master of sin's corruption in my soul just as easily as of death's corruption in my body—can I doubt it?

Linked with Jesus? Then linked with life and immortality. He is Life Eternal, unkillable; He is Energy itself, undying, unquenchable. Let Him flood your being today and lift you above defeat and inertia. So long as He has work for you to do, He can quicken your mortal body here and now.

Jesus always speaks Life. His only opponent is the will of man. Why should we will death rather than life?

A fortiore, logic would say. We reason from the stronger to the weaker: because a man has done the greater, he can do the less. But with Jesus it is not logic, but a Person. He is greater than all His works, and we know it. What He has done is only an earnest of the far greater yet to be done. Our first experience with Jesus tells us we have tapped the Infinite.

His Voice—we have only begun to know its authority. His Life—we have only begun to feel it. We have known the thrill of spiritual life in our souls; we have felt His touch quickening our bodies; we have seen the smile on the face of a loved one who confronted death but found it opening into life. Before us are the reaches of eternity.

> *O could I speak the matchless worth,*
> *O could I sound the glories forth*
> *Which in my Saviour shine!*

DYNAMIC CHRISTIANITY

Read: Rom. 12:1, 2, 9; Heb. 1:8, 9.

Text: *Let love be without dissimulation. Abhor that which is evil.* Rom. 12:9.

The only Christian life that is worth anything has power at its heart; a power that is stronger than dynamite or electricity. But it does not come cheap. We do not get the heavenly current turned on until we make the connection; we do not keep it unless we maintain the contact. We choose between the supernatural dynamic and the human effort that is always inadequate.

The only Christian life that is worth anything is the life that follows Paul's blueprint—and Christ's. Not, "It's right if it works in the 20th century"; but, "It's heaven's own right; therefore it will conquer in the eternities." Some of the specifications seem quite unpractical; the mind must be made over to accept an entirely *new set of values* and dare to live by them—values that come down from above.

These are the new laws of holy living; check up. 1. *Sincere love.* Do not ever let your nice words come from the teeth out. Do not let Satan poison your love with suspicion or resentment. Saint or sinner, he will be yours in the end if you keep on loving; but sooner or later you will lose him and yourself if you stop loving.

2. *Hatred of sin.* There are two charges for every dynamo, positive and negative; there is no power until negative meets positive. To love God truly you must hate sin; to do good you must oppose evil; the closer to God, the stronger the revulsion against Satan. The greatest spiritual need of our day is a keener sense of sin. Till then, no revival.

> *Hath He marks to lead me to Him,*
> *If He be my guide?*
> *In His hands and feet are woundprints,*
> *And His side.*

DYNAMIC CHRISTIANITY

Read: Rom. 12:1, 2, 3, 10, 11; John 13:1-17.

Text: *In honour preferring one another; fervent in spirit; serving the Lord.* Rom. 12:10, 11.

3. *Humility.* Perhaps you prove best the genuineness of your faith in God by gladly giving others their way. It is those who have not much treasure on the other side who must have their reward here. If you are not envious of earthly honors, you show that you are willing to wait—and have something to wait for. You are a spiritual millionaire—why scramble for pennies?

Nothing is more subtle than the temptation to envy another's Christian influence. But you will never be a strong Christian until you learn that you grow in Christian influence only as you grow in love. With every bending of the heart to exalt another, with every glow of spirit over another's achievement, you not only become stronger yourself, but you strengthen the collective power of the church in its fight against sin.

4. *Joyful service.* God puts no premium on laziness. There are no lazy Christians. But the Christian's activity is not that of the squirrel cage. He has the strength of a purposeful life. He knows what he is doing, and why. Plenty of us go through our routine faithfully, but feel the grind. We have a right to the inner glow and the spring in the step.

You cannot humiliate the man who is serving Christ. He glorifies his Master when he takes a slight with spirit erect—and to honor the King is itself an honor.

> *End of faith, as its beginning,*
> *Set our hearts at liberty.*

DYNAMIC CHRISTIANITY

Read: Rom. 12:1, 2, 12, 13; Rev. 3:7-13.

Text: *Patient in tribulation; continuing instant in prayer; given to hospitality.* Rom. 12:12, 13.

5. *Endurance.* We know we have the victory if we can rejoice and hold steady when there is nothing tangible to rejoice over. The world knows it too, and is curious to learn the secret. Perhaps it will help you through your next trial if you can remember that you are on display and that your patience may help you win some soul who is looking on—this may be the opportunity you have been praying for!

There is dynamite in patience. Once you know a person has decided to wait until you give in, you are done for. So the Christian is sure to win; for he has set himself to wait until the devil himself gives in.

6. *Prayer.* The Christian prays about everything; he prays always. When he ceases to pray, he soon ceases to be a Christian. He breathes by prayer; his spiritual life depends on his contact with God. He works by prayer; he fights by way of the throne. Just how much do you count on prayer? That is your spiritual touchstone.

7. *Helpfulness.* No Christian is so small or so insignificant as not to have a ministry of compassion and sympathy in which he can forget himself. He may think he is giving, but he really is gaining—in love, in influence, in friends, in soul stature. When we have no homes or goods we can still keep open house in our hearts. Sometimes a genuine smile or tear is worth more to a soul in need than food and drink.

> *O the unsearchable riches of Christ!*
> *Who would not gladly endure*
> *Trials, afflictions, and crosses on earth,*
> *Riches like these to secure?*

August 30

DYNAMIC CHRISTIANITY

Read: Rom. 12:1, 2, 14-21.

Text: *Be not overcome of evil, but overcome evil with good.* Rom. 12:21.

8. *Perfect trust.* Which, being analyzed and interpreted, shows itself as meekness, forgiveness, magnanimity. The "terrible meek" are invincible because God has undertaken their cause; they need not retaliate. The forgiving will find mercy; God has undertaken their defense. The great-souled who will not stoop to notice an insult have God to fight for them.

The shepherd lad in *Pilgrim's Progress* sang:

> He that is humble ever shall
> Have God to be his guide.

God, who "dwells in the high and holy place," dwells "also with him who is of an humble spirit." God is the lifter-up of humble heads. With God on my side I am utterly strong; and no one can stand against me when God is my lawyer. I have put my case in His hands.

9. *Peace with honor.* I am not responsible to keep "peace at any price"; sometimes I am bound to stand firm for a principle. But with personal matters it is different. There the fight must all come from the other side—and such a fight cannot last long.

10. *Honesty.* Zealous Christians have sometimes broken down at the point of honesty because of their very zeal for God's work. It seems all right at the moment to do a shady thing "for the sake of the cause." Honorable sinners will not excuse this; I wonder if God will.

> God's way is the best way,
> He knoweth the right way;
> I'll trust in Him alway;
> He knoweth the best.

THE GOOD SHEPHERD

Read: John 10:1-9.

Text: *I am the good shepherd, and know my sheep, and am known of mine.* John 10:14.

Joy-bells. Today there are chimes of "joy-bells, ringing in my heart," any one of them enough to chase away the gloom. Listen:

Jesus gives Himself the name of Shepherd.

He knows my name.

He tells me the name of the door to safety.

He always goes before.

He speaks to His sheep so often that they know His voice.

He has proved His love beyond question; for He died for His sheep.

He knows us personally.

His sheep are of infinite variety—and He loves to have them so.

The life He has given us will never end.

> *When we've been there ten thousand years,*
> *Bright shining as the sun,*
> *We've no less days to sing His praise*
> *Than when we first begun.*

No one can make us backslide.

The Father, the Shepherd, the sheep—and I am included!

If you feel disheartened, set any one of the chimes to ringing, and see what happens!

Keep a song in your heart, though your lips cannot sing it;
Keep a song in your heart, though the world may not hear;
Keep a song in your heart, and as faith wafts it skyward,
The Saviour will listen, and heaven draw near.

THE GOOD SHEPHERD

Read: John 10:10-16.

Text: *The sheep follow him: for they know his voice.*
John 10:4.

The Flock: Are all different. Christ does not want to
make us all by one pattern. We Christians are to look
at Christ and be ourselves, not to look at one another and
be woodenly uniform.

Are of many lands. The power of the gospel bursts upon you afresh when you see it work on men of strange
tongues and races just as it does in your own country.
Jesus speaks to the heart directly, and no nation has a
corner on Him. Many men of many tongues will make
up Heaven's chorus, but their voices will blend in the
language of praise. He will understand it.

Are all as peculiar as I! Yet all His own—and He sees
something lovable in every one. Surely I can find it too.

*The Hireling: Is in it for what he gets out of it. Is care-
ful of his own skin.* We cannot judge the gospel of Christ
by faults we see in some ministers. He has already
warned us of counterfeits, and drawn their picture. We
have seen some pastors with the shepherd's heart, and
have known they looked like Jesus.

The Wolf: Is a destroyer—and only a destroyer. Do not
ever let the devil fool you into thinking he wants to do
you any good. He hates God, and always will. And he
hates God's children, and always will. Do not trust him.
He never builds, but tears down. He never blesses, but
always curses.

Is an enemy implacable and strong. Not one of us is a
match for the devil alone—any more than a lamb without
a shepherd is a match for the wolf.

I need Thee every hour; stay Thou near by;
Temptations lose their power when Thou art nigh.

THE GOOD SHEPHERD

Read: Ps. 23.

Text: *The Lord is my shepherd; I shall not want.* Ps. 23:1.

The Shepherd is: Provider. Ever wish you had some one wiser and stronger than you are to take care of you and show you the way through? You can have—even in this new, strange, tangled world—if you have Jesus. You can't count on fuel, food, home, country, even on the value of money. You make plans, but always end by saying, "Well, we don't know how anything will be tomorrow." You can count on Jesus; and with Him you will be safe.

Guide. You can know that Jesus goes before you: to try the path, to select the very best pasture. You can be sure of it even when the food seems to you unpalatable. He will make you strong through every experience, if you let Him choose for you.

If the rough road draws us closer to our Shepherd, it is well worth traveling. Those who have dared trust Him wholly have found Him wholly true. Suppose we too walk a little closer this day.

Security. He will go before to ward off your enemies. Every wolf He will hold at bay. Just as you can sit on a great rock by the sea while the roaring breakers pound in at high tide and seem about to inundate you, yet know you are safe because the command of God to the waves is, "Thus far shalt thou go and no farther," so with the fury of Satan against you. He cannot get at you, however much he roars.

So it is not impossible to "give thanks always for all things."

> *I fear no foe, with Thee at hand to bless;*
> *Ills have no weight, and tears no bitterness.*

ADVENTURING WITH GOD

Read: Gen. 12:1-9.

Text: *Get thee out of thy country . . . . unto a land that I will show thee.* Gen. 12:1.

Venture? Or Opportunity? "All my eggs in one basket?" Yes, if that basket is the will of God.

"Willing to step off the precipice onto nothing?" Yes, if the Everlasting Arms are there to hold you up.

"Adventurous faith?" And the "venture" is *God?* It is not a risk to stake all on Omnipotence.

A contemporary journalist with a Jewish name says the real trouble with the Jew today is that he has imitated the Gentiles, adopted their rule of "adjustment to environment," and so lost out altogether. He used to have God if everything else was taken from him. Now he has put on a new protective coloring. He has compromised his beliefs, half-sophisticate, half-Jew, and has nothing left to suffer for. When he loses money and home he loses everything and is totally adrift. A warning to us. When men begin to save their skins they begin to lose their souls.

Abraham did not "adjust to his environment." He and God made a new environment wherever he went. Try it! Christians are not called to conform; they are called to convict.

There are "good people" for whom the Bible has lost its interest and religion has become tame and a bit monotonous. They turn to other things for their real excitement. It is because they do not know faith as a personal venture; they are merely following the conventional paths marked out by others. Perhaps they even know "what a sanctified person should do," and try to do it. Every day can be alive with the thrill of romance if we will live it fresh with God.

> Lead on, O King Eternal,
>   We follow, not with fears;
> For gladness breaks, like morning,
>   Where'er Thy face appears.

ADVENTURING WITH GOD

Read: Heb. 11: 8-12.

Text: *Abraham believed God, and it was accounted to him for righteousness. Gal. 3: 6.*

Risk? Or Sound Investment? No risk—for God has promised you His protection. You can live a charmed life until your work is done. For God Himself will take care of your enemies.

If you hesitate to "give God all you don't know," you suggest that you are wiser than He—or kinder. In a world like ours I would rather shift the responsibility of life to stronger shoulders than mine!

God is still in the business of calling—and blessing. Many a young man never would have been heard of if he had not answered the call of God and gone out "from his father's house." To draw back from the call that is facing you today is to draw back from blessing.

Sometimes it is easier to say the big "Yes" in the initial leap of faith than to keep saying the small "Yes-es" along the way. Faith wears everyday clothes and proves herself in life's ordinary situations. In the way you answer or keep still today, in the tone of your voice or the curve of your lip, in your thoughts of confidence or self-pity you are "fighting the good fight of faith"—or not.

And harder than to leave family and friends in a spectacular venture of faith is to live among them but not by their standards, walking life's ordinary paths but seeing God, mingling with the crowd but obeying higher standards. To risk the disapproval of your group is not easy; but it pays if it puts God on your side.

> *I gave to God a lagging soul,*
> *Fast losing in the fight.*
> *He gave it back with chart and goal*
> *To climb the steeps of light.*
>
> —C. E. FLYNN

September 5

ADVENTURING WITH GOD

Read: Gen. 17:1-8.

Text: *Fear not, Abram, I am thy shield, and thy exceeding great reward.* Gen. 15:1.

The Returns? Blessing Received. Link your life with God, you link your life with blessing. There is no curse with Him or His. Is it too much to believe that even this sore trial of mine will be turned to blessing, if I am wholly His?

In taking God as my treasure, I have all the real goods of life; for the value of a thing is tested only by its lasting quality. With Him I have character, contentment, spiritual children, eternal life, and eternal country.

Was God partial to Abraham, or may I too be "the friend of God"? That friendship is the greatest reward, and motive for every sacrifice.

The highest friendship is reciprocal: neither side does all the giving. God knows how to give, lavishly; but— marvel indeed—He knows how to receive graciously as well. He makes me feel that I too can give Him something that He needs and wants: my love, my confidence, my service, my devotion. I would not have the friendship one-sided.

Walk with God, and you become a spiritual pioneer. You know the thrill of discovery. You do not say, "I suppose if I'm a Christian I can't do that and I must do this." You have the chart of God's Word and the whisper of the Spirit, and you settle the details of your everyday experience by those principles and that guidance. Your Christian life is not second-hand; others can show you the way, but you and God must make it together.

> *Thy Cross is lifted o'er us,*
> *We journey in its light:*
> *The crown awaits the conquest;*
> *Lead on, O God of might.*

ADVENTURING WITH GOD

Read: Rom. 4:16-25; Gal. 3:8-14.

Text: *So then they which be of faith are blessed with faithful Abraham.* Gal. 3:9.

The Returns? Blessing Given. Some lives have left a trail of evil behind them—I would not live so. I have only one life; I would have its outflow blessing and grace. I may have it so if I will link my life with God.

But humanity of itself has not the resources needed for blessing-giving. We are essentially self-centered, self-absorbed; or we fall short at the critical moment and need to be helped ourselves; or we have not the sort of help that is needed. But we can be channels of His blessing—and that is His rich gift to us.

Every true Christian pioneer leaves behind him the blazed trail and the stretched horizon; for someone else looking at him says, "If he can live a Christian life in his circumstances, I can in mine. If he can stand for Jesus, I can too. If God can take him through, He can take me through."

Link your life with God, and your children will be blessed. The best investment you can make for your children, and the best heritage you can leave them, is the example and the influence of a Christian life.

The wire filament does not lose its individuality when the electricity is turned on, nor the gas jet when the fire burns in it; it only fulfils its purpose and is made beautiful. So we are only half without Christ; we lose ourselves when Christ takes possession, but only to find our real completeness, and our reason for being.

> *My life possessing, my service blessing,*
> *Make me a channel of blessing today.*

HERITAGE

Read: Gen. 25:19-21; 15:2; Gen. 26:25; 22:9; Gen. 26:3, 16-22; 13:8, 9; Gen. 28:1, 2; 24:3, 4; Gen. 26:7; 12: 11-13.

Text: *And he called their names after the names by which his father had called them. Gen. 26:18.*

Young people will follow examples that they believe in —sometimes too closely. Be patient with your young people. After all, they are only reliving your experience, good and bad. You are fortunate if they balance your follies with your good deeds. They might stop with those youthful escapades you have conveniently forgotten!

It is almost terrifying to see how closely the sons follow the father's—or perhaps the grandfather's—pattern. We cannot escape the power of our own influence. What we have done we have done; but its effect is yet to come.

Abraham lies about his wife; Isaac lies about his—and Isaac's son Jacob also lies his way through.

But—

Abraham prays for a son when it seems impossible; so does Isaac.

Abraham builds altars; so does Isaac.

Abraham refuses to fight for his land rights; so does Isaac.

Abraham saves his son from marrying a heathen wife; so does Isaac.

Young people talk a good deal about "living their own lives." Actually they are much impressed by anything genuine in the older generation.

The legend is familiar of the old man who crossed the chasm safely, but turned back to build a bridge across the ravine behind him. Questioned, he told of the lad who was to follow him, who might not know the path so well as he. His answer must be ours:

Good friend, I am building this bridge for him.

HERITAGE

Read: Gen. 26:1-6; 22:1-18.

Text: *Thou shalt call his name Isaac; and I will establish my covenant with him for an everlasting covenant, and with his seed after him.* Gen. 17:19.

Is there such a thing as a "birthright Christian"? In one sense, yes. You are heir to the vision, the prayers, the example, the faith, of a glorious heritage. You are heirs of revelation; the skies above you are full of blessing. In the key sense, no. The inheritance must be claimed in person. There is a blank space left on the deed and you must sign your own name. Every man decides the path his soul shall take.

Who wouldn't rather be a link than a gap? It will show up tomorrow.

The promise is always conditional. No one will make you be a Christian. God waits for a personal confirmation before He takes you on or calls you His. "Alive unto God" are His church—young or old. You can refuse the benefit of your mother's prayers; you can shut yourself off from God's blessing. You will if you just do nothing about your own salvation.

Faith becomes real in the test. The supreme test comes in every Christian's life—in a new form, but quite as soul-shattering. Our fathers' faith became theirs by testing; so must ours become ours.

The bitterest test of faith is the test of waiting. It is hard enough to be patient when we see the way through and know the right forces are at work. But to wait in the dark, to live in patient obedience when everything seems to be going in the other direction, when doors are locked and God has forgotten—that is faith triumphant. But it pays; for God never has forgotten.

> *Tho' earth pass away, His word stands for aye—*
> *The promise unfailing is mine.*

266

HERITAGE

Read: Ps. 91; Isa. 12.

Text: *On earth peace, good will toward men.* Luke 2:14.

"Thy gentleness hath made me great." You can put your life in God's hands completely; He will make you great in His own way—and in your own special way. He will not make you like anybody else; you do not need to be.

It is good to know a "man of good will" (Vulgate version of Luke 2:14); holy and harmless, whose strength is in his gentleness—strength irresistible. Why not lay your plans now to be that kind of person? You don't have to grow into a grouchy old person.

You become effective as you let God fight your personal battles. It is the only way. The man who is fighting to advance himself is fighting for a small cause.

It is a psychological fact: snatch for your own advantage, and other people stiffen up and snatch back; strike the man that has hurt you, and he will hit back twice as hard; complain of poor treatment, and you will get sullen indifference. But smile and be grateful, and you will be treated like a prince. Jesus is right: the meek inherit the earth. Why can't we remember?

The Bible talks about "drawing water out of the wells of salvation." The grace of God is always available, abundant; but we have to tap the supply. The devil has stopped up some of those old wells of joy and peace and love, and praise and testimony and prayer. He would have us grow formal and self-absorbed, frivolous and superficial and sophisticated. Salvation is still simple, spontaneous, from the heart; but we need to dig through some layers of fallow ground before the waters will spring up.

> *I am drinking at the fountain*
> *Where I ever would abide;*
> *For I've tasted life's pure river,*
> *And my soul is satisfied.*

HERITAGE

Read: Prov. 3:1-6; 19-26.

Text: *In all thy ways acknowledge him, and he shall direct thy paths.* Prov. 3:6.

Life is too much for any of us alone; but we do not need to live it alone. No better motto for the young person setting out in life than this: "In all thy ways acknowledge him, and he shall direct thy paths." To live by it means to form some habits and adopt some attitudes. A good morning song: "I know the Lord will make a way for me." A good evening song: "The Lord hath given us room." Twenty people pray, for one who praises. Twenty people acknowledge need, for one who acknowledges deliverance.

You don't feel yourself a very strong Christian? Perhaps you are not the "strong personality" your father was. But you can build altars, and you can dig wells. You can recognize God and maintain a vital contact with heaven; that is your lifeline. And you can do your duty steadily every day, faithful in all earth's common round. With daily altars and daily wells you will find yourself growing strong in the Lord.

Be encouraged by the testimony of those who have followed God down to life's ending.

> *The young cannot look back and say,*
>   *"He led me thus and so;"*
> *The young can only trust to Him,*
>   *And walk by faith; but we,*
> *Those who have traveled longer roads,*
>   *And older grown—can see!*

—MARTHA SNELL NICHOLSON in *Sunday School Times*

To the end of life it will be safe to trust God fully; and your last evening testimony of all will be:

> *Though numerous hosts of mighty foes,*
> *Though earth and hell my way oppose,*
> *He safely leads my soul along—*
> *His loving-kindness, oh, how strong!*

"MARCHING ORDERS"

Read: Acts 13:1-4.

Text: *As they ministered to the Lord, and fasted, the Holy Ghost said, Separate me Barnabas and Saul for the work whereunto I have called them.* Acts 13:2.

Our attitude will determine how much guidance we shall have from the Holy Spirit. Many people never will be called to be missionaries because they have no gospel to carry. Many churches never will have the vision of sending out missionaries because their religion is no bigger than a respectable Sunday morning service. Saving the world is the greatest enterprise open to human beings. I would not be shut out from a fruitful career because I do not know the saving power of Christ in my own life.

The best Christians do not serve a church—ultimately. They are members of a church, but they serve the Lord. So it is possible for the church to get directions from higher up.

We cannot be reminded too often that foreign missions is not a church's enterprise, but God's. He started the missionary movement when He sent Jesus to this unevangelized world; He started missions in India when He stirred the heart of Carey; He started missions in China when He sent out Robert Morrison a century and a half ago. And He started the movement coming westward that took us in, when He sent out Barnabas and Saul. He still is sending. The terrific shaking up of nations He will use to make new highways for His plan of world-wide evangelization.

The man who fasts and prays will not be long in catching a vision of world need. And when a group fasts and prays, something is certain to happen. It would seem we lose immeasurably when we fail to keep our lives open to heaven and God's directions.

Onward, Christian soldiers, marching as to war,
With the cross of Jesus going on before.

"MARCHING ORDERS"

Read: Acts 13:4, 5; 14-16; 42-52.

Text: *Go . . . . and it shall be told thee what thou must do.*
Acts 9:6.

*Obedience in what we know will insure guidance in what
we do not know.* Go as far as you know—and God
will not let you walk off a precipice, nor into a wall. He
will open a door in the wall; He will put solid earth under
your next step. As soon as you need to move He will
show you where to move.

Use the best light you have; if God has larger thoughts,
He will see to it that they get to you somehow. It may be
one step at a time, but those steps will lead to His goal.

We need more simplicity in our Christian work. We
need to do God's work as if it were really God's work
and we were really His servants, His agents, His representatives, His sons conducting business for Him. We
need to look to Him directly for our instructions and for
our enablings.

The work of God is conducted in two planes; rather,
perhaps, by the co-operation of two worlds. God calls
men, and the church separates men. The church sends,
and the Holy Ghost convoys. The missionaries go out,
into the unknown, but holding the hand of God—"safer
than a known way."

Our work is always the same—an all-important work:
"opening the door of faith" to someone bound in darkness.
So long as we are willing to open these locked doors
God will furnish us with keys.

> *Ready to go, ready to stay,*
> *Ready my place to fill;*
> *Ready for service, lowly or great,*
> *Ready to do His will.*

"MARCHING ORDERS"

Read: Acts 14:1-18.

Text: *A great door and effectual is opened unto me, and there are many adversaries.* I Cor. 16:9.

Once in the will of God, we can be guided safely by God's providences. Are we to be guided by our sanctified judgment or by a direct word from God? By both, and where these fail, by "providential circumstances" (only a high-sounding expression for "the things God allows to happen"). He is in control and He will not mock us.

Guiding circumstances are not always pleasant circumstances. Not only the interest of the Gentiles, but also the persecution of the Jews tells Paul that God is sending him to the Gentiles. Afflictions as well as successes will drive us forward in the plan of God, if our sails are set right.

Remember the "two impostors, Praise and Blame." Paul seems more worried by being worshiped than by being stoned. Praise is easier to bear than blame, but it seldom draws us closer to God. And when it means that people see us instead of God, it brings no glory to God.

Christians that are made in the fire are tested—toughened in moral fiber. Paul—and Jesus—never tried to shield their converts nor promised them an easy path. Rough treatment, this "entering through much tribulation"; but it makes strong Christians. Include persecution in your program; then it will not bowl you over.

> *Lord, I would clasp my hand in Thine*
> *Nor ever murmur nor repine;*
> *Content whatever lot I see,*
> *Since 'tis God's hand that leadeth me.*

"MARCHING ORDERS"

Read: Acts 14:19-28.

Text: *They rehearsed all that God had done with them, and how he had opened the door.* Acts 14:27.

If you know God is guiding, you know you can succeed. God accredits the men He sends out—but not by winning them popular favor nor by smoothing their path. He makes things impossibly hard for them, then sends them miracle-working power. He doesn't give them easy circumstances, but He gives powers equal to their circumstances.

Got any rivers you think are uncrossable? . . . .
God specializes in things thought impossible.

And He is your Backer.

God does not give up the cause of foreign missions just because men make war and close mission stations. Neither do missionaries just because they have been called home. Driven out one day, they will be back the next. Stoned today, they will be founding a church tomorrow. And the tomorrows for them will be greater than the yesterdays. God has not abdicated His throne.

The miracle is that wherever the gospel is preached in power, disciples are made and a church is born. When the missionaries leave, the native church still can carry on, for it has divine life in it. The power of the gospel proves itself.

> *God is still on the throne,*
> *And He will remember His own;*
> *His promise is true, He will not forget you—*
> *God is still on the throne.*

September 15

GOD DOES NOT FORGET

Read: Gen. 7:1-10; 23, 24.

Text: *The Lord is not slack concerning his promise.* II
Pet. 3:9.

God does not forget His threatened judgments on evil. "It
came to pass." (Gen. 7:10.) Righteousness delivers—always. Sin pays off in death—always. In the end. And
even now we are permitted sometimes to see God's mills
grinding.

God does not forget his constant care of the good. "I have
seen." (Gen. 7:1.) "Where I really live enemies cannot
come. . . . The strength of God is on the side of right.
This inward certainty overwhelms my unknown future
and I have no fears."—Samuel Young.

God does not forget definite directions for the obedient.
"As the Lord commanded him." (Gen. 6:22; 7:5, 9.) Always His the planning, mine the obeying. Easy to say,
and easy to disregard when the plan includes details that
seem too small to notice. A crack of half an inch could
have sunk the ark.

One of the happiest things is to know that God really
cares about the little details of my life today. He will
help me in my minutes as well as in my days and years.

> *The storms will come, but fear not,*
> *For, Noah, I am nigh;*
> *And through the upper window*
> *You'll see Me standing by.*

GOD DOES NOT FORGET

Read: Gen. 8.

Text: *Behold, I have graven thee upon the palms of my hands; thy walls are continually before me.* Isa. 49:16.

God does not forget His salvation for the trusting. "The Lord shut him in." (Gen. 7:16.) And when you cannot see the way through, do not be so ignorant as to think God is at a loss. Already "He Himself knows what He will do" in your case.

Again we assert it with a shout: "Nothing shall separate us from the love of God!" "Our God whom we serve is able to deliver us; but if not"—we will not question His love.

God does not forget His promised deliverance for the faithful. "The waters assuaged." (Gen. 8:1.) Are you giving up hope? Wait another minute. "In the nick of time," as He sees time, your need will be met. It is the panic of the eleventh hour that ruins most of us.

"Abba, Father." Every language has a familiar word— "Daddy," "Abba"—that represents the prattle of a tiny child. If we are saying "Abba," we are not sophisticated or self-sufficient; we are just simple enough to trust.

> *In the furnace God may prove thee,*
> *Thence to bring thee forth more bright,*
> *But can never cease to love thee;*
> *Thou art precious in His sight.*

274

GOD DOES NOT FORGET

Read: Gen. 9:8-17; Jer. 31:31-37.

Text: *And I will establish my covenant with you, and it [the rainbow] shall be for a token of a covenant between me and the earth.* Gen. 9:11, 13.

God does not forget His covenant with individuals or with dispensations. "My bow in the cloud." (Gen. 9:13.) The rainbow of the New Testament is the promise, "All things work together for good to those who love God." The rainbow of Isaiah is, "Beauty for ashes, the oil of joy for mourning." Where is there another power that will take the ashes of a worn-out life and make them living coals of blessing, or take the storms of devastating sorrow and make them glow with the light of love? Thank God for the hope of the gospel. No Christian life can be a tragedy.

But here we never see the whole rainbow—only half of it. The complete circle John saw surrounding the throne of God. Life has its unanswerable questions; your heart still aches with the pain of them. But God has given you the rainbow arc of hope. Tomorrow you will see the other half.

The rainbow is pure white light broken up into the various colors that are its parts. We should never see them but for the storm. So in the storm of sorrow we may see aspects of Christ the Light that we never could know otherwise.

> *The tide of time shall never*
> *His covenant remove;*
> *His name shall stand forever;*
> *His name to us is Love.*

THE COMFORTER HAS COME

Read: Gen. 1:2; Ps. 51:11; John 3:5-8.

Text: *If ye then, being evil, know how to give good gifts unto your children: how much more shall your heavenly Father give the Holy Spirit to them that ask him?* Luke 11:13.

The Unseen Power. The Holy Spirit is the *divine energy* that produces the spiritual life. The Spirit of God moved that first day of Creation, and life began to stir. Ever since where He is, there is creation; where He is not, is spiritual deadness. The same Spirit has breathed life into my dead soul; I would honor Him. (Gen. 1:2.)

To be abandoned by the Holy Spirit is to be a castaway—a derelict in the moral universe. Prize His whispers and obey His leadings; they are life and hope. And He does not forsake a soul willingly. (Psalm 51:11.)

Our Father knows we have no spiritual capital to run our Christian lives. He knows we have no resources of our own; we must receive from above. The Holy Spirit is His good gift. The power is withheld only until we make the connection, only until we desire enough to ask, only until we realize our need enough to appreciate the supply. (Luke 11:13.)

"Born of the Spirit"—a new life, inward, unseen, real, vital. Have you been trusting to church-going, movie-renouncing, Sunday-school teaching, church work? Outward forms never can make a Christian. (John 3:5.)

The birth of the Spirit is not to be understood, but to be experienced. If we cannot understand it ourselves, we cannot expect our materially-minded friends to understand and approve our actions. We can say, "Try for yourself." (John 3:6-8.)

O spread the tidings round, wherever man is found,
Wherever human hearts and human woes abound . . . .
The Comforter has come!

THE COMFORTER HAS COME

Read: John 16: 7-14.

Text: *It is expedient for you that I go away: for if I go not away, the Comforter will not come unto you; but if I depart, I will send him unto you.* John 16: 7.

The Promised Energizer and Teacher. The Holy Spirit carries on Christ's work through us *by strengthening us.* Better, Jesus said, to have the Comforter ("Strengthener") in their hearts than to have Jesus at their side. For it was better for them to have a miracle done in them than to see miracles done for them. So for us. (John 16: 7).

The Holy Spirit keeps us pure in our hearts, clear in our thinking, steady in our conduct. For He is the *Great Convincer*: "of sin," reproving us when we do wrong; "of righteousness," truing up our standards; "of judgment," making us sensitive to our responsibility to God. We are not adrift spiritually while we have Him. (John 16: 8-11.)

Great "Conserver of Orthodoxy," the theologians have called the Spirit. Yes, for He reminds us of the words of Jesus. He "guides into all truth" and "teaches all things" —not new truth or spectacular actions, as the modernist or the fanatic would have it—always by illuminating "the truth as it is in Christ" and applying it fresh to our ever-changing emergencies. (John 14: 26; 16: 12-14.)

Heavenly Guide, the Holy Spirit always has led individuals and groups, to the glory of God—if they were willing. If we, churches and Christians, would seek His guidance *before* we stumble and lose our way, we should bring less dishonor upon His name. (Isa. 63: 10-14.)

> *Holy Spirit, faithful Guide,*
> *Ever near the Christian's side.*

September 20

THE COMFORTER HAS COME

Read: Acts 2:1-4; 10:44-48; 19:1-7.

Text: *And they were all filled with the Holy Ghost, and began to speak with other tongues, as the Spirit gave them utterance. Acts 2:4.*

The Spirit's Incoming. There is an epochal experience when the divine electric current is turned on. There was a first time that He came to the infant church and a first time that He came to the Gentiles; but always He came to individuals and always to believers, making them fully Christian. The watchword in the apostolic church was "Have ye received the Holy Ghost since ye believed?" Ours can be no less.

The Holy Ghost poured out on individuals (just ordinary people) makes them "prophesy" ("speak forth") and "see visions." It gives them certainty of heavenly realities and a personal revelation of truth. They become established; they become positive factors, workers, soulwinners. (Joel 2:28, 29.)

The Holy Spirit comes suddenly. He comes with a sense of fullness, for it is a great God taking possession of a small temple; He comes with a sense of cleanness, for it is a holy God entering what was defiled and fitting it for His abode. Whatever the varying emotions, by His incoming He purifies my nature and imparts the disposition of Jesus; by His abiding He enables me to make the holy choices that will make holy character. (Acts 15:8, 9.)

Jesus gave the promise to His disciples; Peter extended it to us all. And Jesus prayed for us all. I would rather trust their word than listen to some doubters who say, "That was just for the apostles." (Acts 2:39.)

> *Then let us humbly, boldly press,*
> *Our heritage in Christ possess,*
> *That power from heaven may fall.*

THE COMFORTER HAS COME

Read: Rom. 8: 12-17; 26, 27; Acts 4: 31.

Text: *But ye are not in the flesh, but in the Spirit, if so be that the Spirit of God dwell in you.* Rom. 8: 9.

The Spirit-Filled Life. Watch the Spirit energizing a holy life. It becomes alive, dynamic, positive. The epochal experience is only the beginning; we prove our experience by developing a new Spirit-indwelt life. This means daily choice of the Spirit's leading until *spiritual habits* are built up. "We are debtors to live after the Spirit."

We learn the necessity of keeping under the Spirit's *anointings*. We learn how out of weakness to become strong. There are still fearsome enemies to meet and still human shrinkings. But we learn that prayer will renew boldness and we learn to pray things through. "We kneel how weak; we rise how full of power."

We learn to let the Holy Spirit guide and control our *prayer life*. We stop asking for what we want, and begin to ask what He wants. We stop praying aimlessly and perfunctorily, and let Him teach us the effectual prayer. There is a grip in a Spirit-controlled prayer.

Spirit-filled Christians soon become *intercessors*. The Holy Spirit knows what it means for a soul to be lost, and He knows the worth of the blood of Christ. He fills our prayers with His own intensity.

> *Holy Spirit, all divine,*
> *Dwell within this heart of mine;*
> *Cast down every idol throne,*
> *Reign supreme, and reign alone.*

THE COMFORTER HAS COME

Read: I Cor. 12:1-13.

Text: *But the manifestation of the Spirit is given to every man to profit withal.* I Cor. 12:7.

There is nothing like the baptism with the Holy Spirit for developing one's personal talents. He puts His finger on latent abilities and says, "Do this. I will help you." He always brings with Him a gift, so that the humblest has his own special contribution to make to the Kingdom Has He shown you yours? (I Cor. 12:4.)

The Spirit-filled are bound together in a fellowship that is supernatural—the unity of the body of Christ. You do not wish to harm your brother nor to excel him; you rejoice and sorrow with him. And your spirits leap out to mingle in prayer and achievement. If the church had kept Spirit-filled, there could have been no schisms, and no enemies could have stood before her. When fellowship wears thin, the cure is to pray together for a fresh outpouring of "the communion of the Spirit." (I Cor. 12:12, 13; II Cor. 13:14.)

The Holy Spirit in you gives you the *spirit of worship.* He makes testimony vital, singing God's praises a joy, preaching a message from God, the Bible His letter to you. Sunday is not a dull day; it does not have to be enlivened by pleasure trips—you are "in the Spirit on the Lord's day." (Rev. 1:10.)

The Holy Spirit is the great Trainer for *personal work.* He enables you to say "Come" effectively: He helps you live a life that will attract others to Christ, and He helps you talk naturally about Him to others. (Rev. 22:17.)

> *Your loosened tongues shall speak His praise,*
> *Your lips no more be dumb.*

280

FITTED FOR SERVICE

Read: Mark 1:1-11.

Text: *He shall baptize you with the Holy Ghost.* Mark 1:8.

Personal experience is basic preparation for Christian service. The Christian worker's greatest asset is his testimony. "If you do as I have done, you will receive the blessing I have received"—a tried recipe is more attractive than a sermon. There is always power in a definite testimony.

The sense of God's approval, the witness of the Spirit to sonship, will be the Christian worker's strength. It will be also his recommendation. He is to introduce people to God, and they must recognize that he himself is on good terms with God.

"Be ye clean, that bear the vessels of the Lord." We show small reverence when we do God's work with selfish motives or unclean thoughts. But our only way to make sure of pure service is to accept the cleansing baptism of the Holy Spirit. Jesus told His church to wait for Pentecost.

At the entrance to the path of service stands the Holy Spirit. He works through men. Without Him we can do nothing. He anointed Jesus; He must cleanse us first. But we must learn also the secret of living under His anointing. Most precious is the promise that He will breathe upon our poor words and deeds, and make them living bread for hungry souls.

The dove does not descend visibly today; but God has ways of making the Spirit visible in Christian lives. People recognize the heavenly aura; they feel the certainty and confidence of the man on whom God sets the seal of His approval. They trust Him.

> *'Tis the enduement, power for service;*
> *Fruits for your labor He surely will send.*

FITTED FOR SERVICE

Read: Mark 1:12, 13; Jas. 1:2-5; Isa. 48:10.

Text: *Blessed is the man that endureth temptation: for when he is tried, he shall receive the crown of life.* James 1:12.

Testing is an essential part of the preparation. Count on temptation. It has not taken God by surprise; in fact, it is part of His program. It is your opportunity to prove His grace sufficient. Then your recommendations of grace will have weight.

The enemy will train his strongest guns on the one who sets out to work for God. Do not think there is something wrong if you are tempted as you never have been before. It means the devil is more afraid of what you are going to do.

You think the devil is after you; he is. But God is ahead of him. The Spirit has led you—is still leading you. He knows you will have no strength of Christian character unless you learn to endure temptation. So he cannot let you escape. Satan's temptation is God's testing. I can go through better if I see it so.

So long as there is anything in us that will shake, we are to that extent unstable and unusable. So long as there is the unlaid ghost of a doubt or a hovering dread, to that extent we are unreliable and untrustworthy. So long as there is a hidden fact we dare not face, to that extent we are weak. Temptation conquered is Christian character strengthened.

Strong in the strength which God supplies
Through His eternal Son.

FITTED FOR SERVICE

Read: Mark 1:14-20.

Text: *And straightway they forsook their nets, and followed him.* Mk. 1:18.

Christ's servant must learn obedience. Service is activity, but it is activity under orders. God's time (perhaps not your convenience), God's message (perhaps not the popular), God's call (perhaps not your choice), —and "straightway." I wonder if we Christians would not profit by Army discipline.

Consecration conditions service. You are no longer the center of your world. Your property and your normal interests are secondary; your vision is set on the kingdom of Christ and what God can do through you to advance it. Are you willing? Can you let go? It is the price of service.

Life is all too short to train for Christian service. As long as he lives, the Christian worker should study in the school of Christ. He needs to learn His ways; to think His thoughts, to speak His words, to share His attitudes, to live in His presence. Small good to attempt His work without His vision or His spirit.

Jesus spoke with authority, because He was the Truth, and His every word echoed in some human heart. We must learn of Him—and we have much to learn—if we would bring men to God. For argument does no good; it only hardens. Only truth will convict.

In preparing for Christian service we are preparing to deal with eternal issues and with souls that will live forever. We are sharing the work of Deity. The preparation should be thorough. It should not be haphazard.

> *More about Jesus let me learn,*
> *More of His holy will discern;*
> *Spirit of God my Teacher be.*

GOOD STEWARDS

Read: Matt. 6: 19-30.

Text: *The light of the body is the eye: if therefore thine eye be single, thy whole body shall be full of light.* Matt. 6: 22.

Our spiritual life is the key to our handling of material things. If our hearts are set on things, our hands will clutch them so tightly that no power can unclench them. As usual, Jesus goes to the root of the matter. He devotes one-sixth of His Sermon on the Mount to the Christian's heart attitude toward material things.

The key is complete trust in our Heavenly Father to supply our every need. Such trust comes only with a complete consecration of the will to God. So long as there is a grain of self-will left, we shall be fancying that we need something God sees we should do better without, and worrying or hoarding or scheming to get it. To give oneself unreservedly to God is the first step, the necessary step, toward the right—that is, the Christian—way of handling money.

And the first step toward the covetousness that damns the soul is worry—worry about such "necessary" things as food and clothes. Begin to worry, and you inevitably begin to grab.

Attitudes convert themselves quickly into actions; and attitudes toward God determine attitudes toward men. So before considering right economic relations to people, it might be well to take a long look inward, in the light of Jesus' searching questions. Ask yourself, as He asks you: (1) Where is your *Treasure,* in earth or heaven? (2) Where is your *Gaze* fixed, on material or spiritual things? (3) Who is your *Master,* Christ or money? (4) What is your chief *Interest,* the Kingdom or yourself? (5) What are your *Thoughts,* worries or trust?

> *He will not forget, God will not forget;*
> *Never has one child been forgotten yet.*

GOOD STEWARDS

Read: Luke 12: 13-21.

Text: *A man's life consisteth not in the abundance of the things which he possesseth.* Luke 12:15.

A wrong estimate of life and what it is for will damn our souls. A good many years ago I heard Dr. R. T. Williams preach a sermon on "the rich fool." His definition of *fool* I have never forgotten: "A fool is a man that makes wrong decisions and comes to wrong conclusions." The converse also is true. The one who holds an unsound philosophy of life and what life is for, is certain to act unwisely and unsafely. The utter fool is the man who thinks life can be measured by things possessed—money and what money will buy. "The majority are fools," you say? That will not make it any easier or safer for me to hear God say to me, "Thou fool."

We have so much to do with material things that we come naturally to think that life is all "things," and its object is to get enough for ourselves and our families to eat and drink and wear—on a scale as good as our neighbors. That seems to take all the energy we have, and more. But when all that is done we have not touched the real business of living. For at the end we are to be asked for a soul—what of that? The body for which we worked so hard was only its house—what of the inmate's welfare? Has it been starved?

Rich for myself and poor for God—a bad bargain, since I am giving account to God. A millionaire in the coin of time and bankrupt for eternity—poor calculation, since I have to live forever by eternity's currency.

> *Only one life—'twill soon be past;*
> *Only what's done for God will last.*

GOOD STEWARDS

Read: Luke 16: 9-13; Deut. 8.

Text: *He that is faithful in that which is least is faithful also in much.* Luke 16: 10.

The Christian regards his money as a sacred trust. "What a man does with his money is the real test of his religion." Money is only a symbol. It is the means of exchange by which we get what we want. And what a man wants tells what he is.

The antithesis is not between the miser and the spend-thrift—both are serving Mammon. The contrast is between the master of his money and the slave of his money. Dante represents both prodigal and avaricious as toiling to move heavy weights. Be systematic in dealing with what money you have (and use God's system); for God puts no premium on careless giving.

"What! Eat the Lord's money!" was the indignant reply of the famine-stricken old Indian woman when the native pastor suggested that she keep the contents of her mitebox till she could find work and get something to eat. Should we in America be as shocked at a proposal to "borrow" from our tithe?

Our ability to get money is given us by God and He could cut it off at any time. (Deut. 8: 17, 18.) Gratitude is a basic moral quality. Gratitude, fairness, common decency require that we consult His wishes in the spending of it.

All the world's money really belongs to God; it is only lent to us. (Ps. 50: 7-17.) So He lets us be generous; and so He tests our love.

Failure to pay our tithes (the tithe is still a minimum standard) is robbing God. (Mal. 3: 8-10.) So much is only paying a debt—interest, as it were, on God's loan. After that we can talk of "giving."

> *Take my silver and my gold;*
> *Not a mite would I withhold.*

286

GOOD STEWARDS

Read: Luke 16:10-13; II Cor. 8:1-12.

Text: *I am debtor.* Rom. 1:14.

The Christian first gives himself; his all is God's. The true Christian has taken his money out of his own savings account and transferred it to God's checking account subject to His draft at any time.

Under the old covenant the believer was to give one-tenth and God was to prosper the nine-tenths. The Christian still knows this to be the rule—generally. But he knows too that all he has is God's and that sometimes permanent blessing involves temporary loss. So like those forward-looking Old Covenant saints, Moses, Job, Habakkuk, he will choose God's long-time blessing rather than Mammon's riches of a day.

Moses esteemed Christ's reproach greater riches than Egyptian treasures; Job said, "The Lord gave, and the Lord hath taken away; blessed be the name of the Lord"; Habakkuk declared, "Although the fig tree shall not blossom . . . . yet I will rejoice in the Lord." They did not lose by their choice.

"We must give out of ourselves if our giving is not to be commonplace or superficial. Jesus Himself watched the collection plates and said some givers never felt their gift. And He was not sorry for the woman who gave all."

We are debtors. So long as we see an unrelieved need we have no surplus to spend on ourselves. There are the heathen who need the warmth and food of the gospel, there are the homeless refugees of Europe, there are the unevangelized youth of our town. I think if we opened our eyes wider, we might find ourselves "in the red"— or at least see that we have some bills to pay.

> *I gave, I gave my life for thee—*
> *What hast thou given for Me?*

GOOD STEWARDS

Read: Luke 16:19-26; II Cor. 9:6-8.

Text: *For the love of money is the root of all evil.* I Tim. 6:10.

You can pay too much for some things. Money is danger: necessary stuff, but to be handled as warily as TNT. For it tends to separate a man from God. (Luke 18:18-24.) Almost anything (earthly) can be got with money; money is almost omnipotent. Unless we see heavenly things pretty plainly we come to trust money more than God—and prize money more than God. Our only safety is to weigh values: there are things money cannot buy.

Covetousness is the "evil eye" of the Old Testament. It is "the root of all evil" because the natural man tries so desperately to satisfy his soul with *things.* It cannot be done.

The person who lives for what money can buy is the plaything of money. It will lift him to the top of the "wheel of fortune," then suddenly drop him to the bottom. Just when his heart is most set on his money it will leave him in the lurch. Dives was not bad—only self-centered. He was not dishonest; he just spent his money on himself. But he came out wrong. When he lost his money he lost everything.

We become like the god we worship. If our God is love, we become loving and kind; if our god is money, we become hard and metallic. We cannot be like both!

You do not have to have much money to be ruined by money. You can set your heart on two dollars as tightly as on two million—it works the same. You can become "money-minded" in trying to keep the wolf from the door without trusting God.

> *Jesus calls us from the worship*
> *Of the vain world's golden store.*

GOOD STEWARDS

Read: Luke 12:22, 23; 29-34.

Text: *For where your treasure is, there will your heart be also.* Luke 12:34.

The wise man makes long-time investments. Leaving God out of our financial calculations is cheating ourselves. For we must give in our reckoning to God. "Make all you can and keep all you get" is a poor policy. Covetousness doesn't pay; for it considers only this life.

Death brings the great reversal—of positions, of riches, of honors, of ease. For eternity substitutes the spiritual standard for the material. Let me invest largely in the wealth of the Kingdom. I would not be a pauper forever.

Our scale of values is scheduled for devaluation. Heaven uses a new currency. Across the river the only values are love for men and devotion to Christ. And even here life is not wholly on a cash basis. There is the colored porter who refused a tip because the passenger had called him "my friend." Men will do for love what they will not do for money.

"Foolish," they say, to live for the next world; "foolish" not to look out for Number One. The world and God call different people fools. God has the last word.

Yes, the Christian is accumulating wealth. But he calculates it in terms of saved souls (so he puts his money into the church and missions) and a Christlike character (so he loves instead of hoards). God will be his Banker.

> *Let me hold lightly temporal things;*
> *I who am deathless, I who wear wings.*
> —MARTHA SNELL NICHOLSON

GOOD STEWARDS

Read: Acts 2:41-47; James 5:1-7.

Text: *Be ye doers of the word, and not hearers only, deceiving your own selves.* James 1:22.

Value your money only for the Kingdom's sake. Be glad of all you have that can be given to the church or shared with a brother's need. Wesley said, "Get all you can; save all you can; give all you can." Livingstone said, "I will set no value on anything I have or may possess except in its relation to the kingdom of God."

You will meet again all the money you have given to the work of God. For in the strictest sense it was not given, but invested. You will meet it on the other side of the River in souls redeemed. Oh, no, you did not lose it; you sent it on ahead of you to spend in eternity.

I wonder what it is to be "rich toward God." Always to have God know that whenever He needs help for His work He can come to us and we will do something about it? That we have given Him a checkbook full of signed checks which He can cash as He pleases? Something like that. He is rich toward us; He expects us to be rich toward Him. Joining forces, we can meet the world's need.

Keep simple. Don't let money spoil you. Be honest and fair. Better be poor all your days than take advantage of another person in order to get ahead. You can't take more than your share without injustice to someone. Be humble. You are never any better than another person by virtue of having more money than he has.

Stay "poor in spirit." Don't get the riches complex. Don't get the hoarding complex. Be a channel, not a reservoir.

> *Let me hold lightly things that are mine;*
> *Lord, Thou hast given me all that is Thine.*
> —MARTHA SNELL NICHOLSON

WE KNOW HIM

Read: Luke 24:1-12; John 20:11-18.

Text: *Jesus saith unto her, Mary.* John 20:16.

Real Christians are not guessers; they are knowers. They are unutterably certain. They are not looking for anyone or anything better. They know they have found Reality in the person of Jesus Christ.

The women came to bring spices; they found angels. They came mourning; they went away rejoicing. It was so when I met Jesus. My world has been alight ever since. "Idle tales" perhaps to others, but to me "blessed assurance."

The assurance of salvation that comes to the individual heart is no impression or hallucination. A genuine Christian experience is backed up by the Word of God. What a thrill to open your Bible and find your own story written there.

The fact that someone else "wonders" does not discredit what God has done for you. Soon the doubter may be on the inside looking out; then he will turn into a witness.

We can know Him, intimately, as we know no other friend. It costs in time and devotion, but it is life's *summum bonum.*

> *He lives! He lives!*
> *Christ Jesus lives today.*
> *You ask me how I know He lives?*
> *He lives within my heart.*

WE KNOW HIM

Read: Luke 24:13-32.

Text: *Did not our heart burn within us, while he talked with us by the way?* Luke 24:32.

Jesus makes Himself known to individual hearts in a personal relationship. He comes to those who *talk of Him.* He will not force Himself upon us. If we are too full of our own concerns to care, it is perfectly easy to live in Christian America as heathen, never even knowing there ιs a living Christ. "Indifference is our Public Enemy Number One."

We can *see Him.* Interested in Him, we find He is interested in us. We too can have Him walking by our side along life's dusty way, and all our common days can be a romance.

We can *talk to Him.* No worry is too petty to bring to Him, no problem too big. The extreme reverence which makes God so great that He cannot bother with our small affairs amounts to practical atheism.

We can *hear Him talk.* Much of our relationship with Jesus should consist of silence toward Him. What things He will tell us: practical counsel for everyday matters, comfort for everyday sorrows, light for our eternities— as He makes the Bible a living book. Suppose I should miss all this by my chattering.

We can *entertain Him.* Let us not treat Jesus shabbily. We set before our other guests the best we have. "Give the best you have to the Best you know."

We can *eat with Him*—in daily communion. Communion is a rare art; but we need it sorely. Some part of our prayers must be more than asking, or we shall starve spiritually while going through the forms of prayer.

> *What a privilege to carry*
> *Everything to God in prayer.*

WE KNOW HIM

Read: Luke 24:33-36; Matt. 18:20; Mal. 3:16-18.

Text: *And as they thus spake, Jesus himself stood in the midst of them.* Luke 24:36.

Jesus makes Himself known today by manifesting His Presence when a group of believers meet together. How is His presence manifested? You know, who have gone to church or prayer meeting worn out, and come away exhilarated. You say, "His presence was real in that service." Let us not be satisfied with any service which lacks that reality. For He said He would come.

It is to a group of believers who are *talking of Him* that He manifests His presence. There are many gatherings of so-called worshipers that Jesus never visits because they do not know Him personally and they never speak of Him in His house. The testimony meeting is unknown, for there is nothing to testify to; the sermon is an essay on current affairs and never mentions Him; the singing is an unintelligible anthem—what room for Him? We believe in the type of service where Jesus will feel at home. But to have such services we must keep Him fresh in our personal experience.

Jesus comes! How good to recognize that Presence. Perhaps it is in a song: "His yoke is easy, His burden is light." Perhaps in a prayer, when you realize the speaker is looking into the face of Christ, and you too catch a glimpse. Perhaps in a faltering, broken word of testimony when your own heart joins and you say, "Me, too, Lord. You did that for me, and I thank You." Jesus is there, and there is a strange blending of hearts in His presence.

> *The love of Jesus, what it is,*
> *None but His loved ones know.*

WE KNOW HIM

Read: Luke 24:36-44; John 13:1-17.

Text: *Peace be unto you.* Luke 24:36.

When He comes, He speaks peace. Body weary, mind fagged and anxious, heart sick with foreboding—but with His peace comes inner poise, rest, calm. Why or how you cannot explain, but with Him there, all is well.

Jesus puts a premium on the fellowship of Christians. There is a sense in which He *explains Himself* to the group as He does not to the one who worships alone. Some Bible truth we never shall find for ourselves. The doctrinal sermon will never be out of date.

Jesus *proves Himself* and His saving power as His disciples unite in faith and desire. The revival meeting will never be out of date.

Jesus *answers our questions* as we meet with other Christians. Haven't you proved it? I have. Pray about some problem Sunday morning; then go to church and find the answer in the sermon. His way is just as simple as that.

Jesus *eats with* the group in the sacrament of the Lord's Supper. Human good fellowship may come through "church suppers"; Christian fellowship must have Christ in it.

When Jesus comes, the tempter's power is broken;
When Jesus comes, the tears are wiped away.
He takes the gloom and fills the life with gladness,
For all is changed when Jesus comes to stay.

WE KNOW HIM

Read: Luke 24:45-48.

Text: *And that repentance and remission of sins should be preached in his name among all nations.* Luke 24:47.

Jesus expects us to keep Him alive in an evangelistic program. We can have the *burning heart.* The love I feel is the force that moves me. I want my life's compulsion to be His.

We will tell others if we know—and are excited enough. That is not just woman nature; it is human nature. That instinct too shall be used for Him.

This is His plan for making His resurrection vital to the world; and it is only as we fulfil His program that He promises His continued presence with us. It is of no use to try to imagine that Jesus is real in our lives if we are not keeping faith with Him. We are fooling ourselves that we know Him if we are not interested in what He is interested in.

Here is the program—to be breathed through and through with the living Christ: (1) Preaching, (2) Holiness, (3) Missions, (4) Witnessing. An evangelistic church—is it like your church?

The Three P's of the Great Commission—the Power, the Presence, the Program—are a good outline to live by for the rest of our lives, if we remember that those three P's are vitally connected; we cannot have any one unless we will have all three. The Power we crave comes only through the Presence; we cannot keep the power if we lose the contact. And both are given us to carry on the Program; we cannot have them to use selfishly.

Tell the blessed story of the cross of Jesus;
Tell the blessed story of the hallowed cross.

THE LOYALTY OF OBEDIENCE

Read: Matt. 16:21-27.

Text: *For whosoever will save his life shall lose it; and whosoever will lose his life for my sake shall find it.* Matt. 16:25.

When Christianity was born, it was born in full armor. The issues were clear-cut; the line was sharply drawn. When a man became a Christian he accepted a mighty challenge; he staked everything upon a single throw. He knew when he "left all and followed Jesus." Today it seems we can "accept Christ" and "join the church" with hardly a ripple made in our inner or our outer life. The difference is with us, not with the standards.

There is a twofold loyalty required of the Christian: a loyalty of spirit and a loyalty of conduct; a loyalty to the Person of Christ and a loyalty to His commands; a loyalty that is born in a moment and a loyalty that will be tested and developed throughout a lifetime; the loyalty of a crisis experience and the loyalty of a life process; the loyalty of obedience to the two Great Commandments and the loyalty of obedience to their numberless minor implications; the loyalty that gives up all other loves for Christ and the loyalty that will give unquestioning obedience to His every wish, as it becomes known.

In conversion the center of a man's life is transferred from self; but not, as some idealists would have it, from self to others. When a man is truly converted and sanctified wholly, his life finds its center in God and His will. The First Commandment first, "Thou shalt love the Lord thy God with all thy heart;" then, "The second is like unto it: thou shalt love thy neighbour as thyself."

> *The Son of God goes forth to war—*
> *Who follows in His train?*

THE LOYALTY OF OBEDIENCE

Read: Matt. 6: 31-34.

Text: *But seek ye first the kingdom of God, and his righteousness; and all these things shall be added unto you.* Matt. 6: 33.

God First. The standard by which we should test our loyalty is God's measuring-stick, not ours; His way of looking at things, not ours. He says, "Love God with all your soul and strength;" we tend to say, "Love God, of course, but not at too much expense to your own comfort." He says, "Seek first the kingdom of God;" we tend to say, "The Kingdom, of course, but not at the expense of your old age."

God first in our thoughts—is there any activity we enjoy that we cannot share with Him? Any song, any music, any picture, any book, any magazine? Or don't we want to know what He thinks about it?

"Some of self and some of Thee" are not deliberately the words of any justified heart. From the moment the soul touches Christ its purpose is to give Him all. We don't plan for even a minor disloyalty and stay Christian at all.

Jesus doesn't mean that we shall not have to get clothes and food—and sometimes find the getting difficult and perplexing. He does mean that if we will take Him simply and literally, He has ways of taking care of us that we never should have dreamed of. Not always an easy way, sometimes good hard work, but no torturesome worry. "Bear my burdens," He says, "and I'll bear yours." "Trust," He says, "not worry." "Live in the present," He says, "not in the future." Why do we choose the hard way?

It amounts to atheism to have a God, then live as if there were no God.

> *Is your all on the altar of sacrifice laid,*
> *Your heart does the Spirit control?*

297

October 10

THE LOYALTY OF OBEDIENCE

Read: Matt. 7:12-20.

Text: *This commandment have we from him, That he who loveth God love his brother also.* I John 4:21.

The Golden Rule. God is generous to us; therefore He expects us to be generous to others. He spares us no good thing—nothing that we really should wish if we could see everything; therefore the Golden Rule. For we are His representatives; we are disloyal if by our actions we misrepresent His character.

The Second Commandment springs from the first as its corollary. They belong together. Your love for God is spurious if you are selfish with your neighbor. Your love for your neighbor is unreliable and essentially spurious—for it has a grain of self at its heart—if it is not grounded in love for God. "What God hath joined" we are not wise to separate.

Jesus' Sayings. Jesus dares to put before us the bare literalnesses of following Him. We cover them up with a misty haze of vague generalities, and ease ourselves through and out of the embarrassing facts.

Jesus says, Face the fact that you tend to be easy on yourself and hard on others. But that would make you a hypocrite. If all the facts were in, you are probably worse than they are. The only way to be sincere is to save your opinion till you know every circumstance and every motive—which will be never.

Jesus says, Face the fact that the right way is not the popular way, and that you are likely to find yourself in the minority if you take it. But also the fact that you can't take the way of least resistance and come out right in the end. Most insistent of all dilemmas: the narrow way is the only path to life.

> *Must Jesus bear the cross alone,*
> *And all the world go free?*

THE LOYALTY OF OBEDIENCE

Read: Matt. 7:21-29.

Text: *Not everyone that saith unto me, Lord, Lord, shall enter into the kingdom of heaven; but he that doeth the will of my Father which is in heaven.* Matt. 7:21.

Jesus' Sayings. Jesus says, Face the fact that you cannot trust every preacher who shows you an easy way. You must test every theory by Jesus' truth. Perhaps the preaching you like is not the preaching you need.

Jesus says, Face the fact that every insincerity is doomed, but that naked truth will win out in the end. Ally yourself with what you know to be right, however tempting and profitable the shading compromise seems.

Jesus says, Face the bare fact that it won't do you any good to testify beautifully, pray fervently, or even preach a "straight gospel" if you do not live consistently. Face the fact that it will do you no good to have a reputation for saintliness or piety or even for success in Christian work if in your heart you know you are untrue to light.

Jesus says, Face the fact that truth is not relative, but absolute. There are not many teachers, but One. Face the fact that you who have heard cannot evade responsibility to do.

And Jesus—not some sensational preacher—Jesus says, Face the unpleasant fact of the Judgment ahead. Face the fact of the coming storm. Face the fact that you must either prepare or go down in the flood, and that you prepare by simple obedience. If you obey, there is nothing to fear; if you neglect, there is everything to fear.

> *Assured if I my trust betray,*
> *I shall forever die.*

THEN LOVE

Read: I John 3:10-15.

Text: *He that loveth not his brother abideth in death.*
  I John 3:14.

You would keep out of Satan's clutches? Then love.
There is a world of love and a world of hate, a world of
life and a world of death. Love belongs to the world of
God and life; hate belongs to the world of the devil and
death. Thank God if you have escaped from that world
of destruction—and stay free.

Love is eternal life begun; hate is eternal death begun. Beware of allowing the first trace of hatred to
spring up in your heart. A grudge, a shadow of resentment or envy allowed to linger will work like slow poison.

Hate hurts most the hater himself. Any murderer
harms himself more than the man he kills.

You would prove your religion genuine? Then love. Love
cannot be worked up. But vital contact kept with God
gives us an inexhaustible supply if we will use it. You
have had the experience of being treated meanly—so
meanly that there was nothing to do but hit back—and
finding almost to your surprise that you could say and do
kind things instead? That power was of God.

Are you not glad you let God sanctify you wholly and
make your love perfect? You did not realize then how
badly you would need in some day of emergency a love
that had no trace of gall. Terrible if when you wanted to
show Christ to some sinner who had wronged you, the
bitterness of Satan had come out instead.

If you love God perfectly, why so many fears? Do
not save all your confidence for the great Day of Judgment.

> *Holy Spirit, love divine!*
> *Glow within this heart of mine;*
> *Kindle every high desire;*
> *Perish self in Thy pure fire!*

October 13

THEN LOVE

Read: I John 2:8-11; 4:7, 8; 19-21.

Text: *Every one that loveth is born of God, and knoweth God. I John 4:7.*

You would have power with men? Then love.

> *Thou hast no power, nor may'st conceive of mine—*
> *But love I gave thee, with myself to love.*
>
> —BROWNING

Love is the greatest gift of Christ's cross; and love is power, the greatest power in all the universe. Life is too much for you? You cannot get ahead? Try loving—genuinely loving—and doing the works of love.

You remember the woman whose pastor advised her to kill her husband. (He had been cruel to her and she had asked advice.) "Kill him with kindness. Return good for evil." Try killing all your enemies—with love. It is easier than it sounds.

You would be truly great? Then love. There are not too many in our world to do the loving, and our brothers and sisters in Christ have many to hurt and wound them. Let us be among the lovers.

"You do not have to be smart to put holes in the profession of anyone. It takes love to cover." The little girl who told her mother one night that she had been a peacemaker that day because she "heard something and didn't tell it" had achieved more than many of us do!

"You will find as you look back upon your life that the moments that stand out above everything else are the moments when you have done things in a spirit of love."—Henry Drummond.

> *Jesus, Thine all-victorious love*
> *Shed in my heart abroad.*

October 14

THEN LOVE

Read: I John 3:16-19; 4:9-16.

Text: *Let us not love in word, neither in tongue; but in deed and in truth. I John 3:18.*

You would be truly Christlike? Then love. Love is negative—the absence of hate. Love is positive—the laying down of life. Perfect love is both.

"He sought for others the good he desired for himself. Let him pass on."—Golden Rule of the Egyptians. Is your love as active as this?

You would show God to others? Then love. The president of a church-affiliated college, when asked (by some who knew his personal views) why he did not take a certain rather positive stand on a disputed issue in a General Assembly, replied, "I'm not just So-and-So (using his own name); I'm the president of ———— College." Every true Christian should have a similar controlling principle: "I'm not just myself; I'm representing God. I'm loving as God loves, acting as God would act. I stand in the place of God to those who cannot see Him."

Talk less and love more? Love is more than flabby sentimentalism. Plan less and love more? Love is more than barren theorizing or even brilliant execution. Love is the work of the Spirit of God in our hearts. There is no "substitute just as good."

> Take thy first walk with God!
>   Let Him go forth with thee;
> By stream, or sea, or mountain path,
>   Seek still His company.
>
> Thy first transaction be
>   With God Himself above;
> So shall thy business prosper well,
>   And all thy day be love.
>
> —H. Bonar

302

October 15

OUR COMMISSION

Read: Matt. 28:16-20.

Text: *Go ye, therefore, and teach all nations.* Matt. 28:19.

Jesus left His work incomplete, but not unprovided for. That is, if we do not forget or grow careless. Every age has its share of redeemed souls to bring in, to make good the Atonement. And every individual has his share. "A charge to keep I have."

Jesus left His work unfinished—why? He believed the Redeemer's kingdom would mean more to us if we had a share in gathering the souls that will make it up. Does it mean that much to you? His was the first great co-operative enterprise; He counted on something in you that would measure up to His trust.

That last appointment of Jesus with the disciples was a vital one; so important as to be crucial. If they had not kept it, what of His purchased redemption? The appointment is still being made; everyone who calls himself a disciple must keep an appointment with Christ and hear personally that last charge. Have I kept my appointment? Or am I behind schedule time?

The same job is ours today. There are more heathen today than when Jesus left our earth. And today the nations are thinking of everything else but saving souls. Has our opportunity gone? Not so long as we have breath to speak and a heart to pray. If the hundred and twenty could make an impact on their pagan world, we need not despair.

The boundless trust of Jesus! He has placed in our hands His reputation and the success of that enterprise for which He gave His life.

Beware lest, slothful to fulfil thy mission,
Thou lose one jewel that should deck His crown.

OUR RESOURCES

Read: Acts 1: 1-11; Acts 4: 23-31.

Text: *And they were all filled with the Holy Ghost, and they spake the word of God with boldness. Acts 4: 31.*

We should do Christ's work in Christ's way. As the disciples toiled in fishing all that weary night and "caught nothing," so earnest Christians can labor faithfully with meager results. But let them be filled with the Holy Spirit as He directed clearly, and the result is steady, constant fruitfulness. Strange, how insistent we are on "working for God" and how satisfied, when without the dynamic power of the Holy Spirit to work for us and through us, our real accomplishment may be nil.

Yes, you have done it, and I have done it: worked, toiled, ground on to get something done we felt we should do, thinking we had not time to stop for prayer. There was nothing "heavenly" about the day; and as its hours wore on we began to realize there was something wrong —we were not making headway. Then we took time out to talk with God. The anointing of the Lord came upon us, the wheels of life were oiled, the Spirit Himself thought with us and through us, our words and acts had a new grip—there was no waste motion. As of a day, so of a Christian life. "Time out" first to "be filled with the Spirit."

Those hidden weak spots that will give way in the strain—the subtle self-will, the unconscious insincerity, the "innocent" vanity—only the searching, burning Holy Spirit can discover, and fortify us for the battle for souls. For the very souls we are trying to save feel our weakness and will be repelled by our failures.

> *The power, the power,*
> *Gives victory over sin and purity within—*
> *The power they had at Pentecost.*

JESUS INTERCEDING

Read: John 17; Rom. 8:34.

Text: *Father, I will that they also, whom thou hast given me, be with me where I am. John 17:24.*

My Complete Saviour. The hour of all the ages was the hour of Calvary. There Jesus gave His life to save me. But He did still more; He prayed for me. The passion is steeped in intercession; the sacrifice is made efficacious by prayer. He took no chances with my soul.

Jesus prayed that I should be kept from the world's evil. Let me not fear the gathering power of unknown evil. His prayer will be a wall of fire about me.

He prayed that I should be sanctified wholly. I do not have to believe the doubters nor the devil, who say the experience is not for me.

He prayed that I might be a good witness. He prayed that through my holy life others should believe in His power to save from sin. Though it seems to me that I do little for Him, I can spread His Kingdom by living true today.

He prayed that His joy should be mine. He knows I need a song in my heart. Even today when life's disappointments are clutching at my heart and the whole world I have known is falling in ruins, His joy remains when all else goes.

He prayed that we should be one: the Father and the great body of sanctified believers and I. I am not a solitary. I belong. Let me not cherish a suspicion nor raise a barrier between any fellow Christian and myself.

I am glad He prayed for me; I need to know He prays today. I will keep on believing in Him. His prayer is for those who believe.

He ever lives above, for me to intercede,
His all-redeeming love, His precious Blood to plead.

October 18

JESUS INTERCEDING

Read: Luke 11:1-13.

Text: *Men ought always to pray, and not to faint.* Luke 18:1.

My Perfect Example. He shows me that I, too, must intercede. Jesus knew the unspeakable glory of heaven; He was Himself the brightest of all its lights. Yet He won new glory through the cross of shame. And our glory will come as we bear with Him the burden of lost souls. There is no joy, no honor, to compare with this.

The evangelist who not only delivers the message but stays by at the altar, the personal worker who not only invites the sinner but prays him through to God—these men are following the Christ who not only provided the ransom but pleaded with the Father. As He went all the way, so may the salvation of every soul stir us to our depths.

Man shares with God in the salvation of souls. God is always seeking, and by the working of His Spirit He will open men's hearts so that truth they would otherwise have let pass unheeded shocks them into attention. So it was with us who are saved; so it can be with our unsaved friends if we pray for that special grip of conviction.

Probably no one is saved unless someone has prayed for him. Why we do not know, but for some reason it seems to take that to get God and a soul together. Lord, help me remember that all my work for others is unfinished until I have prayed for them. Teach me even to distrust my work unless it is steeped in prayer.

Restraining prayer, we cease to fight.

JESUS INTERCEDING

Read: Luke 18:1-8; I John 5:16; I Sam. 12:23.

Text: *If ye shall ask any thing in my name, I will do it.*
John 14:14.

My Perfect Example. He shows me how I must intercede.
To intercede is to pray "in His name"; that is, in unity
with Him: for the same things, and in the same spirit.
And His intercessory prayer shows me how He is praying
today at the Father's right hand. I can check on my prayer life.

To intercede, I must forget myself. Only the wholly
consecrated man or woman can truly intercede; for to intercede is to identify myself with another's need; to intercede is to accept a "prayer job" for someone's soul, and
complete that job; to intercede is to realize that a soul is
headed for eternal death, unless I pray through; to intercede is to get God and a human soul together.

You have prayed earnestly and long for that son's
salvation or that husband's, yet no answer comes? Can
it be that you have prayed selfishly, because you wanted
so desperately to see him at his best and truly happy?
Even in prayer we may have idols. The intercession that
prevails is for God's glory.

I cannot live as I please, then all of a sudden wake up
and pray with power. Only when I am living for God's
glory can I pray for God's glory.

But then I can pray with the faith that is confident.
Jesus said, "I will." So may we, reverently, if we have
no other will but His.

> *Satan trembles when he sees*
> *The weakest saint upon his knees.*

JESUS INTERCEDING

Read: Heb. 7:23-28.

Text: *He ever liveth to make intercession for them.* Heb.
7:25.

My Great Prayer Partner. So long as our prayers all
center about ourselves, many of Christ's promises are
blank to us. It is only as we take up the work of intercession He committed to us, that we shall learn the full
meaning of His words and His fellowship.

Jesus' prayer of intercession was different from any
prayer of intercession I can ever pray. But I can know
that to my little faith is added the mighty "faith of the
Son of God." We are working together when I pray.

Jesus couples Himself with us. He calls us Christians to fellowship with Him. He—and we—are to "sanctify ourselves." The work of saving men is to be our first
business. He—and we—are to be "glorified." When the
battle is over, there will be the Father's presence and a
place at His side. He will not be ashamed to present us at
court. He—and we—are to be "one with the Father"; we
both are "loved"; we both are "sent."

If we have chosen to be sanctified wholly, we have
chosen to share with Jesus in His deepest interests and
His highest glory. Let us not fancy that we can live an
independent life on our own resources. We are forever
identified with Him.

> *I have a Saviour; He's pleading in glory—*
> *For you I am praying, I'm praying for you.*

GOD LAYS HOLD OF A MAN

Read: Gen. 28:10; Luke 15:11-15; Jonah 1:3.

Text: *Whither shall I flee from thy presence?* Ps. 139:7.

"Though like a wanderer, the sun gone down." Scene One—*The Wanderer.* It is the first scene in the spiritual drama of every one of us. We deserved nothing of God; we were sinners and pursued by our sins. Why should God pay any attention to us?

Every sinner is a fugitive from justice, an outcast from home. If only he could see himself as he is! The Hound of Heaven, the Seeking Shepherd, follows with love instead of judgment. Can he stop us?

Never lose hope for the unsaved person you are praying for. When he has wandered farthest, God is on his track. When he seems most unconcerned, God is stabbing him wide awake.

God is good not to let us succeed too well without Him. Perhaps there's a reason if things have all gone wrong in your life!

"Pleasure at the expense of duty is but a brief forgetting, an indulging in dreams which will be shattered by the least gleam of consciousness bringing remorse in its wake."—J. L. Borgerhoff.

Fear is the curse of all humanity. Even when we think we are carving out our own success and doing very well, down at the core of our subconscious selves is fear—fear of death, fear of life, fear of people, fear of ourselves, fear of the future, fear of the present. At the root of fear is sin. A great testimony, that of David's: "I sought the Lord, and he heard me, and delivered me from all my fears."

> *I was a wandering sheep,*
> *I did not love the fold,*
> *I did not love my Shepherd's voice,*
> *I would not be controlled.*

GOD LAYS HOLD OF A MAN

Read: Gen. 28:11; Ps. 139:1-12.

Text: *The darkness and the light are both alike to thee.*
Ps. 139:12.

"*Darkness be over me, my rest a stone; yet . . . .*" *Scene
Two—Darkness Before Dawn.* How many mothers have
sent their boys away into the world—helpless to follow
them. Remember that God has unexpected ways of reaching souls. Monica, Augustine's mother, wept when her
son went away in the opposite direction from her prayers. Yet in that unlikely environment of pagan Rome
he met the man who led him to God.

It is the man who has least to recommend him naturally
that often stands the best chance of finding God. Esau
is probably attractive and good-natured, the general
favorite; but only his mother sees much good in Jacob.
His sense of inferiority develops an aggressiveness and a
sly shrewdness—he must help himself, for nobody else
will; but it also tells him that he isn't enough for himself—he needs God. His one asset is his appreciation of
God. But the man who has that is never hopeless.

Many a man has seemed to be going fast in the wrong
direction; but away underneath, where others cannot see,
he has been saying, "If ever I'm a Christian, I want to be
a Christian like Father." "Some day I'm going to preach."
"What would I care about money if I could have peace
with God?" We cannot know these thoughts; God can.
A dim half-choice in the darkness He reads, and respects.

God does not have to have perfect stuff to make His
saints out of. I'm glad—aren't you?

> *I heard the voice of Jesus say,*
> *I am this dark world's light;*
> *Look unto Me, thy morn shall rise,*
> *And all thy day be bright.*

GOD LAYS HOLD OF A MAN

Read: Gen. 28:12-15; Ps. 139:17-24.

Text: *How precious also are thy thoughts unto me, O God! how great is the sum of them.* Ps. 139:17.

"In my dreams I'd be nearer, my God, to Thee." Scene Three—The Shining Ladder. God makes a way into every life that really wants Him. The ladder is let down; men do not build it up. "While we were yet sinners, Christ died for us."

God speaks a language that men understand. He makes an offer that practical men—even good traders—recognize as good business. He offers a better way to safety and success than scheming; He offers spiritual values that are ahead of the material. He offers to make a man His man; and that means blessing stretching out of time into eternity.

Man has a spiritual hunger that answers to this proposition. He knows that God is right. Everyone who turns God down does so in defiance of his own nature. "He that despiseth me wrongeth his own soul."

It is amazing how low motives a man can have in seeking God, and yet be accepted. God knows He can make a man right if only He can get hold of him.

God is more interested in men—always—than they are in Him, or in their best good. He was interested in you—that's how He found you. He still is.

God always is finding ways to keep His promises. Our fears are wasted energy; our faith will bring results.

> *The Shepherd sought His sheep;*
> *The Father sought His child;*
> *He followed me o'er vale and hill,*
> *O'er deserts waste and wild.*

October 24

GOD LAYS HOLD OF A MAN

Read: Gen. 28:16-22.

Text: *I am still with thee.* Ps. 139:18.

"There let the way appear, steps unto heaven." Scene Four—The Altar. The presence of God realized makes a demand on the sinner. When I see God I must worship; "every knee shall bow." Happy if I build my own altar now. When I see God I must give. I cannot discharge my debt—it is too great; but I give the tenth as sign that all I have belongs to Him and is subject to His demand.

The presence of God recognized and reckoned with brings security and peace. Ernie Pyle in his *Brave Men* told of the feeling of men on the hospital ship who were leaving the combat zone for home: "the quiet composure of men . . . . in the clasp of a strange new safety" describes even better the heart of the one who has come to live in the presence and protection of God.

One small boy knelt at the altar. What happened? A life principle was put in his heart which penetrated his whole being, which fought off spiritual disease and made him immune to sin through years of infection, which energized him to deeds of Christian heroism for decades, which spread healing and sunshine to bruised, infected and darkened lives in two continents, which drew hundreds of souls by its magnetism out of the quicksands of sin and attracted them to the Saviour, which finally burst the bands of death and transformed a corrupt body to glorious immortality. The Kingdom is in me, in you— life!

> *I looked to Jesus, and I found*
> *In Him my Star, my Sun;*
> *And in that light of life I'll walk,*
> *Till traveling days are done.*

VISION BEFORE SERVICE

Read: Isa. 6.

Text: *I saw also the Lord . . . . high and lifted up.* Isa. 6:1.

We need the vision. Is your prayer life so vital that it makes others hungry? Jesus' was; and He said we could follow Him.

These things that we see and handle every day are not the real, lasting things. How busy we are with them, how buried in them. Heavenly realities exist unnoticed, unseen; one day we shall stand face to face with them and be astonished—or confounded.

Heavenly realities exist, and some men see them. But they are picked men, men who appreciate God and spiritual things. And they prepare the way for the vision by waiting on God.

Our truest moments are those rare times when reality bursts through the veil and we see things in the light of eternity—shining clear through the mists of earth, sure and certain beyond all possibility of doubt. Just living will blur their distinctness and make them seem unreal. The cares of this life will choke our spiritual breath; we must fight sometimes as a drowning man would fight for air, to keep time for God to speak to us and make eternal reality seem real.

It is on an intimate relationship with Jesus that we must ultimately rely for keeping. To abide in Him we must concentrate on Him.

> *Thou callest me to seek Thy face—*
> *'Tis all I wish to seek.*

October 26

VISION BEFORE SERVICE

Read: Matt. 17:1; 6:6; Luke 9:28, 29.

Text: *Come ye yourselves apart.* Mark 6:31.

We can have the vision. The vision does not come unsought. You must tear yourself away from the pressure of earth if you are ever to see the eternal reality. The vision comes "on the mountain"; it comes "at prayer." But not by "saying prayers."

"Satan will always find something that ought to be done when it is time to pray, if it is only arranging a window blind." He will show us some opportunity to serve and help someone—good in itself. Jesus had to go up into a mountain to get away from His duties and even His opportunities, in order to get a fresh message from heaven.

Set apart a time to go and meet God. He will not disappoint you; He will show you truths new and old; He will show you His glory. We shall never know what we have missed by failing to make and keep some appointments with God.

"Shut the door. Shut the door to sight and sound; shut the door to haste and strain; shut the door to insincerity and selfish ends; shut the door to unbelief; shut the door to indifference and slothfulness; shut the door to the opinion of others—and PRAY."—*The Other Sheep.* So the vision will have a chance to reach you.

Spirit-filled prayer is the best safeguard against backsliding; there most truly am I "kept for the Master's use" and share His thoughts. There Satan finds no place.

"You might as well try to contaminate a sunbeam as a soul that keeps close to Christ."—H. C. Morrison.

> *Dear Lord and Father of mankind,*
> *Forgive our feverish ways.*—WHITTIER

VISION BEFORE SERVICE

Read: Luke 9:29-33.

Text: *I saw him; I fell at his feet.* Rev. 1:17.

The vision is blessing manifold. "There is always a blessing in prayer." But what do you call a blessing? For one thing, blessing is the "glory," the manifest presence of God: to know God Himself has touched you, God Himself has filled you. When you really pray you are meeting God; when a prayer meeting fulfils its end, God is there.

There is joy aplenty in the blessing. Foolish to say emotions are not stirred to their depths when God manifests Himself. There are moments of delight so intense that we too would "build three tabernacles." Strange Christians who would not prefer the prayer meeting when God is present to any other gathering or entertainment.

But the heart of the blessing is the residuum of truth it leaves behind. You do not go to the prayer meeting merely to be made to feel good. You go to learn of God That is the test of the genuineness of the blessing experience: what did it mean?

To see Jesus the *Son of God,* equal with God—this is a knowledge that comes of personal experience. All my life I have read it; but one day it flashes alive in my spirit. "I saw Him; He touched me; I fell at His feet." Then I worship. This is the cornerstone of Christianity. Admiration is not enough for Jesus; He claims worship.

> *Oh, sweet wonder, oh, sweet wonder,*
> *Jesus, the Son of God!*

October 28

VISION BEFORE SERVICE

Read: Luke 9:34-40.

Text: *On the next day, when they were come down from the hill, much people met him. Luke 9:37.*

The greatest of all visions—have you ever had it? Jesus the Man of Sorrows (dedicated to the cross) is Christ the divine Son of God. If you have seen that, you have seen the heart of the gospel. The *Cross* is the theme of all the redeemed, in heaven and on earth. Stooping is greatness; the mark of shame is the badge of glory.

To understand God's *dispensations;* to know that His times and seasons are exact, that His clock strikes with unerring precision; to see that He is still ordering His plans so that events fit perfectly—this is a revelation we need today. The closer to God, the less confusion in our thinking about world events.

The vision will be tested. It is what we do next day that counts; the blessing is strength for the future. Just as real as the vision is the pressure of human need. Commensurate with privilege is responsibility. Confronting the ideal is always the challenge of the practical. But if the vision was genuine, it is equal to the demand of duty.

"Face your facts"—it is a good motto. "Don't dodge." "You cannot run away from a weakness"—or a temptation, or a duty. You can try to, but it will follow you—and dog your steps until you settle with it.

> *Give me, Lord, the mind of Jesus,*
> *Make me holy as He is;*
> *May I prove I've been with Jesus,*
> *Who is all my righteousness.*

October 29

VISION BEFORE SERVICE

Read: Matt. 17: 14-21.

Text: *I can do all things through Christ which strengtheneth me.* Phil. 4: 13.

Bless me, Lord, and make me a blessing. To get your own doubts and fears and uncertainties settled is the best and the basic preparation for helping others. You will stand as a tower of strength in a world that is dying of fear and uncertainty. "You cannot always *do* something to help your friends, but you can always *be* something to help them if your own lamp of faith and love shines clear."

People all around us have needs that are breaking their hearts, and they look to Christ's followers for help. In a world of distress we are expected to stand in His stead. We cannot hold up unless we have superhuman resources through contact with Christ. All that is human in us will crumple, asking sympathy for ourselves.

The visionless disciples failed before a real need. Did a person ever appeal to you for soul help when you were not "prayed up" yourself? Did some younger Christian ever look to you for an example when your own steps were faltering? Suppose your big challenge or your big opportunity should come the day you were "out of touch with your Lord."

We Christians are citizens of two worlds. We must be at home in both. In the one we are receivers, in the other we are givers; in the one we are but children and learners, in the other we are to quit us like men and do exploits. We prevail below in proportion as we have learned above.

> *O use me, Lord, use even me,*
> *Just as Thou wilt, and when and where.*

317

A PATH TO THE HEARTS OF MEN

Read: John 4:1-10.

Text: *There cometh a woman of Samaria to draw water:
Jesus saith unto her, Give me to drink.* John 4:7.

Jesus was a day-by-day soul-winner. Personal work
must be an important study for every Christian. We
must not forget the worth of the single soul. Hand-picked
fruit is usually sound!

Jesus is the lover of the individual. Interested in
people, yes—but not as "specimens." He is interested to
save and to help. Jesus took plenty of time with one soul,
and that when He was tired and thirsty. Then the woman
went back and told a whole city. Some of our "big"
acts will shrink; some of the "small" acts will multiply
to infinity. Which are the truly great?

Remember "Pat Tanahan." One evangelist said a
person could know he was well up the road to sainthood
if he was willing to be interrupted in his most pressing
work by any "Pat Tanahan" who wanted just to talk.
That sounds like the real soul-winner. For Pat Tanahan
has a soul, and some day he will turn for help to some
one he believes is interested in him. And never doubt
that *everybody* needs Jesus. There is a hunger in every
human soul—and a path to it.

When shall we learn that no one sect or nationality
has a corner on salvation? There is no one religious or
social conditioning which must build up to finding our
Saviour. He is for Samaritans as well as for Jews; for
Roman Catholics as well as for Protestants; for rich and
cultured as well as for poor and ignorant. There are
spiritually "neglected rich."

> *There's a path to the hearts of men,*
> *It begins in the heart of God;*
> *It was made by the blessed Son*
> *And marked by atoning Blood.*

318

A PATH TO THE HEARTS OF MEN

Read: John 4:11-15.

Text: *The water that I shall give him shall be in him a well of water springing up into everlasting life.* John 4:14.

The method of personal work? The personal work that counts is done *en route* to somewhere else. You talk of Christ and His salvation naturally; you talk to those whose paths cross yours. It is most effective so because it comes out of your life and into theirs directly. Salvation is nothing if not vital.

"But I never see the opportunity till it is past, and then I wish I had said something." How can we recognize an opportunity when it comes? How make an opportunity? To Jesus an opportunity was both given and made. A needy soul was an opportunity given. A conversation directed was an opportunity made.

"Buying up opportunities" does not always mean talking religion. Jesus saw into the heart and knew when talking would help; we do not. Some would-be "personal workers" have made nuisances of themselves by chattering ceaselessly and indiscriminately. The best way to know when to speak and when not to speak is to ask the Holy Spirit to make the opportunity and then show it to you.

In a conversation all topics can lead to Jesus Christ— if you think enough about Him. The Holy Spirit will direct both minds, if we ask Him.

All the methods of the "fisherman" we can see in Jesus' approach to people, but most of all the fisherman's enthusiasm. It takes tact to win souls, but it takes more love for Christ and souls.

> *Help me the slow of heart to move*
> *By some clear winning word of love;*
> *Teach me the wayward feet to stay,*
> *And guide them in the homeward way.*

A PATH TO THE HEARTS OF MEN

Read: John 4:16-30.

Text: *Come, see a man which told me all things that ever I did: is not this the Christ?* John 4:29.

Not everybody will be a soul-winner. No mechanical following of formulas will open to you the door of another human heart. People must somehow feel your love and interest. So you will need something of Jesus' vision of souls, their hunger and their need. And something of His love.

You will need something of His passion for the will of God. If you have that, no business of your own will seem more important than talking with—and listening to—a person who needs help. Souls cannot be won in a hurry—and they know when you are in a hurry!

The true soul-winner is not in a hurry; he would rather save one than count a hundred. The true soul-winner is honest; he does not smooth over sin and tell a man he is not so bad. For he knows that men must be made to realize their deep need—or what they get by way of salvation will be only a passing relief.

Part of the soul-winner's secret is his self-effacement. His job is to introduce to Jesus and then step out of the picture. Keep praying for the soul you have won, keep helping—but don't keep him leaning on you or following you. That is to ruin all you have done.

Our own spiritual life must never be allowed to become formal while we are working to save others. Prayer is a vital part of personal work. Only Jesus can talk to hearts with authority, and it is through human lips that He must speak to their hearts. That does not come by chance.

What thou hast not by suffering bought,
Presume not thou to teach.

November 2

A PATH TO THE HEARTS OF MEN

Read: John 4: 31-42.

Text: *Lift up your eyes, and look on the fields; for they are white already to harvest.* John 4: 35.

Everybody can be a soul-winner. Sometimes an ordinary layman will succeed in winning a soul to Christ where a minister would fail. They think it is his job; he is paid for it. But they know you are not a professional salesman of the gospel. If you talk about it every day, it must be genuine.

Love Jesus, keep a good Christian experience, know your Bible, have a good prayer-list and work it, love people enough, then follow the Spirit's guidance and your own heart. There is all the difference in the world between a school-made professional "soul-winner" and a real seeker of lost men and women.

Two simple tools for saving souls are in every hand, simple and effective. They are prayer, made of breath and heart's desire; and testimony, made of breath and heart's praise.

"What are you doing with your religion? God stands by daring us to undertake, and to trust Him with the issue. But we are afraid. We draw back, and thus we never know." The men and women who are great soul-winners will tell you that their success did not come to them out of study about how to do it. "No, it came to them only out of doing. Ability to walk comes by walking. So do something!"—Peter Marshall.

Soon the time for reaping will be over;
  Soon we'll gather for the harvest-home;
May the Lord of harvest smile upon us,
  May we hear His blessed, "Child, well done!"

321

JESUS' USE OF POWER

Read: Mark 5:21-34.

Text: *And as many as touched him were made whole.*
Mark 6:56.

Jesus' use of power is uncalculating. Jesus seemed reckless in spending His power. He did not husband it for tomorrow's larger need, nor for some great person's benefit. It seemed to flow from Him for every one in need, and it always found the right place. It still is flowing to meet faith wherever it finds it.

Let God pour His blessing through you; He will. Don't be afraid to preach your best sermon to a small group. God will give you a better one for the large audience when the time comes. Don't grudge your best efforts nor hoard your strength. Live a life of blessing always. There is plenty of power available.

Jesus could have been impatient at His interruptions. On His way to a great ruler's to do a big piece of work that would make His reputation, He is stopped—by a woman. No one is insignificant to Jesus, no time inopportune. I am glad, for I needed Him and needed Him in a hurry; I still do. And if I am going to be a channel of His power, I cannot be less generous than He.

> *Just one touch as He moves along,*
> *Pushed and pressed by the jostling throng;*
> *Just one touch, and the weak was strong,*
> *Cured by the Healer divine.*

JESUS' USE OF POWER

Read: Mark 5:1-15.

Text: *I honour my Father .... and I seek not mine own glory.* John 8:49, 50.

Jesus' use of power is unselfish. Power can be used for self, or for others; Jesus always used His power for others. He raised Lazarus, but He went to the cross Himself. Power can be used for display, or for human need; Jesus always used His power to meet a human need. He fed the multitudes, but He would not give the Pharisees a sign to justify Himself. He is our Example.

Jesus helps all classes, regardless of the social effect on Himself: the rich and the outcast, man and woman— all are equally important to Him. We stand before Him as human souls. And his regard imparts to us something of His own dignity. We are worth saving.

To Jesus, power is incidental. All Jesus' miracles had a spiritual purpose and preached a spiritual sermon. They fulfilled prophecy; they showed God to men. Power is safe only under divine control. Talents will curse unless consecrated.

Jesus did not prize power for the sake of power. That is the devil's spirit. Jesus did not prize power at all. He prized the honor of the Father's name, He prized the souls of men; and He valued power as a means to one of those ends.

"Getting things done" is not so important as what you are doing and why you are doing it. Cultivate your best ability, but with it cultivate love and heart-likeness to Christ.

> O to grace how great a debtor
> Daily I'm constrained to be;
> Let that grace now like a fetter
> Bind my yielded heart to Thee.

SENT AS HE WAS SENT

Read: Mark 1:23-34.

Text: *I must work the works of him that sent me, while it is day.* John 9:4.

If my life is to be like Jesus', it will be a busy life. What is wrong about card-playing and movie-going? For one thing, they are time-wasters, time-stealers, time-killers. There is a subtle fascination in them that claims more and more time. Jesus had no time to kill; and your life is planned poorly if you find much time hanging heavy on your hands.

The world is full of needs and sorrows and weakness. People seem to scent out the man or the woman who is strong and poised, who has a Source of supply that does not give out; they are quick to come for help with their burdens and problems. And when they do not come of their own accord, the urge in the Christian's heart sends him out seeking lost men who do not realize their lostness. The representative of Christ finds plenty of work.

Jesus' life was a *ministry.* He was among us as one who served. Do you ever wish to be relieved of the many demands and calls for help? wish to be waited on for a day or so? wish that you could do the leaning instead of being leaned on? Remember Jesus.

Fundamental in Jesus' ministry is suffering. He is not the gracious philanthropist tossing coins out of his bounty. He shared our griefs and our temptations. He came not to make a life, but to give one. He came not to achieve, but to lay down. He came to open a stream into the heart of humanity.

> Bless me, Lord, and make me a blessing;
> I'll gladly Thy message convey.
> Use me to help some poor, needy soul,
> And make me a blessing today.

SENT AS HE WAS SENT

Read: Luke 4: 14-22; Isa. 61: 1-3.

Text: *The Spirit of the Lord is upon me, because he hath anointed me to preach the gospel to the poor.* Luke 4: 18.

Jesus was always ready. He needed no urging. "Forthwith," "straightway," He always responded. He never grudged time nor resented an interruption.

Jesus always was *unselfish.* He never expected a return, always gave glory to God, always turned men's eyes upward.

Jesus was *impartial.* He healed rich as well as poor, poor as well as rich. He never failed foreign missions in His zeal for home missions. All "cases" were interesting to Him.

Jesus was *compassionate.* He never became professional in His healing or preaching: never lost sight of human souls in the routine of activities, never taught without a tender heart, never got so used to suffering and sin that He ceased to suffer in sympathy.

Jesus always felt *responsible to His Father.* "I must" was always on His lips. He lived in the will of God. He worked with the sense of vocation.

Jesus was *sincere.* He told the truth even when it hurt both others and Himself. He was faithful enough to hurt if by hurting He could heal.

Jesus was *Servant of all* but *independent of all.* His service never made Him servile, for He knew He was Son of God. He never allowed His spirit to become dominated by any human being.

Jesus was *confident* of His power. He was Master of devils. He knew it, and they knew it. He knew that however strong power from below may be, power from above is stronger.

> *It is the way the Master went;*
> *Should not the servant tread it still?*

SENT AS HE WAS SENT

Read: Mark 1: 35-39.

Text: *And it came to pass in those days, that he went out into a mountain to pray, and continued all night in prayer to God. Luke 6: 12.*

Jesus was always busy, but never driven by His work. Pressure from without must be equaled by strength within. The horizontal plane must be balanced by the vertical. The demand of human needs must be met by the supply of contact with God. Jesus took no vacations from work, but He took much time out for prayer. Strange that He should recognize this need when some of us seem to feel sufficient of ourselves.

The ancient Greeks had caught sight of a truth, in their myth of Antaeus. Every time this giant was felled, he rose with new strength; for he had touched his mother, Earth. We know that it is contact with Heaven, not earth, that will pour fresh strength into our spiritual veins. We know, but sometimes we forget.

Jesus did not have time for prayer; He made time. He took time for prayer. Even when pressed by His work, by necessary work, even when it was cruel to turn His back on suffering, He found it necessary to pray. The busier He was, the more He needed prayer. If Christ had no independent resources of power apart from contact with the Father, how about us?

The path of prayer Thyself hast trod:
Lord, teach us how to pray.

November 8

SENT AS HE WAS SENT

Read: Luke 4:38-44.

Text: *But Martha was cumbered about much serving.*
Luke 10:40.

Jesus' body grew tired in His work, but He never let His spirit grow tired. "God never asks of us such busy labor as leaves no time for quiet resting at His feet." There is no power in feverish activity.

> *"I must have quiet hands," saith He,*
> *"Wherewith to work My works through thee."*

Sometimes our work crowds upon us, even our work for God, and assumes such proportions that we begin to feel we are doing it. Our works are lifeless without His touch on our hands.

"God sets His seal only on what belongs to Him." He works miracles through the lives of men—but only through lives that have died out to their own choices. There is a time to rest, but there is also a time to bear the strain of fasting and watching. A Christian life is not built by rigid rule; it must be flexible in the hands of Christ.

It is an old song, but it always finds a response in some honest heart; for the experience of which it tells is all too common:

> *I was working in the temple*
> *With the Saviour by my side,*
> *Where the multitude assembled*
> *In its misery and pride.*
> *Glancing upward from my labor,*
> *I just caught His distant smile:*
> *"You have placed your work between us;*
> *Come and talk with Me a while."*

BOUGHT WITH A PRICE

Read: I Peter 1:17-21.

Text: *Ye were not redeemed with corruptible things, as silver and gold . . . . but with the precious blood of Christ.* I Pet. 1:18, 19.

Jesus came to die. His life finds its full meaning only in His death. Jesus' death was not accidental, not incidental. It was deeply and fundamentally essential. Calvary had to be. It had to be just as it was. For it had to be *right*.

God had not forgotten when He let Jesus go to the cross. Nor was He arbitrary in His demand. He was planning in love and wisdom, planning the only way that would deal adequately with all the facts. Tragic, cruel, heart-breaking, impossible; but adequate—Christ the Lord of Glory crucified.

Sin must be dealt with; God could not overlook it. Calvary is adequate. Jesus' death proves the awful reality of sin. If you are tempted to dally with sin, or to wonder if the well-meaning sinner is really lost, take a look at Calvary. If sin is a light thing, why the Cross?

God must punish sin, yet save man from it. His own Son, voluntarily paying the full penalty in man's place, set man free—justly, rightly, honorably, beautifully— and the personal relationship resulting eclipsed the evil of sin. "Where sin abounded, grace did much more abound." The Cross is God's answer to sin.

Has my sin been dealt with—through the Cross?

> *I am redeemed, but not with silver,*
> *I am bought, but not with gold;*
> *Bought with a price, the blood of Jesus,*
> *Precious price of wealth untold.*

BOUGHT WITH A PRICE

Read: Mark 15: 22-39.

Text: *And he was numbered with the transgressors.*
Mark 15: 28.

Man must be shown the nature of sin. Calvary shows it. If you are tempted to trifle with sin or to excuse it, look at the Cross. Sin is not negligible. It took Christ's death to meet it.

Sin hates God; it will kill His very Son. Sin is essentially enmity against God. The nails and the spear and the cruel jeers show me what I am harboring when I keep inbred sin in my heart.

Sin is death-bringing. Calvary shows me what the end of sin will be. In Jesus' cry, "My God, why hast thou forsaken me?" I feel the horror of separation from God. That is the bitterness of the sinner's death.

Have I seen sin as it is—on the Cross?

Man must be shown the love of God. Calvary shows it. Our God is not to be worshiped through fear or barter or form. He is not to be guessed at nor groped after in the dark nor placated unwillingly. A warm personal bond is to link earth with heaven. The Cross reveals a God who loves: God taking the initiative and seeking out man in his need.

The Cross shows love to the uttermost. It is unbelievable that the Creator should die for the creature; but it is true. Jesus went beyond the utmost bounds of thought. He went the limit—that no man should be able to question His love or to think himself too great a sinner.

Have I seen love as it is in the Cross?

When I survey the wondrous Cross
On which the Prince of Glory died,
My richest gain I count but loss,
And pour contempt on all my pride.

BOUGHT WITH A PRICE

Read: I Cor. 1:17-31.

Text: *Christ crucified . . . . the power of God and the wisdom of God.* I Cor. 1:23, 24.

Man must be shown his need of God. Calvary shows it. We feel that we can make ourselves good enough, surely as good as the average. If we do the best we know, somehow we shall be all right. The Cross confronts us with the fact that man's best was not good enough. God had to do something about it; God came to us.

The Cross tells us that we are helpless to win salvation. Jesus paid it all. He would not have died if there had been any other way. First of all, I must make connections with Him. I must be lifted; I cannot lift myself.

Have I seen my only hope for salvation in the Cross?

Man needed to be shown the best way of living. He needed to be given a working philosophy of life. He needed to be taught true values. Calvary met his need.

The Cross teaches the glory of humility. The Son of God, when He lived on earth, chose to give up His own rights; He chose to save others rather than Himself. He chose to let the rich and ambitious ride over Him if they would; He chose to "answer not a word." He chose to do the will of God; God was bound to exalt Him.

The Cross shows that we win by yielding, we rise by stooping, we are great by serving. We are without excuse if we choose earthly standards; for we have seen Jesus die.

The Cross shows us that a man is not measured by his honors nor by his humiliations. No insult can degrade a great spirit.

Have I chosen the philosophy of the Cross?

> *In the cross of Christ I glory,*
> *Towering o'er the wrecks of time.*

330

BOUGHT WITH A PRICE

Read: John 18:33-37; 19:6-11.

Text: *That through death he might destroy him that had the power of death, that is, the devil.* Heb. 2:14.

Man needed to see Satan defeated. In his fight with the powers of evil he needs both an Example and a Saviour. Calvary is not a tragedy finally; it is the greatest victory man has ever seen.

The Cross shows that Christ is not dependent on Satan. He does not have to take Satan's interpretation of winning the world. He does not care about great wealth or material power. In *The Robe* Lloyd Douglas has Emperor Tiberius say, in a flash of insight, "When Christians begin to ride horseback, they will lose their power—they will be like everybody else." Christ's conquest is of the spirit.

Christ does not have to use Satan's weapons: deceit, hate, force, trickery. If He did, He would be building Satan's kingdom instead of His own. He conquers by love, kindness, forgiveness, obedience, faith. His conquest is not artificial, forced, temporary; His conquest is eternal, written into the nature of human hearts.

Christ does not have to make terms with Satan. The Cross shows Satan doing his worst—and Jesus doing better. We do not have to compromise and dicker with evil—only stick to Jesus and the Cross, forever and always.

Have I seen the way of the Cross as my way to victory?

> *Then I bid farewell to the way of the world—*
> *The way of the Cross leads home.*

THE COST OF DISCIPLESHIP

Read: Matt. 19:16-21.

Text: *Jesus said unto him, If thou wilt be perfect, go and sell that thou hast, and give to the poor, and thou shalt have treasure in heaven: and come and follow me.* Matt. 19:21.

There is a drawing power in Jesus. We all would qualify as His disciples—if the tuition is not too high.

His terms? He asks for all your riches. Morality is not enough. If you have high principles, the world will find no fault with you. If, in addition, you are reverent and Sabbath-keeping, they will label you a good Christian. But there can be all this and no Christ; and Christianity can not leave out Christ.

A lovable personality is not enough. Some people seem "naturally good." They are far easier to live with than are many Christians. Everybody loves them and they seem to love everybody. Yet they are as ignorant of Christ as if they never had heard His name. Christians have met Christ and are devoted to Him.

It costs to be Christ's disciple. It costs that one last thing you are depending on, that one last thing that gives you self-confidence, that one last thing that for you makes life livable. For if there is one thing you have to have more than you have to have Jesus, some day in a pinch you will sell out Jesus for that.

You are not rich, you say. Not in money, perhaps. Your wealth is the thing you hold dearest. And for you that is the price, for at the crucial moment that would loom larger than Jesus and keep you from following Him. "My only hope must be in Jesus."

> *There is no other Saviour given—*
> *No other name in earth or heaven,*
> *My guilty, dying soul to save.*

THE COST OF DISCIPLESHIP

Read: Luke 9:57-62; II Cor. 6:1-10.

Text: *No man, having put his hand to the plough, and looking back, is fit for the kingdom of God. Luke 9:62.*

But Jesus is not arbitrary in His terms. Jesus is dealing with spirits who had sold themselves to Satan and have been bought back at infinite cost. They must not hold their redemption cheap, or they will be coarse-grained, ungrateful, unfit for fellowship with Him and with the Father. What costs us little we value little.

Jesus is dealing with spirits that have been warped by selfishness and self-will. We are not saved until we are rid of self. We must pay the price of a yielded will.

Spirits are saved only when they are purged. Salvation is not buying cheap an entrance to heaven; salvation is having something done to us. Jesus must do it—but we must let Him have us to work on.

The initial price is only the beginning. The same self-abandonment must hold through to the end. The disciple is a learner from Christ. His motive now is love of Christ; his program is following Christ. It is a poor follower who is always looking back to what he has left—or like Bunyan's waterman, facing one way and rowing the other.

The bare repeating of theological formulas or even Bible truth doesn't seem to grip men's hearts. Truth passed through lives comes alive to men; so do not squirm or question overmuch when persecution or suffering for Jesus' sake comes your way. If you had had to pay little you could hardly preach to those who must lose their all to follow Christ.

Every price you pay will help you ransom some soul later.

> *Refining fire, go through my heart,*
> *Illuminate my soul;*
> *Scatter Thy life through every part*
> *And sanctify the whole.*

THE COST OF DISCIPLESHIP

Read: Matt. 19:22-26.

Text: *But what things were gain to me, those I counted loss for Christ.* Phil. 3:7.

It costs everything, but it is cheap at any price. Dr. J. B. Chapman, writing on "Cheap Religion," makes the point that you usually get what you pay for. If you don't want to pay much for your religion you'll get a poor brand. Cheap religion is cheap. Salvation costs high; but it is a bargain at any price.

"The great refusal" is the refusal to enter into life. Anyone who turns from eternal life "goes away sorrowful"; he has made a poor bargain. He has exchanged eternity for time—and he never can make up his loss.

The price is your all; but He gives it back—that and more. And if you do not give it, it spoils on your hands. To keep a sweetheart you turn Jesus down, and the married life you build is likely to be bitter with heartache. To keep your money you turn from Jesus, but that money will never buy you satisfaction. Better give your treasures to Jesus; He knows just what will satisfy you. God never takes a thing from you but He gives you something better—it is good philosophy, and experience bears it out.

Christ knows the path to real greatness and He will lead us in it. He knows the path is entered through self-surrender; and He will not cheat us by letting us think we can find an easier way.

> *Oh, the cross has wondrous glory!*
> *Oft I've proved this to be true;*
> *When I'm in the way so narrow,*
> *I can see a pathway thro';*
> *And how sweetly Jesus whispers:*
> *Take the cross, thou need'st not fear,*
> *For I've tried the way before thee,*
> *And the glory lingers near.*

THE COST OF DISCIPLESHIP

Read: Matt. 19:27-30; Phil. 3:12-14.

Text: *These are they which follow the Lamb whithersoever he goeth. These were redeemed from among men,
being the firstfruits unto God and to the Lamb.* Rev.
14:4.

Following Jesus—where will He lead? Self-surrender is
only the door. On the other side, what? Not a blind
alley with nothing beyond; not the edge of an abyss with
the next step death. Surrender to Jesus is the first step
of an endless adventure with Him.

The steps of this journey are readily traced. Count on
every one: the wilderness of temptation, the mount of
vision, the valley of service, the dazzle of passing popularity, the garden of intercession, the night of betrayal,
the judgment hall of injustice, the cross—and the resurrection morning! Jesus knows well every step; He knows
He is calling us to a rugged way. Yet He dares to insist,
for He knows the glory of the end.

And the thrill of the journey itself. Who would live a
torpid, indifferent, earthbound life when he might breast
the winds and storm the stars? Following in His train
we know reality and achieve the triumphs that will ring
through the ages.

> *Finding, following, keeping, struggling,*
> *Is He sure to bless?*
> *Saints, apostles, prophets, martyrs*
> *Answer, "Yes!"*

November 17

THE FINAL TRIUMPH

Read: II Cor. 11:13-15; I Pet. 5:8-11.

Text: *Satan, which deceiveth the whole world.* Rev. 12:9.

The Adversary. The devil is a powerful foe. But see him as he is and strip him of his one weapon, *deceit*, he has no power at all. He is a liar first and always, the spirit of untruth, as God is the Truth. Test what he says by the revealed Word of God, and he cannot fool you.

The devil deceives you as to *true values*. He is the prince of this world and of course he wishes to sell his wares. So he makes you think this world's goods—money, fame, pleasure—are valuable, and the next world's goods —character, love, the approval of God—are worthless. He has an axe to grind; do not trust him.

The devil is the spirit of *unreality*. He tries to make the things of God seem unreal and far away, heaven a fable, eternal life vague and uncertain—but the temporal nothings of today all-important. The day is coming when eternal verities will be manifest and will mean more than all the world to us.

This is a day when it seems Satan is let loose to deceive the whole earth. Some evil power would seem to control the minds of men—else how would such masses credit the manifest lies of communists, atheists, easy-going optimists, shallow propagandists, when the tried Word of God is so simple and sure a way to peace? His day is short—thank God that it has been given you to discern his lies.

> *The prince of darkness grim—*
> *We tremble not for him;*
> *His rage we can endure,*
> *For lo! his doom is sure,*
> *One little word shall fell him.*

THE FINAL TRIUMPH

Read: Gen. 3:1-5; Rom. 8:33, 34.

Text: *The accuser .... is cast down.* Rev. 12:10.

The devil is the accusing spirit. He has no use for goodness himself, and he cannot bear it in others. (So Goethe's Mephistopheles is the mocking spirit. He sneers at all goodness, questions all sincerity, makes a man feel ashamed of his own good impulses.) That voice which casts slurs on your purest actions, insinuates that you did them from mean motives, and after you have done your best tells you you are good for nothing, that is the voice of Satan. It is more deadly than the temptation to outbreaking sin, for it is more subtle.

The devil *accuses us to God.* He sees our weaknesses more clearly than we do ourselves, sees how far short we fall of the ideal, and complains of us to God. (See Job 1.) Thank God for our Intercessor at the throne, who pleads His blood.

The devil *accuses God to us.* In the Garden of Eden he told Eve that God was unfair and untrue. The next time he tells you that you can sin with safety (for God does not mean His warnings), or that you will not be happy in the will of God (for God is keeping the best things from you), recognize the voice of the accuser.

The devil *accuses our Christian brethren to us.* He would focus our attention on their faults and weaknesses, and give them a mean slant. "Love thinketh no evil." The devil enlarges, magnifies, distorts, poisons. "Love covers."

> *I will praise my dear Redeemer,*
> *His triumphant power I'll tell;*
> *How the victory He giveth*
> *Over sin and death and hell.*

THE FINAL TRIUMPH

Read: Rev. 12: 7-12.

Text: *And I say also unto thee, That thou art Peter, and
upon this rock I will build my church; and the gates of
hell shall not prevail against it.* Matt. 16: 18.

The Assurance of Victory. Whenever Satan can be faced
in a fair fight, he is certain to be defeated. It looks today
as if that fight were approaching. But as evil conditions
come to a head we need not despair. "When all these
things begin to come to pass, lift up your heads, for your
redemption draweth nigh." God will conquer; right will
prevail.

Today's facts must be interpreted in the light of eternal
truth. Facts become truth only when seen in true perspective. See to the end, you see evil headed for destruction.
As of old, God's promise is to roll the sea away. He will
drive back the tides of sin. His honor is pledged.

We fight a winning battle. We may be one of the despised minority here; we shall be on the winning side at
last. "There are too many tomorrows for me to accept as
final any slight, or defeat, or failure that may come today."
—J. B. Chapman. And we shall see the cause we love
triumph at last.

One good minister is known by his reassuring slogan,
"Drive on." Discouragements, uncertainties, shortcomings, hurts, misunderstandings—our days are full of
them, and any one accepted and brooded over can block
our march to the Celestial City. Satan would straddle
quite over the whole breadth of the way and shake these
in our faces to frighten us back; but Jesus says, "Give it
to Me—and drive on!"

> *Called unto holiness, bride of the Lamb,*
> *Waiting the Bridegroom's returning again;*
> *Lift up your heads! for the day draweth near*
> *When in His beauty the King shall appear.*

THE FINAL TRIUMPH

Read: I John 5:1-5.

Text: *And they overcame him by the blood of the Lamb, and by the word of their testimony; and they loved not their lives unto the death. Rev. 12:11.*

The Price of Victory. No victory without a personal faith in the Blood. We shall be overcomers on the other side only if we have been overcomers here. But there is no temptation in which a conscious claiming of the merits of Calvary will not bring a speedy victory. Satan knows he was worsted there and he literally flees at the reminder.

You will overcome by your testimony. Testifying keeps your experience bright. Many a one could confess with truth, "I didn't tell about it, and it was not long until I had nothing to tell about."

Sometimes the testimony that defeats must be a silent one. An army officer had been persecuting a young Christian private. One rainy night when the young man came in tired and wet and knelt to pray, the officer threw his heavy, muddy boots at him, hitting him each side of the head. The private went on praying. In the morning the sergeant found the boots beautifully polished standing by the side of his bed. His heart was broken, and he was converted that day.

The conditions of victory are three: faith in the Blood, testimony, unquestioning obedience. With those three we can live simply, normally, without strain, in a world full of the enemy's pitfalls, and come through victorious. There is no guesswork as to the outcome of the Christian life.

God thy strength is with thee, causing thee to stand;
Heaven's allied armies wait at thy command.

THE FINAL TRIUMPH

Read: Rev. 5:9, 10; 14:2, 3; 15:2-4.

Text: *And they sung as it were a new song before the throne.* Rev. 14:3.

The Song of Victory. What music on the harps of God! But they must be played by the fingers of redeemed souls.

Have you learned to sing the "new song"? The vast choir of all the ages is made up of separate voices. Every one has learned for himself the meaning of Calvary's triumph over Satan in personal deliverance from sin. Practice a little today!

> *Oh, the new, new song, oh, the new, new song!*
> *I can sing it now with the ransomed throng:*
> *Power and dominion to Him that shall reign,*
> *Glory and praise to the Lamb that was slain!*

The song of Moses and the Lamb—mightiest of all conceivable themes! Song of the two great covenants, song of the two great deliverances from bondage (of Pharaoh and of Satan), song of the gift of the law and the gift of the gospel, song of God's justice and His love, song that climaxes all God's dealings with man—true and righteous altogether, song of permanent victory. If I should miss that song, I should miss all that man was made for!

> *Lo, He stands the mighty Conqueror,*
> *Since He rent the veil in two!*

WORKING FOR GOD

Read: Neh. 1.

Text: *Neither told I any man what my God had put in my heart to do at Jerusalem. Neh. 2:12.*

The story of high enterprise for the kingdom of God is the same in every age. The conditions of building are the same: the obstacles, the uncertainties, the enemies, the methods, the victories. The men are the same; and their God is the same. Note the familiar phrases in those "dead" books of *Ezra* and *Nehemiah*—dead only because unread; actually the living memoirs of two great men of God, our eternal contemporaries.

The man and the crisis. Great crises make great men. Rather, great men change great crises to great conquests.

"Jerusalem lieth waste . . . . That we be no more a reproach." (Neh. 2:17.) The challenge comes afresh. The devil always is tearing down; always there is some waste place to be built up. And every waste place—every defunct church, every barren altar, every lukewarm service —is a reproach that should shock us into action. Those who care much for God are jealous for His name.

"My God hath put in my heart" . . . . "All whose spirit God had raised." (Neh. 2:12; Ezra 1:5.) The initiative comes from God. That urge to do something for God, that special concern over some particular need—it is God speaking. Better listen; He has a promise for your waste place. We should do more for God if we listened more.

> *Lift high His royal banner;*
> *It must not suffer loss.*

341

WORKING FOR GOD

Read: Neh. 2:1-8.

Text: *Here am I.* Isa. 6:8.

The man and the crisis. "A man is come to seek the welfare of Jerusalem." (Neh. 2:10.) And what a man! Resolution, strong convictions, practical good sense, executive ability, knowledge of men and how to deal with them, vast resources of indignation and of devotion—all energized and fused to white heat by love for the cause of God. God knows how to fit the man to the crisis.

"Ezra had prepared his heart to seek the law of the Lord .... and to teach." (Ezra 7:10.) If you plan to be a minister of God, study the Bible; digest the Bible. Learn all you can from books and from the experiences of life; and true every one by the standards of God. So make His Word a part of you. It takes a seasoned spirit to teach God's Word fitly.

God will help you prepare ahead of time for commissions that He foresees, but you do not. How often He has stirred you up to "go to school," to "take a course," to study some particular line of truth, to enter upon some special course of training. You did not know why; but when you were prepared, timed as by clockwork the call came and you were ready. When all the records are read out there will be some shouting over God's timing.

"Will you give the Lord 50% or even 75% of the man you could be? If you keep consecrated you will not miss God's plan for your life."—F. W. Nease.

> *Speak, my Lord; speak, my Lord;*
> *Speak, and I will answer, "Lord, send me."*

November 24

WORKING FOR GOD

Read: Ezra 8:21-23.

Text: *Call unto me, and I will answer thee, and shew thee great and mighty things, which thou knowest not.* Jer. 33:3.

Victory Tactics. Pray. "I mourned certain days, and fasted, and prayed." (Neh. 1:4.) "And it came to pass." (Neh. 2:1.) "Every emergency is a call to prayer." "We can do nothing until we have prayed; after we have prayed we can do all things."

Before you have "prayed through" about a situation, how worried and weak and irresolute you are; after you have prayed, how quiet and confident and strong. Have you prayed through about your waste place? Prayer is the first step toward victory—and a sure step.

Trust and obey. "The good hand of my God was upon me." (Neh. 2:8, 18; Ezra 7:6, 9, 28; 8:18, 22, 31.) The refrain of the advance: "The hand of my God upon me." That Hand will open locked doors; that Hand will shield from danger. The essential secret of victory is to let God work. If you know you are in the will of God, you can trust surely the safe-conduct of God.

"I was ashamed to require of the king a band of soldiers." (Ezra 8:22.)—because he had "bragged on the Lord." One argument for testimony. Declare your faith publicly, positively; it is good leverage for faith in the hour when things seem not to be going so well. You are safe. God will not let you down if you obey and trust.

One step at a time, and the way is revealed. "As thou goest the way shall open up before thee." Blessed exhilaration of keeping step with the Guide who knows!

In the strength of the Lord let me labor and pray,
Let me watch as a winner of souls.

343

November 25

WORKING FOR GOD

Read: Neh. 4.

Text: *Nevertheless we made our prayer unto our God, and set a watch against them day and night.* Neh. 4:9.

Victory Tactics. Co-operate with God. "God will prosper us; . . . . we will arise and build." (Neh. 2:20.) Here is true co-operation between God and man. Genuine faith leads to action. After we have prayed and believed, we are pretty certain to do something. And our efforts are successful in proportion as they are blessed.

"We made our prayer unto our God, and set a watch against them." (Neh. 4:9.) Trust in God never rules out common sense; nor does it lie down on God. We do the best we are capable of; God completes our incompleteness. I don't expect God to pass my examinations for me when I have been too lazy to study.

"Our God shall fight for us." (Neh. 4:20.) "I am doing a great work, so that I cannot come down." (Neh. 6:3.) "Trust in God as if everything depended on Him; then work as if everything depended on you." You'll make it together. "I know that we two shall win—Jesus and I."

Co-operate with one another. "The people had a mind to work." (Neh. 4:6.) "All of us to the wall, every one unto his work." (Neh. 4:15.) It takes only a small unguarded spot to let in the enemy. Let there be no gap at "your small corner."

After all, there is something you can do that even the preacher cannot do. There are people you can reach that the preacher cannot. They do not go to hear him. Perhaps this is where such things as house-to-house visitation come in, and the testimony of a shining life in the shop.

> *One more day's work for Jesus!*
> *How sweet the work has been . . . .*
> *Lord, if I may, I'll serve another day.*

November 26

WORKING FOR GOD

Read: Neh. 8—9:3.

Text: *Neither be ye sorry; for the joy of the Lord is your strength.* Neh. 8:10.

The Victory. Nothing new. Back to the eternal, unchangeable values that have been thrown away. Back to the old revivals: the temple, the Word, separation from the world, the joy of the Lord.

There have been great revivals; but how quickly the effect has worn off. To our shame, repeatedly we have had to acknowledge that the light that shone so clear during the revival has faded into the light of common day. The truth has oozed away as from a leaky vessel. Is God's truth too common, too familiar? Seventy years of doing without taught the Jews the worth of what they had despised.

If Hitler and Hirohito had won, should we today be learning to our sorrow how we prize the privileges of Christian fellowship, Christian preaching, the Word of God, freedom to live according to conscience? Thank God they did not win, and these treasures still are ours. What are we doing with them?

There are many things a Christian can do without. There are some things he has to have. The returning exiles can do without the gold of the first temple, but not the glory. The things we have to have are the things they had to have: a city (the Christian Church); a temple (worship, contact with God); the book of the law (God's Word, the Bible); separation from the heathen (a clean-cut, holy life). These we must maintain, however complicated living becomes. These must occupy the center of our lives, whatever else we lose.

He hath sounded forth the trumpet that shall never call retreat,
He is sifting out the souls of men before His Judgment Seat.
Oh, be swift my soul to answer Him, be jubilant my feet.
Our God is marching on!

345

THERE IS HELP

Read: Mark 8:1-9; John 6:5-14.

Text: *He himself knew what he would do.* John 6:6.

There is help. Through Christ there is always a way to meet the need of the person who looks to you in desperation. The way may not be apparent. It will probably take all there is of you to find it. But, having Christ, you have the inwrought, divinely instinctive knowledge that resources are available.

Jesus will. For Jesus cares. Jesus has His eye on every person who suffers temporally for following Him. It is for these He performs temporal miracles. If He is first in your thought and your care, you have small cause to worry about finances. In some way He will see that you do not lose by your loyalty.

Jesus always recognized that people have bodies. He sympathized with physical aches and pains and hungers. They were not the big thing, but they were a real thing. We, His followers, can well learn of Him in our quest for souls. Plain human sympathy opens many heart doors.

Jesus knows. Things do not just happen with Him. Nor is He taken by surprise. Nor does He barely scrape through. Where we are excited and nervous and anxious, He is calm and sure. He knows what He will do and His plans are deliberate. He is not walking on thin ice, nor are we when we depend on Him. There is the eternal Rock beneath a trusting soul.

Jesus can. One miracle does not exhaust Jesus. Miracles are the usual with Him. Walking with Him, we come to expect miracles. If we are not daily confronting the impossible and seeing it melt away, perhaps we have cause to fear we are not too close to Him?

> *Oh, then to the Rock let me fly,*
> *To the Rock that is higher than I.*

November 28

THERE IS HELP

Read: Mark 6:30-38.

Text: *Give ye them to eat.* Mark 6:37.

We must. We shall always find ourselves surrounded by needy people. "Nothing to eat." Need is almost a definition of humanity; so many individuals, so many separate needs. Most people are uncertain, helpless, hungry; vaguely or actively unsatisfied, not knowing where to turn for supply. We who have found satisfaction in Christ forget what it is like not to have Him.

We shall always have a responsibility to the hungry about us. "Give ye them to eat." We cannot evade need nor make excuses that will pass.

"But I was resting"—yet even on a vacation we can spread blessing.

"Send them away"—but that doesn't sound much like Jesus' "Come." He never allowed a soul to turn away disappointed.

"Let them buy for themselves"—but what they will buy is not the bread that satisfies.

All these are our alibis. Jesus still looks straight into our eyes and says, "Give ye them to eat."

But we shall never have enough in our own resources. "How many have ye?" Is He mocking us? However much we can muster of natural means is ridiculously inadequate. It must be "blessed" to meet the need of souls.

No cause to pride myself on my gifts and graces; unblessed and unanointed, they fall infinitely short. Four thousand with seven loaves and a few fishes, or five thousand with five loaves and two fishes—the miracle is as great whatever the human figures.

> To serve the present age,
> My calling to fulfil,
> Oh, may it all my powers engage
> To do my Master's will.

347

THERE IS HELP

Read: Mark 6: 39-52.

Text: *He blessed, and brake the loaves, and gave them to his disciples to set before them.* Mark 6: 41.

We can. We shall always have enough, with His resources. "They did eat and were filled." When shall we learn that His supply never gives out—only our faith. He never stops giving; we only stop receiving, and giving. When shall we learn that His arithmetic is all multiplying: grace and peace and wisdom, strength and comfort and hope, and all good seed.

We shall always receive so long as we keep giving. "He gave to his disciples to set before them." When you have to give counsel and are at your wits' end, send up a prayer, turn over your mind to Him—and He will fill your mouth with wisdom beyond your own. Weary and exhausted, set out in His name to answer another call—you will find the energy coming. He will not fail you. "To them that have no might He increaseth strength"—to use for Him. Mueller's God still lives, and He is ours for our peculiar responsibility—and opportunity.

Shall we always be scared by the latest problem? "They considered not the miracle." But this one seems different. It is different, but it is guaranteed by "the God of all grace." The God who rolled back the Red Sea will not be nonplused by a Jordan River. And the Christ who saved from starving can save from drowning.

> *All the rivers of Thy grace I claim,*
> *Over every promise write my name.*

TESTS FOR CHURCH MEMBERS

Read: Matt. 5:1-12; Luke 11:41-52.

Text: *Behold, I set before you this day a blessing and a curse.* Deut. 11:26.

"Blessed" or *"Woe"?* *"The unexamined life is not worth living."* Jesus began His ministry with eight "Blesseds." He ends it with eight "Woes"; for He has seen some people vote themselves out of salvation. The "Blesseds" are the standards of heaven; the "Woes" are for those who have evaded, made excuses, and finally chosen the standards of this world. We have the privilege of patterning our lives by either set of values.

Jesus' "woes" are for church members, strange as it may seem. Church membership does not save a man; in fact, church membership is all too often made a substitute for salvation. Tragic, if my good standing in the church should actually keep me out of heaven!

Criticism for the Critics. *"If we would judge ourselves, we should not be judged."* Criticism is not worth paying much attention to unless you know what standard of judgment is used. Anyone can criticize by his own standard—and people "take it whence it comes." If we are given to criticizing, possibly we should check up on our standard. We may be as far off as the Pharisees were— and look as foolish and as wrong.

Jesus' standard of criticism is the only sound one. He disregards nonessentials, but insists on essentials. He strips off the trappings, and goes straight to the core of the matter. Only He knows what is essential; for He is our final Judge. I would hear His words.

We would see Jesus: this is all we're needing;
Strength, joy, and willingness come with the sight.

December 1

TESTS FOR CHURCH MEMBERS

Read: Luke 11:37-41; Ps. 26:1-8.

Text: *Search me, O God, and know my heart: try me, and know my thoughts.* Ps. 139:23.

Essentials versus Nonessentials. How sane and beautiful Jesus' analysis of essentials. Not church membership, but turning from sin. Not family relationship with good people or belonging to a chosen race, but walking in the light of God for yourself, finding the will of God and doing it. Not sensational marvels, but everyday obedience to the Word of God. His standard commends itself to my thinking as well as to my conscience.

Sincerity. Nonessential to Jesus are formalities, refinements, "nice ways." Essential are love of the heart, kindness, genuineness. The church of Christ is no place for snobbishness or the class spirit. And reverence is not all a matter of hushed aisles and organ music.

"He that dares not say an ill-natured word or do an unreasonable thing, because he considers God as everywhere present, performs a better devotion than he that dares not miss the church."—William Law.

One prime duty of the Christian leader is to uphold the standards of the Christian church. But he will do it even better by his example than by his preaching. Always the sheep have wanted a shepherd who would lead them, of whom they could know that, "First he wroghte, and afterwards he taughte."

"I'm not putting any shoddy timbers into this boat; I have to float in it myself."—Paul Hill.

May Thy will, not mine be done;
May Thy will and mine be one.

TESTS FOR CHURCH MEMBERS

Read: Luke 11:42-46.

Text: *Blessed are the pure in heart: for they shall see God.* Matt. 5:8.

Essentials versus Nonessentials. Purity. Of what good is a dirty dish—no matter how pretty its design or decoration? It was made to hold clean food, to be 'eaten from. And what good is a Christian whose heart is not right? He was not made to please other people; he was made for a holy God to indwell and to use. Lord, make me sincere in my inmost thought, a vessel meet for the Master's use.

Love. Tithing is right; but a tither can rob God if he gives only money and no love.

The true Christian never asks, "What am I to get out of this?", never wants to see people bowing down to him, never wants to dominate. He has the passion of giving and serving.

Humility. "Humility is not thinking you are little, but thinking little of yourself."

Renunciation of self-dependence is the first step in the Christian life, and it will be the last—and all the steps between.

Right relations to persons. After all, one's conscience cannot be really clear toward God and very guilty toward men. For six of the Ten Commandments and a good share of the Sermon on the Mount deal with our relations to men.

Persons are more important than things.

The cup of water given for Thee
Still holds the freshness of Thy grace.

TESTS FOR CHURCH MEMBERS

Read: Luke 11:33-36; 47-52.

Text: *Well done, thou good and faithful servant.* Matt. 25:21.

Essentials versus Nonessentials. Love of the truth. It is an easier thing to build a memorial church or a memorial hospital or a memorial mission than to live a memorial life. Sons and daughters of holy men have lauded their "fathers" to the skies after breaking their hearts by disloyalty to the "faith" for which they lived and died. To perpetuate the fathers' spirit of faith and devotion is the only sincere way to show our appreciation.

One inescapable essential of true religion is a true appreciation of the light of God. "Light is meant to walk in, not to look at."

Walk through one day with yourself and watch your decisions. Are they made on the basis of what you believe is the Bible standard, or on the basis of what is customary in your church or your group? Jesus was not very respectful of "the traditions of men."

Faithfulness. Tremendous responsibility to be entrusted with the gospel in our generation! What are we doing with the Bible truth that has been preached to us all our days? Our refusal to live by it might shut off the light from someone else.

"Stand thou firm as a beaten anvil; for it is the part of a good soldier to be flayed alive, yet conquer!" (Early Christian saying.) Jesus is our Pattern. You cannot always escape opposition; but if you know you are right, you have the endorsement of God, and can stand firm for truth against its enemies. Thou therefore endure criticism as a good soldier.

Speak the word of power to me,
Even me.

THE SIXTH COMMANDMENT

Read: Matt. 5:21, 22.

Text: *Thou shalt not kill.* Ex. 20:13.

The Principle. Right relation to other personalities. A young preacher said that the biggest thing he had learned in his first years as a pastor was to love people. It was a great lesson—and learnable. Everyone is lovable if you can see him as he sees himself—or better, as God sees him. God will help you see that way. Personality—plain, ordinary human nature—is God's masterpiece. He loves it. Better be careful how you treat it.

Anger is not always wrong; it is sometimes a duty. But anger is wrong when it has a shade of personal grievance; and it is pretty hard to steer clear of personalities in this world.

Contempt and scorn have in them the seeds of death. Do not identify yourself with them, for fear you die with them. To live you must love.

The "*Raca*" attitude that holds my neighbor cheap, the "Fool" attitude that despises him, both make it impossible to treat him fairly or to love him as myself. If I could see from his point of view, he is as good and as wise as I. If I do not try, I am the loser. Charles Lamb once said to a friend, "I do not like that man." "Why?" was the natural question. "Because I do not know him."

We can't be Christian and be careless of confused, antagonistic relations with other people. We should start loving, and loving hard.

Touched by a loving heart, wakened by kindness.
Chords that were broken will vibrate once more.

December 5

THE SIXTH COMMANDMENT

Read: Matt. 5: 23-26.

Text: *All things whatsoever ye would that men should do to you, do ye even so to them.* Matt. 7:12.

The Practice. Do the impossible, through grace. "Impossible to love my enemies!" "Helpless before my temper!" "Jesus could 'bless them that cursed,' but I can't." True. A man cannot make himself react to circumstances as Jesus did, by pretending or even by willing to be like Him. But God will give us the disposition to love instead of hate; and repeated practice will grow into habit, and habit into a character of holy love.

There is only one way to show God's grace in your life; that is by trying situations. We are put here to live with people; every day is one test after another. And every failure tells the world that God's grace is less than He promised.

Life is full of causes for anger. In social life, the contempt of personal insults; in business life, the injustice of extortion and sharp dealing; in political life, the oppression of tyranny and partiality. Everywhere imposition and unfairness. The Christian must meet this, not with the world's weapon of retaliation, but with the Christian weapon of love. Not easy when it is you that suffer. But love wins.

The worst obstruction to the blessing that should flow from my life to others is the harbored grudge. No love can get around it or through it. It is potential murder. Whether I am nursing the grudge or causing the grudge, I am responsible for its existence. For if I follow Bible directions, I can melt it away. If I refuse, I take on myself the guilt.

> *Write Thy new name upon my heart,*
> *Thy new, best name of Love.*

THE SIXTH COMMANDMENT

Read: Matt. 5: 38-45.

Text: *But I say unto you, Love your enemies.* Matt. 5: 44.

The Plus. *"Perfect as your Father."* *More than your duty.* Don't fight, kill, hit back, retaliate, resent—but more: make peace, do kind things, go more than half way, give more than is asked. Don't hate, curse, persecute—but more: love, be kind, bless. Take the offensive. Overcome evil with good.

Better than a publican—of course. Control yourself when people treat you unjustly; don't follow your impulses and give way to anger. *Better than a Pharisee.* Don't just be decent, polite, self-controlled; priding yourself that you never lose your temper, but inwardly resentful. *Better than "human."* Pour out kindness on the kind and the unkind. Kill your murderers by love.

Godlike. Children of the Father, we have a family tradition to uphold: rain on the evil and the good. Following Jesus, we have an Example: blessing when reviled. Born again, we have a new nature: love.

Conquering. Love conquers, retaliation loses—always. If you use the weapons of the wrongdoer you come down to his level. If you use the Christian weapons you immediately make yourself your enemy's superior; and he feels your strength. You never can succeed by hitting back; you never can fail by loving.

More, because *changed* within. It takes a sanctified heart to keep the Commandment Jesus' way. With His power within, what He tells us to do we can do.

> *I've borne, I've borne it all for thee—*
> *What hast thou borne for Me?*

I TOO SHALL LIVE

Read: I Cor. 15: 44-49.

Text: *As we have borne the image of the earthy, we shall also bear the image of the heavenly. I Cor. 15: 49.*

There is a spiritual body. My body takes too much of my time to attend to its needs—when there are so many more important things I could be doing. Just feeding it and clothing it require energies that I need sorely for thought and prayer and work for the Kingdom. It seems I could do better service with a less demanding body.

This body does its best for me; I am grateful that I have a voice and hands and feet to use for Jesus. But it is all too slow for my eager spirit. My best endeavors often fall short through my body's bungles. Surely my Lord deserves a better temple; His grace deserves a better witness.

This body has been a wonderful piece of mechanism, but it is wearing out. God created it marvelously adapted to its environment: ear and eye, digestive and reproductive systems, the heart with its ceaseless pumping. But little by little, its parts are breaking down. I am slipping out into eternity; my spirit will need a house adapted to its new environment. The same Creator has not lost His skill. I will trust Him. The fine adaptation of means to ends in my natural body tells me my new spiritual body will be just as well adapted to heavenly air and heavenly food.

Every lack in my natural body will be corrected in my spiritual body. For gradual decay, ever-fresh, undecaying life; for weakness, frailty, inadequacy, the power of ever-quickening energy. The curse of sin will be gone; the power of an endless life released.

I know, I know, I have another building;
I know, I know, 'tis not made with hands.

December 8

I TOO SHALL LIVE

Read: I Cor. 15: 41-44.

Text: *It is sown in corruption; it is raised in incorruption.*
I Cor. 15: 42.

Not buried, but sown. Those friends whom we have loved, those bodies so dear to us even after life has left them—we have not seen the last of them when they are put in the ground. They will spring up again, radiant, transformed, warm with life. The God who cares through the winter for the wheat seed sown in autumn will care for them till the resurrection spring morning.

It is when the dead hear the voice of Christ that they shall come forth from their graves. His is the quickening energy. It should not be hard for Christians to believe in the resurrection of the body. They have felt the stir of His eternal life in their souls.

Even here we may feel in our bodies the quickening energy of Christ—earnest of resurrection power. Test it next time you are "too tired to go to prayer meeting." Go, and find renewed freshness. Test it next time you face a day with no strength for its duties. Draw from Him "strength as your day."

In the resurrection, as in all else, we follow our Leader. As we have walked in His image, we shall be raised in His image. Jesus Christ had a natural body and a resurrection body; so shall we have. He took flesh, and He was glorified; so we. He is "the firstfruits"; we come after.

> *I shall be like Him, I shall be like Him,*
> *And in His beauty shall shine.*

December 9

I TOO SHALL LIVE

Read: I Cor. 15: 50-53.

Text: *We shall all be changed.* I Cor. 15: 51.

"I have a rendezvous with Life." We are headed for a great event, an inevitable event. For the principle of corruption is the result of sin. In entire sanctification it is banished from the spirit, but our bodies still suffer the effects of the curse. We can't drag those about in heaven. Somewhere, some time, there must be a transformation; and God has the hour slated.

Death is certain for us all. But just as certain is the resurrection afterward. When the Christian faces death, he does not face a blank wall. There is an open door—to life.

We are slated for freedom. We have known it in our spirits, but our bodies have always felt the clogging weight of human limitations. Some day soul and body will respond to the same upward pull. Our body too is to have wings.

We are slated for glory. We have not yet proved all of God's good purposes for us. Justified, adopted, regenerated, sanctified—we are yet to be glorified. "It doth not yet appear what we shall be, but . . . . we shall be like him."

We are slated for incorruption. No more decay, no more disease, but eternal health. Before us, if we are true, are endless vistas of growth and beauty and grace and service. We have an eternity to do successfully the thing we love to do.

> *Living forever where sorrowless days,*
> *Days never ending are fragrant with praise.*

I TOO SHALL LIVE

Read: I Cor. 15: 54-58.

Text: *Death is swallowed up in victory.* I Cor. 15: 54.

"Death, thou shalt die!" Death has "swallowed up the generations of men"; eternity shall "gulp him down, so that he is endlessly lost and absorbed in its illimitable waste." We shall see no more of death. "How glorious a time to the righteous, when the inhabitant shall no more say, I am sick; when . . . . there shall be no more death. This time must come. Hallelujah! The Lord God Omnipotent reigneth."—A. Clarke.

For the Christian death *is* victory; Jesus has already conquered the last enemy for us. And when Jesus wins, He does it overwhelmingly. Not only are we not death's victims; death serves us, for it opens the door to our glory.

That lingering dread of death that is so human—let hope crowd it out; hope and faith and loving confidence in our Lord. "Through fear of death subject to bondage?" Get a pure heart, then remember how we speak truly of the saints who have gone on: "entered into joy," "passed to their eternal reward," "translated."

Corollaries of the Resurrection.

Let me live every day in relation to the resurrection. It has meaning for me today.

Let me be steadfast. Let me settle all my weight on the promise of the resurrection. It pays to serve Jesus.

Let me be fruitful. I want to fill my quota for this stage of life before I go to the next. And the reward for faithfulness is great.

Let me be encouraged. I'm facing the dawn!

> *There waits for me a glad tomorrow,*
> *Where gates of pearl swing open wide.*

December 11

LOOKING AHEAD

Read: Eph. 1:3-12.

Text: *Looking unto Jesus, the author and finisher of our faith. Heb. 12:2.*

Our life view should include the future. A man is a fool who lives only for the day—yet millions in "Christian America" are doing that: earning, eating, drinking, dressing, perhaps movie-going, perhaps church-going, but all with blind sight. It could be so with some of us.

Most people do not dare to look ahead. The future holds so much they do not want to think of: old age, sickness, loneliness, death, the strange unknown beyond, or, if they have been taught rightly, the Judgment, eternity. No wonder they bury themselves in the present. Only Christians can face the facts of the future, with resources to meet every eventuality.

We know better than to base our hope for the future on circumstances—they are often distressing and the best circumstances may change; even on the prophecies and forecasts of the optimists—they have been known to be mistaken. We refuse to depend on chance. We know better: our future is as bright as the promises of God. Our basis of hope is Christ Himself.

God always says, "Look to the end." The devil dares not. Christ is the Omega as well as the Alpha; He is "Finisher of our faith" as well as "Author."

Lead, kindly Light, amid the encircling gloom,
Lead Thou me on.

December 12

LOOKING AHEAD

Read: Matt. 16:13-20.

Text: *We see not yet all things put under him. But we see Jesus.* Heb. 2:8, 9.

When we look ahead, what do we see? We see Jesus— and Victory. Jesus is building through the centuries a church, a church of those who really know Him as the Eternal Son of God, who have learned to overcome through the blood of the Lamb and the word of their testimony. That is the company of the overcomers. They are Christ's eternal *comitatus,* conquering through the ages to come.

He has promised me victory for today, strength as my day. But as I win my victories this day, let me look up and look ahead. I am training for eternal victory. I am qualifying as an overcomer. I am verifying His promise that the gates of hell shall not prevail against His church. His church is a "glorious shining army" because its members are individually "clad in garments pure and white." His church shall prevail finally against the gates of hell because its members every one prevail against hell's devices in their own lives.

In this fearfully shaken world there are some things that "cannot be shaken." They are safe from the atomic bomb. The love of God, the blood of Christ, the presence of the Holy Spirit, the Word of God, the assurance of final victory over evil—these will abide unchanged. Are they enough? They were enough for that London congregation who gathered amid the ruins of their bombed church and sang:

> *In heavenly love abiding*
> *No change my heart shall fear;*
> *And safe is such confiding,*
> *For nothing changes here.*

LOOKING AHEAD

Read: II Tim. 4: 6-8.

Text: *Be ye stedfast, unmoveable, always abounding in the work of the Lord, forasmuch as ye know that your labour is not in vain in the Lord.* I Cor. 15: 58.

When we look ahead, we see Jesus—and a sure reward. We are not looking for pay for our work for God. We serve because we love; we love Him and we love His cause. But there are times when we cannot see results; the wheels drag; the enemy whispers that we are failures and all our efforts are wasted. Then we need to see light at the end. It is there.

How do we know that our work for Christ—however small and insignificant—cannot end in failure? Because it has eternal life in it. It is linked with Jesus and His resurrection; it is of eternity and not of time; it is seed sown to the Spirit and shall be reaped as life everlasting. Jesus Himself seemed a failure; but He rose!

We have foretastes here of the final revelation and the coming vindication of our hidden, "little" work. Foreign missions were considered by the sophisticated a harmless employment for unmarried women and queer, visionary, anemic men. But the fire of war tried missions, as the fire will try all work, "of what sort it is." The service men of World War II could not say enough good of the results of missions in the South Pacific; all agreed that the achievements of the missionary cause had been immensely significant for our victory and for world peace. There are many such surprises ahead for faithful Christians.

> *When our labor's ended,*
> *He will bid us welcome;*
> *We shall come rejoicing,*
> *Bringing in the sheaves.*

December 14

LOOKING AHEAD

Read: I John 3:1-3; John 14:1-4.

Text: *I go to prepare a place for you.* John 14:2.

When we look ahead we see Jesus—and home. The New Testament does not extend much hope that world affairs ever will be straightened out by human efforts nor that world confusion ever will turn to permanent peace. It does not encourage us to hope that this will ever be a world where Christians will feel at home. But it does tell us that Jesus is coming back and that when He comes He will make all things new. Chances and changes past, we shall be at home.

The future is not a leap in the dark; the future is in our Father's hands. What He is working out we do not know exactly—our interpretations are faulty at best. We do know that if we live by God's salvation program we shall fit into His dispensation program.

We see home. There is a "building of God" ready; what difference what happens to this body? We do not clutch too hard after houses and lands here. We know death will not end it all, and need not be dreaded. We look forward to a personal welcome home "after the day is done."

We have a beautiful song, *Zion's Hill*—but a sad song, it seems, sung always at the funerals of dearly loved ones. Change the conjunction, and it becomes a hymn of hope, a shout of victory, a song of home:

Some day the wheels of mortal life shall all stand still,
BUT I shall go to dwell on Zion's Hill.

LOOKING AHEAD

Read: II Pet. 3:14-18; Ps. 17:15; Jude 24, 25.

Text: *We know that, when he shall appear, we shall be like him; for we shall see him as he is.* I John 3:2.

When we look ahead we see Jesus—and Christlikeness. Of all the privileges that belong to sons of God this is the greatest: that we can share the family resemblance. Not the golden streets, not deliverance from tears and pain and hell, but a nature so transparent that Jesus can see His face reflected and be satisfied to call us His own. Heart holiness a duty? Far more, a gift of His marvelous grace.

My heart can be wholly sanctified down here, so that I can live blameless before God. Yet my faulty mind and body too often misrepresent my heart; I appear to people far from faultless. But I have an appointment with Jesus. I am to meet Him one day and be presented to the Father faultless. This is a sure promise to all the sanctified who have gone outside the camp with Him, bearing His reproach. It is their great day.

"Without faith our human problems are difficult of solution. Lack of confidence in ourselves is often due to the absence of a strong religious faith."—Generalissimo Chiang Kai-shek. We Christians should be ashamed to be fearful and irresolute. Note the Bible phrases: "Ye know." "According to his promise we look." "We know." "We have a strong confidence"—in God and His Christ.

> *So we'll go marching onward*
> *To Him—unafraid.*

December 16

HIS BANNER, LOVE

Read: Ex. 13:17-19; Ps. 107:1-8.

Text: *And he led them forth by the right way, that they might go to a city of habitation.* Ps. 107:7.

The Long Way Around. Not yours the choice, but God's. Not the way your wisdom would have dictated, but confidence in His judgment. Divine guidance is the distinguishing mark of the Christian life—or should be.

God is never in a hurry. Can we learn it when it seems there is such need for haste? Better done right than done soon, is always His thought.

There are reasons for His delays: protection, preparation, patience; look for one of these three P's when His way seems a slow way. He is protecting you from some unseen dangers; He is preparing you to do better work when the right time comes; He is developing in you the patience and fortitude of a strong character. He is wise.

Madame Chiang Kai-shek compares God's view *versus* ours to the airplane view of the mountains and valleys *versus* the foot-traveler's. For making maps and planning campaigns we need perspective.

"God doesn't reveal to us the details of His plan for tomorrow; He reveals to us His Person—what He is today. He chose for us the better part."

> *The feet that wait for God, 'tis they*
> *Are soonest at the goal.*—Selected.

December 17

HIS BANNER, LOVE

Read: Ex. 13:20-22; Ex. 14:19, 20; Num. 9:15-23.

Text: *I will lead them in paths that they have not known.*
Isa. 42:16.

The Pillar of Fire. Our night seems black. The cry for guidance and safe leadership is the greatest of our age. In its bewilderment the world should be able to look to Christians and find them certain and unafraid in this dark hour. They should see the pillar of fire.

A little boy, whose father had put him to bed and now sat reading in the hall outside the door, called and asked, "Daddy, is your face turned towards me?" All we need to know in our darkest hours is that our Father's face is turned towards us. It always is, and it is light.

The Pillar of Cloud. In the day of prosperity we are not driven to seek guidance as in the night of sorrow and adversity. We think the way is clear. Truth is, we need it most when we miss it least. In self-confident, God-forgetful hours we make our missteps. Every day I need the assurance of His actual presence.

Following God in the ordinary everydays builds character. After all, we must be guided most often by the principles of truth that are not very spectacular. Christian habits are dependable in the crisis, and they must be built up in day-by-day choices.

Ask God in the morning to direct your day's events. Make it a definite part of your morning devotions. He will do it. And if you remember He is choosing for you, irritations will be transformed to peace, and vexations to testimonies of His grace.

> Let the fiery, cloudy pillar
> Lead me all my journey through:
> Strong Deliverer,
> Be Thou still my strength and shield.

December 18

HIS BANNER, LOVE

Read: Ex. 14:13-31.

Text: *Fear ye not, stand still and see the salvation of the Lord. Ex. 14:13.*

Dry Land in the Midst of the Sea. That impossible situation—you know it. Tangled relationship that cannot be unsnarled; stronghold of Satan that cannot be taken; misunderstanding, habit, problem too much for you. He still says, "Commit," "Trust," "Rest in the Lord," "Stand still and see!" Before your eyes the mountain does melt away. You are on the other side of the sea. There is power in His guidance.

As Annie Johnson Flint reminds us, He leads us not *around* but *through* the sea. He does not deliver us *from* difficulties but *out of* difficulties. For a testimony to the onlookers. Worldlings have troubles too; they must see in us the Power that takes us through. They too need it.

"As thou goest, the way shall open up before thee." Someone reminds us that those "steps of the good man" that are "ordered of the Lord" cover only two-and-a-half feet each. So much we need to see at a time. The important fact is that as we take what seems the last step we really do see the next. He does not fail us. And looking back, how clear the vision. "Ebenezer"—"Hitherto the Lord hath helped us."

And His hand shall lead you through, clear through,
Till the night of your fear is past.

—A. J. Flint*

HIS BANNER, LOVE

Read: Ex: 15:13-18.

Text: *Thou shalt bring them in, and plant them in the mountain of thine inheritance. Ex. 15:17.*

Brought In and Planted. To be guided of God means to be led into satisfactions you never would have dreamed of and achievements you never would have thought yourself capable of. You are not "cramping your style" in following Him. "He brought me into a large place."

"Up and down?" "Can't get established?" Perhaps because you have not learned to follow Him for yourself instead of listening to the say-so of your crowd. He has a work and a fellowship just for you. He wants to "plant" you in your own place.

The Mountain of His Holiness: the Sanctuary. Holiness is first. To be led of the Lord we must be separated to Him. All guidance is in the way of a holy life. If you don't know what to do, says E. Stanley Jones, ask first what is the Christlike thing to do. You can be certain that He will never guide in any other direction.

The Holy Ghost is the one authorized Guide of Christians today. If the church had not so largely forgotten Him, they would be more sure of the way, more separate from the world. Jesus left Him to us as Guide into all truth, Reminder and Interpreter of His words, our divine Greatheart, "Christ in us" to keep us to the very end. We are not orphans unless we choose to be.

> *You shall sing His praise in a better place,*
> *A place that His hand hath made.*

> —A. J. Flint*

IF JESUS HAD NOT COME

Read: Matt. 2:1-12.

Text: *Whereby the dayspring from on high hath visited us.* Luke 1:78.

If Jesus had not come, Christmas would only be "merry." Christmas gladness has its counterfeit in pagan reveling: drunkenness instead of the upward look, unrestraint for self-control, selfishness instead of good will. Jesus takes every human faculty and raises it to its highest level; He lifts life to its best possibility; He gives the genuine of which anything else is only the counterfeit.

No Star of Hope. We are creatures of hope, but we cannot be creators of hope. Without a guiding star we lose our way. Jesus gives us a future. He pulls us out of the miry clay of our own failures and our own resources.

No finding shepherds, no worshiping Magi. All over the world from the beginning of time, human hearts have been seeking rest, human minds have been seeking truth. But there are no finders outside of Christ. Only in Him does the spirit rest; only at His feet does the human heart worship in satisfaction.

No heavenly message, no word from God to man, no revelation of His good will. And I must grope in darkness as the heathen do, unsatisfied, sin-burdened, bewildered. lost. After two thousand years are we keeping the message from them?

No good tidings, no gospel, no message for the lost, no testimony to saving grace. I must preach only law and no love. But:

> *We have heard a joyful sound,*
> *Jesus saves, Jesus saves!*
> *Tell to sinners all around,*
> *Jesus saves, Jesus saves!*

IF JESUS HAD NOT COME

Read: Luke 2: 8-20.

Text: *And she shall bring forth a son, and thou shalt call his name JESUS; for he shall save his people from their sins.* Matt. 1: 21.

If Jesus had not come, no carols; for no song of salvation to sing. No hymns of praise; for no deliverance. Go through your hymnal and count the sacred songs you must lose if Jesus had not come: "Joy to the World," "Hark! the Herald Angels Sing," "Rock of Ages," "Jesus, Lover of My Soul"—but why begin? His coming set earth's joybells ringing. He keeps a song singing in my heart.

No Saviour. However self-confident men are, they cannot lift themselves to God by their own bootstraps. Sin is real and it is too strong for us. But since He came there is a path clear between the Cross and every seeking sinner. He came to save.

No Lamb slain, no atoning Blood, no cleansing fountain. Suppose I could not sing:

> *There is a fountain filled with blood*
> *Drawn from Immanuel's veins,*
> *And sinners plunged beneath that flood*
> *Lose all their guilty stains.*

No Prince of Peace. War is the devil's schedule: for nations, for families, for human hearts. I choose Christ's better way of conquering by love.

No victory over Satan. I can always put the enemy to flight if I call on the name of Jesus.

> *The soul that on Jesus hath leaned for repose*
> *I will not, I will not desert to his foes.*

December 22

IF JESUS HAD NOT COME

Read: John 14:1-19.

Text: *Let not your heart be troubled: ye believe in God, believe also in me.* John 14:1.

If Jesus had not come, no gifts, for no unselfish love. Apart from Christ men are self-centered and self-seeking. It was Jesus who set the givers above the getters.

No cross, no law of sacrifice, to tell us of life through death, of the corn of wheat that falling into the ground brings forth much fruit; to show us that only as we lose ourselves in a cause can we find our fullest self-realization.

No beautiful law of service, so that we know we are greatest when we serve and strongest when we love. For He, the King of kings, came as the Servant of all.

No comfort in sorrow. For it is Jesus who said, "I will not leave you comfortless"; He who sent the Comforter, He who in your darkest hours has always been closer than breathing, to whisper, "No, never alone."

No joy that lasts through the deepest trial. No transformation of life's ashes to beauty, life's mourning to concentrated joy, life's gloom to praise. No supernatural spring of gladness. He willed us *His joy.*

No peace of spirit that abides through life's tempests and earthquakes, that persists whether the tribulation be soul-shattering calamity or irritating pinpricks and "spiritual mosquitoes." He willed us *His peace*—and it passeth understanding.

No security. The angel said, "Fear not." Think how many times those about you were afraid, and you, too, should have been afraid; but you knew Christ held your hand.

> *Peace in the day of hurry,*
> *Wisdom in time of stress;*
> *Resting my heart from worry,*
> *My Joy, my Righteousness—*
> *Today He is this to me—Wonderful!*

IF JESUS HAD NOT COME

Read: Isa. 9:1-7; Luke 1:76-79.

Text: *And his name shall be called Wonderful, Counsellor, The mighty God, The everlasting Father, The Prince of Peace. Isa. 9:6.*

If Jesus had not come, no "blessed assurance," no unfailing certainty, no infinite, limitless confidence. For the longer we live and know Jesus, the more we find there is no question for which He does not have the answer, no life situation for which He is not the perfect Example, no demand for which He does not provide grace— no need of time or eternity that is not fully met in Him. Jesus never fails—He cannot fail.

No anchor cast within the veil, no name written in heaven, no Advocate above, no faith for His second coming—I must live a life bounded by today's horizon.

No marriage supper, no song of Moses and the Lamb when we who have accepted His love and His grace shall be claimed as His bride and see His face, and go no more out forever.

No constant Friend who knows me when all others fail to understand. No Healer of my bruised soul, no Counselor who knows me and knows the way. No "Well of water, ever springing," no Bread of Life with just the spiritual food I need—but why try to tell it? Why try to picture a world with the Light gone out?

No faith-keeping God, no Holy Bible, no steadfast Word. For the Old Testament Scriptures are full of the promise of His coming. God's honor was staked upon it.

> *Hope in a world despairing;*
> *Guide—I His steps can trace;*
> *Light, by His glad appearing;*
> *Home, when I see His face.*
> *Forever He'll be to me—Wonderful!*

THE JOY OF CHRISTMAS

Read: John 1:1-5.

Text: *Behold, I bring you good tidings of great joy, which shall be to all people.* Luke 2:10.

The Song of Christmas has in it respect for womanhood, consideration for childhood, deference to old age, reverence for personality; good neighborliness, friendliness, helpfulness. It has in it the fatherhood of God and the brotherhood of Christian men. It has in it the sublime music of all the Christian hymns you have heard since you were born. It has love, joy, peace; longsuffering, gentleness, goodness; faith, meekness, temperance. It has freedom from care if you will take it, freedom from fear if you will claim it; liberty of spirit is there, and there only. It has joy through righteousness. If we will live by that song we may get many pleasant by-products, or we may not; but if we refuse to live by it we shall surely get fear and hate, and war and death.

All real joy for all time for all peoples was wrapped up in that one Babe. He was the Sign. The angel's word was true. In Jesus—His words, His blood, Himself—is the only joy without a sting. And peace was there: peace, "the possession of adequate resources." He is the one Secret for every emergency life can bring. To have Him is to possess unfailing resources.

The joy of Christmas has a solid basis of eternal verities, infinite in their reach, beyond our full comprehension. If we realized the full import of the truths of our salvation, we could not contain ourselves for joy and praise. We are dull of spirit because we are finite of mind.

> *Joy to the world! the Lord is come;*
> *Let earth receive her King.*

THE JOY OF CHRISTMAS

Read: Heb. 1:1-12.

Text: *For unto you is born this day in the city of David a Saviour, which is Christ the Lord.* Luke 2:11.

Our Infinite Sources of Joy. Jesus' coming was *God shining through* into our dark world. The brightness of His glory—that is, Himself—we cannot conceive; our human gaze could not endure it. But we caught a glimpse when He came veiled in flesh. And that glimpse brought us the good news of a better world, a world of light, an eternal brightness beyond. Nothing can rob us of that knowledge. His coming told us of heaven.

Jesus' coming showed us "the express image of His (God's) person." He brought us the good news of a *holy God.* Other gods of the nations are cruel, vile, hateful and retaliative; He is kind, morally spotless, all love. Others are arbitrary; He is just. And because He is holy, we see that we too should be holy. The vision of His holiness gives us a vision of possible moral rightness for ourselves and a loathing of our moral degradation. No better Christmas gift than the beauty of holiness.

Jesus' errand was *salvation.* He Himself "purged our sins." And that makes Christianity a singing religion instead of a sinning religion, a praising religion instead of a wailing religion. The Christless religions have a sense of sin, but no sense of a Saviour. They know they are wrong, but they have no dynamic to make them right. Let me not mock my mighty Saviour by naming His name, then living in sin.

> *Hark! the herald angels sing,*
> *Glory to the newborn King;*
> *Peace on earth and mercy mild,*
> *God and sinners reconciled.*

THE JOY OF CHRISTMAS

Read: I John 1:1-4.

Text: *In him was life; and the life was the light of men.*
John 1:4.

Jesus spoke the Word of Eternal Life. His coming "brought life and immortality to light." He gave the answer to our inner cry for *immortality* when He said, "He that believeth in me shall never die." He did more. He *is* the Life; and as men touch Him they feel the thrill of a new, different, divine energy from above, a life that cannot die. We have the earnest already. We have power to walk the world in white as we shall walk the streets of heaven. We *have* eternal life.

Jesus' coming told us of a possible *fellowship for men with God the Father.* Fellowship in character, fellowship in understanding, fellowship in interests. Impossible, for see how great the distance! No, for the Son has bridged the gap. He came to show us that God would stoop; He came to show us that He would lift. He came the long, long way,

> *From glory to my need,*
> *From God to me.*

And by the blood of His cross,

> *From sinking sand He lifted me,*
> *With tender hand He lifted me.*

That divine fellowship is real today.

There are two kinds of Christmas joy. We can substitute, if we will, the world's cheap gaiety for the Christian's real joy; we shall do so unconsciously if we are not careful. Shall we not rather find a place of worship, and pray that its infinite realities shall grip us with new meaning? We shall need its deep joy throughout the coming years—for ourselves and for others who will look to us for strength.

> *O come to us, abide with us,*
> *Our Lord Emmanuel.*

LIFE AT ITS BEST

Read: Eph. 4: 11-20.

Text: *Till we all come . . . . unto the measure of the stature of the fulness of Christ. Eph. 4: 13.*

What have you set out to do with your life? You have only one to spend. What is your slogan? "Getting by"? "As good as the rest"? "Can't do that and be sanctified"? Or are you reaching out for "the measure of the stature of the fulness of Christ"? Let us all lift up our eyes, and stretch our souls, and look truth full in the face—truth and Jesus.

How much truth we have seen even in the past year, what possibilities of Christian strength and usefulness we have admitted. We shall need it all, for we have an infinite reach before us—an infinite reach and a glad goal: likeness to Him. "Recognized ideals are imperative."

Are the sails of my soul really set for the goal of Christlikeness? Or am I one of the crowd that drifts? Surely Jesus died to make us more than drifters, or even merry-go-rounders.

When Jesus went to heaven He did not leave us orphans. He left us the Holy Spirit as His executive. He is to guide us into all truth. He is to bear in our lives the fruit of Christlikeness.

Between the best moral life of good works and the humblest Christian life there is a great gulf fixed. The Christian life throughout is dependent on divine grace— that no flesh should glory. From first to last it is of the Spirit.

Oh, the unsearchable riches of Christ!
Wealth that can never be told.

December 28

LIFE AT ITS BEST

Read: Col. 3:1-7.

Text: *Christ liveth in me: and the life which I now live in the flesh I live by the faith of the Son of God, who loved me, and gave himself for me.* Gal. 2:20.

The best Christian life is spontaneous. Live in the Spirit. Have I made a good start? Have I received the Holy Spirit's cleansing baptism? A holy heart is not the end, but the beginning.

To plan to live a Christian life without that second crisis of entire sanctification is to plan to live short of God's program. The inner clash between God's will and self-will may be average Christian experience; it isn't normal. The only way that works is to declare bankruptcy and let the Holy Spirit take full control.

A holy heart has had to be made holy. We don't stumble into holiness; no "specially good" person comes by it naturally. We have to be convicted by the Spirit of our unlikeness to a holy God; we have to want holiness above all else, and seek it definitely and insistently. Once our heart is made right we have a right start.

The self-twist which is carnality shows up in pride (self-sufficiency), in worldliness (self-indulgence), and in what someone has called lovelessness, or spiritual coldness (self-centeredness). The Spirit will purge out these dispositions and bear His own fruit in a disposition to the humility of longsuffering, gentleness, meekness; to the self-control of goodness, faith, temperance; to the warmth of love, joy, peace. There will be temptations as before, but now the heart will take the side of God.

Lo, the great King of kings, with healing in His wings.
To every captive soul a full deliverance brings—
The Comforter has come.

377

LIFE AT ITS BEST

Read: Gal. 5: 22-26.

Text: *For every man shall bear his own burden.* Gal. 6: 5.

The best Christian life is practical. Walk in the Spirit. Is my holy heart manifesting itself in a holy character? If we are to make headway, we must be in stable equilibrium. Love puts us there. We do not elevate ourselves and so run the risk of falling, nor depress others and so prepare pits for our own feet. Perfect love is the best possible social adjuster.

Treatment of Self. Develop spiritual poise. Perhaps none of us can look at himself impartially. All of us have some dealings with that old "idol of the cave": we see things from our own point of view; we are the center of our own world. But perfect love is in essence humility: setting a true value on oneself. Practice it. Do not be offended because you are not appreciated. In the long run everyone will get his just deserts. God has pledged Himself to that.

Develop a healthy self-reliance. Prove what you are worth. Do honest work. Don't be a leaner; learn to settle your own problems with God. Don't be a parasite; contribute, wherever you are, rather than drain resources.

Develop the giving attitude. Tithe regularly and systematically, from principle rather than convenience. The church has given you all that is of greatest value; the tithe begins to pay your debt. Then give; give when giving means sacrifice, just to keep your fellowship with the God who sacrificed. Give good works, give your testimony, give your prayers. Keep the current flowing out as well as in. Otherwise, stagnation.

> *Give of your best to the Master:*
> *Give Him first place in your heart;*
> *Give Him first place in your service;*
> *Consecrate every part.*

LIFE AT ITS BEST

Read: Gal. 6:1-4.

Text: *Bear ye one another's burdens, and so fulfill the law of Christ.* Gal. 6:2.

Walk in the Spirit. Is my holy heart manifesting itself in my dealings with others? A holy heart must express itself in a holy life. Hands, feet and voice all do heart errands—always. The Spirit's fruit will mature or else dry up. The Spirit's life will move the body—else paralysis.

Treatment of Others. Perfect love for our neighbor exists in the sanctified heart potentially. It is developed by agitation under stress. It exerts power under pressure. It is made positive, active by life's demands and strains. I react to my neighbor's honors, to his faults, to his burdens; and as I react in love, my love is strengthened. I become more like the Christ whose every contact brought forth from Him nothing but pure love.

My neighbor gets ahead of me in my special field—an opportunity for my love to be glad in his gladness, for my lips to say kind things to him and to others about him—sincerely. I could depreciate his achievement. But love will grow as I exercise it here.

My neighbor falls—an opportunity for love to help him up. How? By prayer for him—in secret, probably. Not by spreading the story, even to my close friends. Not by cherishing a superior feeling. For the failure of a brother Christian is an occasion for love to catch a fresh glimpse of the Cross and to remember that *my* sins nailed Christ there. Love will grow as it says, "There, but for the grace of God, go I."

> *More like the Master I would ever be;*
> *More of His meekness, more humility.*

LIFE AT ITS BEST

Read: Gal. 6: 7-10.

Text: *He that soweth to the Spirit shall of the Spirit reap life everlasting.* Gal. 6: 8.

The best Christian life is purposeful. Sow to the Spirit. Three questions and three imperatives, if we really wish to make progress.

What are the priorities of your life? *Be spiritual.* It is easy to say, "God first." The test comes when two claims actually conflict, and we must choose between doing the thing that will give us a material satisfaction and the thing that will give us soul development—between pleasing ourselves and pleasing Jesus. Have we decided our priorities, and do we maintain them?

Are you investing or spending? *Be positive.* The law of growth is sowing, not scattering. We all spend our energies on something. This little poem is searching:

> *I read in a Book*
> *Of a Man called Christ*
> *Who went about doing good.*
> *To me it is very disconcerting*
> *That I am so easily satisfied*
> *With just going about.*
>
> *—Sunday School Times*

Do you have fainting spells? *Be steady.* "Be follower of them who through faith and patience inherit the promise." With all your best and God's best there will be stretches of apparent failure. Then remember the weapon, All Prayer; keep the contact with heaven clear and a heavenly current flowing. "If you pray, you will not faint. If you faint, you have not prayed."

In one of Schubert's symphonies the directions for the conductor read on one page, "As loud as possible." And a little farther on, "Still louder!" More than our best in the coming year by the grace of God!

> *Stand up, stand up for Jesus,*
> *The strife will not be long;*
> *This day the noise of battle,*
> *The next the victor's song.*